ESSENTIALS OF FOOD SAFETY AND SANITATION

David McSwane, H.S.D.

Nancy Rue, Ph.D.

Richard Linton, Ph.D.

Prentice Hall
Upper Saddle River, NJ 07458

Library of Congress Cataloging-in-Publication Data
McSwane, David Zachary,
    Esssentials of food safety and sanitation / David McSwane, Nancy
Rue, Richard Linton.
        p.   cm.
    ISBN 0-13-532136-0 (pbk.)
    1. Food service—Sanitation. 2. Food service—Safety measures. 3.
Food handling—Safety measures I. Rue, Nancy, II. Linton, Richard. III.
Title
TX911.3.S3M38   1998
363.72'96—dc21   97-20689
                                                                 CIP

Production Editor: *Adele M. Kupchik*
Managing Editor: *Mary Carnis*
Camera-ready Copy Editor: *Karen J. Hall*
Developmental Editor: *Anna Graf Williams, Ph.D.*
Acquisitions Editor: *Neil Marquardt*
Director of Manufacturing and Production: *Bruce Johnson*
Manufacturing Buyer: *Ed O'Dougherty*
Marketing Manager: *Frank Mortimer, Jr.*
Editorial Assistant: *Rose Mary Florio*
Printer/Binder: *R.R. Donnelley & Sons*
Cover Design: *Marianne Frasco*
Cover Illustration: *John Wise*

©1998 by Prentice-Hall, Inc.
Simon & Schuster/A Viacom Company
Upper Saddle River, New Jersey 07458

Printed in the United States of America

10   9   8   7   6   5   4   3   2   1

ISBN 0-13-532136-0

Prentice-Hall International (UK) Limited, *London*
Prentice-Hall of Australia Pty. Limited, *Sydney*
Prentice-Hall Canada Inc., *Toronto*
Prentice-Hall Hispanoamericana, S.A., *Mexico*
Prentice-Hall of India Private Limited, *New Delhi*
Prentice-Hall of Japan, Inc., *Tokyo*
Simon & Schuster Asia Pte. Ltd., *Singapore*
Editora Prentice-Hall do Brasil, Ltda., *Rio de Janeiro*

CONTENTS

Contents

CHAPTER 4—FOLLOWING THE FOOD PRODUCT FLOW

Contents

CHAPTER 5—THE HAZARD ANALYSIS CRITICAL CONTROL POINT (HACCP) SYSTEM: A SAFETY ASSURANCE PROCESS

CHAPTER 6—FACILITIES, EQUIPMENT, AND UTENSILS

Contents

CHAPTER 7—CLEANING AND SANITIZING OPERATIONS

Contents

CHAPTER 8—ENVIRONMENTAL SANITATION AND MAINTENANCE

CHAPTER 9—ACCIDENT PREVENTION AND CRISIS MANAGEMENT

Contents

APPENDIX A

Contents

Preface

There are many challenges facing the food industry. The list of disease-causing agents continues to grow, along with the number of foods linked to foodborne illness. Americans now eat a variety of exotic and ready-to-eat foods that were not on the menu fifty years ago. At the same time, the expectation of safe and wholesome food is at an all-time high. In response to growing public pressure, government agencies are expanding regulations to assure the safety of our food supply.

As a successful food manager or supervisor, you are expected to do more than make a profit or meet your budget. You must anticipate the situations that might threaten your customer's health and well-being. It is your responsibility to implement the ontrols that prevent foodborne illness. You need to know how to apply food safety principles and practices to the flow of food.

One of the most important tasks you face is to train and supervise food workers. Your knowledge is useless if you do not teach employees the correct way to handle food. Learn to recognize any break in standard operating procedure that might endanger food safety. Avoid the problems related to embarrassment, loss of reputation, and financial harm that accompany a foodborne disease outbreak.

Some state and local jurisdictions have passed legislation to require certification of one or more food managers in each establishment. Other jurisdictions are considering doing the same. Most certification programs require candidates to pass a written examination to measure knowledge of food safety and sanitation principles and practices. Some jurisdictions require completion of a food safety course before taking the exam.

Several different examinations are available for certification. In some cases, state and county regulatory agencies have developed their own examinations that apply specifically to their jurisdictions. There is, however, growing support for a nationally recognized examination and credential for food safety. If a national test is recognized by local agencies, a local examination might not be the better choice.

Current examinations (other than state and local tests) to certify food managers are available from:

▲ Professional Testing Inc. (PTI)

▲ Educational Foundation of the National Restaurant Association (EF)

▲ Chauncy Group

▲ National Assessment Institute (NAI)

Addresses for these groups are listed in Chapter 10.

When you want or need to become certified, check with your local regulatory agency to learn what they require. If you are pursuing a degree in hospitality management, culinary arts, or a related field ask your teacher or advisor for information and recommendations.

A card to request information or a test from PTI is included with this book. The authors selected the PTI examination because, like this text, it is based on the Food and Drug Administration's model *Food Code* which sets standards for all types of food establishments. The exam is also keyed to a new job task analysis derived from a survey sent to 2,500 food industry professionals.

The team of McSwane, Rue, and Linton wanted to produce a book to accompany the FDA's model *Food Code*. We trust that you will find this text accurate, comprehensive, and, most of all, useful.

David Z. McSwane, H.S.D., Registered Environmental Health Specialist, is an associate professor of Public and Environmental Affairs at Indiana University. He has over 25 years of experience in food safety and sanitation working in state and local regulatory agencies and is a consultant to the food industry. Dr. McSwane has published numerous articles and presented papers on a variety of subjects related to food safety.

Dr. McSwane is a nationally recognized trainer in food safety and sanitation. He has taught courses at the university level and for regulatory agencies, food establishments, food industry trade associations, vocational schools, and environmental health associations throughout the United States. Dr. McSwane is the past chair of the Industry Affiliate of the National Environmental Health Association and a former member of the Applied Foodservice Sanitation Advisory Board for the Educational Foundation of the National Restaurant Association. He has been a correspondent for the *Food Protection Report*, and is a member of the Environmental and Public Health Council at Underwriters Laboratories Inc. and the Automatic Merchandising Association.

Nancy Roberts Rue, Ph.D., R. N., has a background in teaching in technical education. Her doctorate is in educational leadership and curriculum and instruction from the University of Florida. With thirty years of experience in higher education and evaluation at Indiana University and St. Petersburg Junior College, she is dedicated to the task of building educational materials that meet the needs of those who want to learn.

Dr. Rue wrote the *Handbook for Safe Food Service Management* while serving as director of the Certified Professional Food Manager program at National Assessment Institute. The Handbook was designed to give entry level food managers a single source for study and focused on need-to-know information. She is now an independent writer and consultant on training and development techniques.

Richard Linton, Ph. D., is an assistant professor of Food Safety at Purdue University. His main area of expertise is the development and implementation of food safety and food quality programs, specifically in Hazard Analysis Critical Control Point (HACCP) systems. He is currently serving as chair of the HACCP Committee of the Conference for Food Protection. Dr. Linton spent twelve years working in retail food establishments. In recent years, he has concentrated on educating food handlers and managers from all segments of the industry across the nation.

There are several reference books available in the field of food safety. However, most of these resources are directed toward a particular type of food establishment. The authors of Essentials of Food Safety and Sanitation believe there is need for a text that applies food safety principles to all food establishments, regardless of type. Chapter 4, The Flow of Food, is the focal point. It clearly defines the important strategies for handling food from receiving until it is placed in the hands of the consumer. Chapter 5 follows with a comprehensive description about how to apply the Hazard Analysis Critical Control Point (HACCP) system to the process.

The authors wish all readers continued success in their food safety and sanitation activities. Regardless of where you work, you must always remember—*foodborne illness is a preventable disease*. Follow the basic rules of food safety and head for a satisfying career in the food industry.

Acknowledgments

The authors wish to thank their families, colleagues, and staff who, through their support and patience, helped us write this book. Jennifer Harris and her talent with the computer were invaluable as we struggled to put all of the information together. John Wise clearly demonstrates that one picture is worth a thousand words. His ability to translate a concept visually, is his gift. In the final days, Anna Graf Williams, Ph.D., and Karen J. Hall from Learnovation[sm], camera-ready publishing and developmental editors, gave us the extra advice and encouragement that made the book come alive.

Lawrence Pong, Registered Environmental Health Specialist, and Principal Inspector for the San Francisco City and County Health Department, reviewed the chapters as we wrote. His attention to details and injection of real world situations helped immensely. Many other food professionals have contributed to the manuscript through their reviews and suggestions. We want to thank them all.

1 FOOD SAFETY AND SANITATION MANAGEMENT

Is It REALLY Safe?

*Fourteen people in Pennsylvania were made ill after eating pie that had been highly contaminated with **Salmonella enteritidis**. Several of the victims were hospitalized, and a man in his forties, who was otherwise in good health, died as a result of the foodborne illness.*

In this outbreak, cream, custard, and meringue pies were made using ingredients from shell eggs. The pies were baked in a restaurant bakery and were stored for two and a half hours in a walk-in cooler before being transported in the trunk of a car to a private company outing. The pies were consumed three to six hours later. Leftover pie was consumed later that evening and the next day after having been kept unrefrigerated for as long as 21 hours.

*A **foodborne disease outbreak** occurs when two or more people become ill after eating a common food that is identified as the source of the illness. Several foodborne disease outbreaks involving **Salmonella enteritidis (SE)** have occurred in the United States.*

Objectives

After reading this chapter, you should be able to:

▲ Recognize the importance of food safety and sanitation as the basis for preventing foodborne illness

▲ State the problems caused by foodborne illness for both the individuals who become ill and the food establishment blamed for the incident

▲ Identify trends in menus and consumer use of food products prepared in food establishments

▲ Explain the purpose of government regulation (federal, state, and local) in the food industry

▲ Recognize the types of food establishments used in this text and the influence of the *Food Code* on these operations

▲ Recognize the term Hazard Analysis Critical Control Point system (HACCP), as a means to protect food from contamination

▲ Recognize the trend toward foodservice sanitation certification

Essential Terms

Clean	Foodborne Illness
Contamination	Microorganisms
	Germs
Food Code	Microbes
Food establishments	Sanitation
Foodborne disease outbreak	Sanitary

New Challenges Present New Opportunities

The food industry is one of America's largest enterprises. It employs about one-quarter of the nation's workforce and produces 20% of America's Gross Domestic Product (GDP). Billions of dollars worth of food are sold each year. Americans have made food a prominent part of business and recreational activities.

The food industry is made up of businesses that produce, manufacture, transport, and distribute food for people in the United States and throughout the world. Food production involves the many activities that occur on farms, on ranches, in orchards and in fishing operations. Food manufacturing takes the raw materials harvested by producers and converts them into forms suitable for distribution and sale. The retail distribution system consists of the many food operations that store, prepare, package, serve, vend, or otherwise provide food for human consumption. The term **food establishment** refers to facilities that are involved in food distribution. A list of food establishments is presented in Figure 1.1

Quick Service	Supermarkets
Full Service	Delicatessens
Employee Feeding	Transportation (planes, trains, ships, etc.)
Schools	Caterers
Hospitals	Convenience Stores
Lodging	Child Care
Colleges and Universities	Elder Care (*Meals on Wheels*)
Military Bases	Prisons and Jails
Nursing Homes	Bars
Contract Services	**Stadium Concessions**

Figure 1.1—Types of Food Establishments

Food establishments, and the clients they serve, are very different. As you study problems related to food safety, keep this diversity in mind.

The size and diversity of the food industry has made it virtually impossible for regulatory officials to continuously monitor all aspects of food safety. Therefore, food safety programs must involve governmental agencies and the food industry working closely together to assure the safety of our food supply.

Food Safety—Why All the Fuss?

Everyone knows that the United States has one of the safest food supplies in the world. So why all the fuss? The answer is simple, foodborne illness happens, and it adversely affects the health of millions of Americans every year. The Centers for Disease Control and Prevention (CDC), a federal agency, estimates that between 24 and 81 million people become ill each year from eating contaminated food. These illnesses cause 10,000 needless deaths. (Source: the FDA *Food Code*).

Foodborne illness also has a major economic impact on America. The annual cost of foodborne illness is estimated to be between $7.7 and $23 billion. Foodborne illness is the sickness which occurs when contaminated food is eaten (the FDA *Food Code*). These costs occur in the form of medical expenses, lost work, and reduced productivity by victims of the illness, legal fees, punitive damages, increased insurance premiums, lost business, and loss of reputation. Consumer confidence also goes down when a foodborne disease outbreak is reported. **Foodborne** illness impairs performance and causes discomfort. A foodborne disease outbreak will have a negative impact on the owners, managers, and employees of the food establishment where it occurred and the rest of the food industry as well.

Why Me?

You may be asking yourself, "What does all of this have to do with me?" The answer is PLENTY. Customer opinion surveys show that cleanliness and food quality are the top two reasons people use when choosing a place to eat and shop for food. Consumers expect their food to taste good and *not* make them sick. It is the responsibility of every food establishment owner, manager, and employee to prepare and serve safe and wholesome food and preserve their clients' confidence.

CDC reports show that in most foodborne illness outbreaks, the mishandling occurred within food establishments (restaurants, markets, schools, churches, camps, institutions and vending locations), where foods are prepared and served for public consumption.

The nature of food and the extent to which it is handled make the opportunity for contamination commonplace. Most cases of foodborne illness are caused by foods that have been:

▲ exposed to unsafe temperatures

▲ handled by infected food handlers who practice poor personal hygiene

▲ exposed to cross contamination

Each of these factors will be discussed in more detail in later chapters of this book.

As a food manager, you must realize that **foodborne illness is preventable if the basic rules of food safety are routinely followed**. Figure 1.2 shows key elements of food safety.

Prevention of foodborne illness must be a goal in every food establishment.

Figure I.2—Elements of Safe Food

Changing Trends in Food Consumption and Choices

Today's menus reflect changing appetites among Americans. Ethnic foods are becoming quite popular, and their exotic ingredients often create new food safety challenges. Whether it's Tai food at a local restaurant or sushi at a major league baseball stadium, people have a wider variety of food to choose from in restaurants, grocery stores, and all other places where we get prepared food.

Menu trends also include common items presented in another fashion—pork is touted as "the other white meat" to appeal to health conscious consumers. Juiciness and sweetness of "pink in the center" pork may enhance taste, but the risk of passing on a viable parasite that causes trichinosis is high. We used to recommend cooking pork to an internal temperature of 150°F (66°C) to destroy this parasite. But that was before *E. coli* 0157:H7 bacteria came on the scene. Now the recommended cooking temperature for pork is 155°F (668°C) or above. This higher temperature destroys both the trichinosis parasite and *E. coli 0157:H7* bacteria that may be present in the raw meat. But when you cook pork to 155°F (68°C) or above, the meat is no longer pink inside. Knowledge of basic food safety principles, as applied to different ingredients and methods of packaging, is critical to safe food management.

Consumers have less time to prepare food because more of them are working outside the home. As a result, they are buying more ready-to-eat food or products that require little handling. More than half of the food eaten by Americans is "fixed" in food processing plants, restaurants, supermarkets, delicatessens, cafeterias, institutions, and other sites outside the home. These foods are produced using a variety of processing, holding, and serving methods. All of these methods help protect foods from contamination.

The Problem: Foodborne Illness

Foodborne illness is a disease caused by the consumption of contaminated food. A **foodborne disease outbreak** is defined as an incident in which two or more people experience a similar illness after eating a common food. In addition, epidemiological analysis confirms the food as the source of the illness.

Recent outbreaks of foodborne illness have been caused by:

▲ *E. coli* 0157:H7 bacteria in lettuce and unpasteurized apple cider

▲ *Salmonella spp.* in alfalfa sprouts and ice cream

▲ Hepatitis A virus in raw and lightly cooked oysters

Most cases of foodborne illness occur in retail food establishments where ready-to-eat foods are prepared and served to the public.

The leading factors that contribute to foodborne illness are temperature abuse, poor personal hygiene practices, and cross contamination.

A growing number of people are especially susceptible to foodborne illness. These include:

▲ the very young

▲ the elderly

▲ pregnant or lactating women

▲ people with impaired immune systems due to cancer, AIDS, diabetes, or medications that suppress response to infection

Foodborne illness can cause severe reactions, even death, to those individuals in these high risk categories. The availability of a safe food supply is critical to these people.

Outbreaks of foodborne illness receive widespread media attention. Newspapers, television, and radio have become sensitive to issues surrounding food safety. As a result, public awareness about the problem, and how it occurs, has increased dramatically in the last few years.

Contamination

Whether a food item is prepared "from scratch" or arrives in a ready-to-eat form, there are opportunities for it to become contaminated before it is consumed. **Contamination** is the presence of substances or conditions in the food that can be harmful to humans. Figure 1.3 shows the agents that cause most foodborne illnesses.

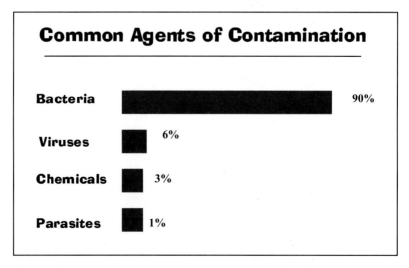

Common Agents of Contamination

Bacteria   90%

Viruses   6%

Chemicals   3%

Parasites   1%

Figure 1.3—Types of Contamination
Source: Surveillance for Foodborne Disease Outbreaks—United States, 1988-1992)

Foods can become contaminated at a variety of points as the food flows from the farm to the table. Raw foods can be contaminated at the farm, ranch, or on board a ship. Contamination can also occur as foods are handled during processing and distribution. Measures to prevent and control contamination must begin when food is harvested and continue until the food is consumed.

Figure 1.4 shows some of the more common sources of contamination such as soil, water, air, plants, animals and humans. Contaminants present an "invisible challenge" because you can't see them with the naked eye. Many types of food contamination can cause illness without changing the appearance, taste, or odor of food.

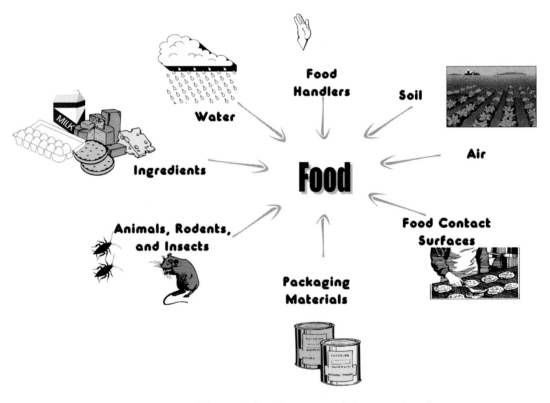

Figure 1.4—Sources of Contamination

Germs can be transferred from one food item to another by **cross contamination**. This happens when microbes from a raw food are transferred to a cooked or ready-to-eat food via contaminated hands, equipment, or utensils.

Microorganisms (Germs or Microbes)

Microorganisms (often called **germs** or **microbes**) are the most common types of food contamination. Germs and microbes are the general terms for microorganisms, including bacteria and viruses. These tiny creatures can only be seen with the aid of a microscope. They are everywhere around us—in soil, water, air, and in and on plants and animals (including humans). The microorganisms that cause most foodborne illness are bacteria, viruses, and protozoans. These organisms get their energy from the food in which they live and reproduce—often the same foods we eat.

Other types of microorganisms are yeasts and molds. These organisms, along with some types of bacteria, are responsible for food spoiling. When foods spoil, they break down causing deterioration of taste, odor, and appearance. Spoilage is a common reason that foods are thrown away. This loss can cause a serious economic hardship for food establishments.

The Food Flow

Food products, and the ingredients used to make them, "flow" through a food establishment. The food flow begins with the purchase of safe and wholesome foods from approved sources. Once the food is delivered, it then flows through receiving into storage. The final stages in the food flow are preparation and service. Preparation and service include all the activities that occur between storage and consumption of the food by your guests.

Preparation steps frequently involve thawing, cooking, cooling, reheating, hot-holding, and cold-holding. Improper food preparation and service can lead to foodborne illness. For potentially hazardous foods (they support bacterial growth), time and temperature must be monitored and controlled. Preparation of foods not requiring cooking (ready-to-eat foods) can also involve a lot of contact with your hands or with food contact surfaces. It is always important for you, the food worker, to practice good personal hygiene and use proper handwashing techniques. However, during preparation and service it is crucial!

Since preparation and service are typically the last steps prior to consumption of the food, efficient monitoring and control of contaminants is also critical. As products flow through a food establishment they are handled many times and in many different ways. For all food establishments, controlling food safety and quality is of utmost importance. You must learn to recognize foods that may have been contaminated prior to delivery and understand what is required to keep these products safe until you serve them to your customers.

A New Approach to an Old Problem

Food industry professionals and regulatory officials agree that new ways to protect people from foodborne illness must be found. The *Food Code* recommends using the Hazard Analysis Critical Control Point (HACCP) system as a means of assuring food safety. This innovative system was developed by the Pillsbury Company in the 1960s for the NASA space program. Officials in the space program realized that a foodborne illness in space could present a life threatening situation. Therefore, it was critical that all food used by the astronauts was as near 100% safe as possible.

The HACCP system follows the flow of food through the food establishment and identifies each point where contamination might cause the food to become unsafe. When a problem point is identified, action is taken to make the product safe or, if that is not feasible, the food is discarded. Individual food facilities can control the flow of food by setting up an in-house HACCP program. The HACCP program should be designed to accommodate the types of products served and the production equipment and processes used in the establishment. Records used in conjunction with the HACCP system are kept on file at the food establishment. These records will be periodically reviewed by regulatory inspectors to assure that the system is working properly.

HACCP systems for monitoring food safety have been used in food manufacturing plants for many years. Now, this system is being recommended for use in food establishments as well. A more detailed discussion of HACCP system is presented in Chapter 5.

Facility Planning and Design

A well-planned facility with a suitable layout is essential for the smooth operation of any food establishment. Layout, design, and facilities planning directly influence:

▲ worker safety and productivity

▲ labor and energy costs

▲ customer satisfaction

Some food establishments are located in buildings that were designed and constructed specifically for a food operation. Others are located in buildings that have been converted to accommodate food preparation and service activities. Either way, the better your facility is planned, the easier it will be to achieve your goals and earn a profit.

Keeping It Clean and Sanitary

Customer opinion surveys show that cleanliness is a top consideration when choosing a place to eat or shop for food. Customers' impressions about the cleanliness of an operation are frequently influenced by what they see inside and outside the establishment. Inside and outside, the facility must be clean and free of litter. Customer satisfaction is highest in food establishments that are clean and bright and where quality food products are safely handled and displayed. By increasing customer satisfaction, you will develop a devoted clientele who will regularly patronize your establishment.

It is the responsibility of every person working in the food industry to keep things **clean** and **sanitary**. Effective cleaning of equipment reduces the chances of food contamination during preparation, storage and service (see Figure 1.5). **Cleaning** is concerned with the removal of visible soil from the surfaces of equipment and utensils. **Sanitary** means healthful or hygienic. It involves reducing the number of disease-causing microorganisms to acceptable public health levels. Something that is sanitary is wholesome and poses little or no risk to human health.

Good sanitation minimizes attraction of pests, increases life of equipment, improves employee morale and efficiency, and is important from other aesthetic considerations.

Poor performance by the cleanup crew may result in dirty utensils and equipment which could harm customers and hinder business. Sanitation practices must be employed at all times to protect the health and well-being of customers.

CLEAN

SANITARY

Figure 1.5—Clean looks good—Sanitary makes sure it's safe

Accident Prevention and Crisis Management

An accident prevention program is a must in every food establishment. The cost of accidents may mean the difference between profit and loss. Beyond financial responsibilities, the loss of a worker's skills can disrupt operations and cause additional stress on other employees. Ensuring a safe environment for employees and consumers requires continuous monitoring but the rewards make it worth the effort.

Human error will always be a factor in food establishments; but, training and proper equipment can help employees avoid accidents. Pan handles sticking over the edge of the stove, poorly stacked boxes in hallways or store rooms, spilled food, and many other situations can lead to serious injuries. For example, a fall on a wet floor can cause expenses running into the thousands for lost time, worker's compensation, and medical care.

In food establishments, another kind of crisis occurs when water supplies, electricity, or sewer systems are disrupted. Food codes contain specific instructions on how to operate when basic services are lost. Public health departments can help when you are not sure how to proceed.

Storms, tornados, hurricanes, or floods cause conditions that require changes to maintain food service. A good disaster plan is invaluable in times of need. Managers and supervisors are expected to know how to handle these and other emergencies, if they should occur.

Education and Training Key to Food Safety

The prevention of foodborne illness begins with the knowledge of where contaminants come from and how they get into food. You are not expected to become a food scientist, but a working knowledge of what causes foodborne illness is valuable information. If you know the correct way to manage food safety and sanitation, but your employees do not know correct food handling procedures—the program will fail.

The importance of training employees for food service positions is heightened because of the global nature of our food supply. Control of factors during growth, harvest, and shipping is not always possible when food is produced in so many different parts of the world. Also, an error in time/temperature management, cross contamination, or personal health and hygiene of food handlers can cost a life among our vulnerable citizens. As you have learned, storage, preparation, holding, and service procedures are critical in the prevention of foodborne illness. Employees do not come to the job knowing this information. They have to be trained.

Managing the safety of food involves controlling the supply, maintaining sanitary facilities, and training employees to know how to handle food safely. Knowledge, skills, and abilities must focus on food safety practices that will protect the public from foodborne illness. Food safety programs require food managers and food workers who have the knowledge and skills needed to keep food safe. It is not enough that the manager knows food safety— employees must be taught how to perform correctly, too.

The Role of Government in Food Safety

The purpose of government regulation in food safety is to oversee the food-producing system and protect food that is intended for human consumption. Governmental agencies enforce laws and rules to protect food against adulteration and contamination. Regulatory personnel monitor both the process and the product to assure the safety of the food we eat.

Federal, state, and local regulators inspect food products and production facilities as a way of detecting problems. However, there are not enough inspectors and other resources to adequately administer the program. The enormous size of the food industry makes it virtually impossible for regulatory inspectors to effectively monitor all aspects of food safety. Therefore, food safety programs of the future will involve governmental agencies and the food industry working together to assure the safety of our food supply.

The Food Code

In 1993, the U.S. Food and Drug Administration (FDA) published the *Food Code* which replaced three earlier model codes—*The Food Service Sanitation Manual Including a Model Food Service Sanitation Ordinance of 1976, The Vending of Food and Beverages Including a Model Sanitation Ordinance of 1978*, and *The Retail Food Store Sanitation Code of 1982*—with one code. The FDA has made a commitment to revise the *Food Code* every two years, with the assistance of experts from state and local government, industry, professional associations, and colleges and universities. It was determined that a biannual revision was necessary to keep pace with changes that are occurring in food safety and the food industry. The latest version of the code was printed in the spring of 1997. In this text, the *Food Code* will be used as the point of reference.

The *Food Code* is not a law. Rather, it is a set of recommendations intended to be a model for individual states and jurisdictions to use when formulating their own rules and regulations. You will need to obtain a copy of the health rules and regulations that apply to the food establishments in your jurisdiction.

The Role of the Food Industry in Food Safety

The food industry has accepted greater responsibility for overseeing the safety of its own processes and products. Consumers expect and deserve food that is safe to eat. If a food establishment is involved in a foodborne disease outbreak, consumers may retaliate by taking their business elsewhere or seeking legal action. Financial loss and damaged reputation are some of the outcomes of a foodborne disease outbreak that can cause serious harm to the food establishment found responsible for the problem. One means of preventing the harmful effects of a foodborne disease outbreak is to start a food safety assurance program in the food establishment. This helps assure that proper safeguards are used during food production and service. The ability to prove that a food safety system was in place at the time a foodborne disease outbreak occurred has been deemed an acceptable defense in court cases where punitive damages have been sought by victims of foodborne illness.

Food Manager Certification

Several organizations including the Conference for Food Protection, the U.S. Food and Drug Administration, and the trade associations for food retailers have recommended food manager certification as a means of assuring that individuals in responsible charge of food establishments are knowledgeable about food safety. A **certified food manager** is a person who:

▲ is responsible for **identifying hazards** in the day-to-day operation of a food establishment that prepares, packages, serves, vends or otherwise provides food for human consumption

▲ **develops** or **implements** specific policies, procedures, or standards aimed at preventing foodborne illness

▲ **coordinates training, supervises** or **directs food preparation activities,** and **takes corrective action** as needed to protect the health of the consumer

▲ **conducts in-house self-inspection** of daily operations on a periodic basis to see that policies and procedures concerning food safety are being followed

A certified food manager will have to be able to demonstrate knowledge and skills in food protection management including the following areas:

- ▼ identification of foodborne illness
- ▼ describing the relationship between time and temperature and the growth of microorganisms the cause foodborne illness
- ▼ describing the relationship between personal hygiene and food safety
- ▼ describing methods for preventing food contamination from purchasing and receiving
- ▼ recognizing problems and potential solutions associated with facility, equipment, and layout in a food establishment
- ▼ recognize problems and solutions associated with temperature control, preventing cross-contamination, housekeeping and maintenance

Some state and municipal agencies already require certification of food managers, and others are considering it. Currently, Florida, Connecticut, Idaho, Illinois, Texas, Rhode Island, and Wisconsin require food manager certification. Some jurisdictions within 17 other states and the District of Columbia also have mandatory certification.

Most certification programs require managers to pass a written food safety examination. These examinations are designed to link food safety theory to practice. By passing a certification examination, the food manager is able to demonstrate proficiency in food protection management. The following organizations/ agencies offer food sanitation exams for certification:

David Cox, President
Professional Testing Inc.
1200 Hillcrest Street, Suite 300
Orlando, FL 32803-4717
407-894-6405
Fax: 407-894-8164
davcox@juno.com

Anthony W. Mitchell, Ph.D.
National Assessment Institute
5500 Rio Vista Dr.
Clearwater, FL 34620-3144
813-535-3775
Fax: 813-532-9989

Louise Miller
Manager of Certification and Instructional Services
Educational Foundation of the National Restaurant Assn.
250 S. Wacker Drive, Suite 1400
Chicago, IL 60606-5834
1-800-765-2122, ext. 703
Fax: 312-715-1217

Mr. Kevin Hawley
Program Management and Development Senior Associate
Chauncy Group International
Room 349
506 Carnegie Center
Princeton, NJ 08540
609-951-6168
Fax: 609-951-6767

Some managers will seek training before they take a certification examination. Some jurisdictions require training before testing, others want the test alone. Training can involve participating in a formal course, or it could involve using a non-traditional approach such as home study, correspondence, distance learning, and interactive computer programming.

This book has been written as a teaching tool to be used in conjunction with traditional and non-traditional food manager certification programs. Like the manager certification examinations, it links theory to practice. The authors of this book recognize that knowing about food safety is not enough. You must also be able to apply the principles and practices that promote the safety of food preparation and service.

Summary

In the case study presented at the beginning of this chapter you learned that *Salmonella enteritidis* is a common cause of foodborne illness. The bacteria were provided conditions that enabled them to grow. First, the pies were only cooled for two and a half hours after baking. The internal temperatures did not reach acceptable cold storage temperatures (41°F, 5°C or below). Added to that, the pies were "temperature abused" (not refrigerated) during transport and during and after the outing. This provided optimal time and temperature, and the *Salmonella enteritidis* bacteria grew very rapidly under these conditions resulting in high levels of contamination.

Everyone who works in a food establishment must understand that foodborne illness is *preventable*. It is the duty of every food establishment operator, manager, and employee to serve safe and wholesome food to their customers. Failure to do so can have serious financial impact on your establishment, and may cost you your job.

You can protect the health and safety of your customers by developing and implementing effective food safety and sanitation practices within your establishment. In the following chapters, you will learn more about how food is contaminated and what actions are needed to prevent, control and eliminate the agents that most frequently cause foodborne illness and spoilage.

Discussion Questions

1. Discuss the role of government in food safety programs.

2. Define *sanitation, contamination.*

3. List some examples of *food establishments.*

4. Does national news media coverage have any effect on food safety issues?

5. What is a *foodborne disease outbreak?*

6. Discuss menu item trends and what impact they might have on food safety.

7. How does food safety affect the young, elderly, pregnant women, and those with immune system problems?

8. Discuss how certification of food managers could affect food safety?

9. Identify some reasons to implement food safety programs in food establishments.

10. Discuss some reason(s) you are studying food safety and sanitation.

Answers to the multiple choice and true/false questions are provided in Appendix A.

Quiz 1.1 (Multiple Choice)

1. What is the estimated number of cases of foodborne illness that happen in the U.S. each year?

    a. 0-500 thousand

    b. 20-23 million

    c. 24-81 million

    d. 85-100 billion

2. The cost of foodborne illness in the U.S. is estimated to be between:

    a. $7.7 and $23 billion.

    b. $24 and $95 billion.

    c. $3.3 and $900 million.

    d. $35 and $88 million.

3. CDC reports show that in most foodborne illness outbreaks, mishandling of the suspect food occurred within:

    a. the transportation segment of the industry.

    b. the retail segment of the industry.

    c. the food manufacturing segment of the industry.

    d. the food production segment of the industry.

4. Popular food trends and a larger variety of food items from around the world and new methods of preserving or packaging food:

    a. pose new challenges for food safety practices.

    b. have no impact on food safety issues.

    c. decrease the need for new food processing equipment.

    d. are passing fads and require little adjustment in food handling practices.

5. How does the *Food Code* affect individual states and jurisdictions?

    a. The *Code* became a Federal law as soon as it was published.

    b. There is no difference since it was merely an update of the *1976 Code*.

    c. It provides a model for new laws and rules in states and jurisdictions.

    d. It validates current practices.

Quiz 1.2 (True/False)

Answer questions 1-5 with either True or False.

1. The Hazard Analysis Critical Control Point System is only used to monitor food processing in manufacturing plants.

2. Certification of food managers and handlers refers to screening done for health problems.

3. Regulatory agencies are assigned the task of monitoring the production and processing of food from harvest to the consumer.

4. The term Food Establishment includes any site where food is processed, prepared, sold, or served.

5. Bacteria cause most foodborne illnesses.

References/Suggested Readings

Branwart, G.J. (1989). *Basic Food Microbiology*. New York, NY: Van Nostrand and Rheinhold.

Centers for Disease Control and Prevention (1996). *Surveillance for Foodborne Disease Outbreaks—United States, 1988-1992*. Atlanta, GA; U.S. Department of Health and Human Services.

Food and Drug Administration (1997). *1997 Food Code*. Washington, D.C.: United States Public Health Service.

Ronsivalli, L.J., andE.R. Vieira (1992). *Elementary Food Science*. New York, NY: Champan and Hall.

Potter, N., and J. Hotchkiss (1995) *Food Science* (3rd ed.). New York, NY: Chapman and Hall.

Rue, N., and National Assessment Institute, (1994). *Handbook For Safe Food Service Management*. Englewood Cliffs, NJ: Prentice Hall.

Spears, M.C. (1995). *Foodservice Organization: A Managerial Approach* (3rd ed.). Englewood Cliffs, NJ: Prentice Hall.

2 HAZARDS TO FOOD SAFETY

A Case of Bad Potato Salad

In Albuquerque, New Mexico, a well-known food establishment, identified as Restaurant A, had been packing customers in for years. The owners took pride in keeping the establishment spotlessly clean and serving thousands of thick juicy steaks and gigantic Idaho potatoes daily.

When some baked potatoes were left at closing time, they were stored on a kitchen counter or shelf overnight. The next morning, the salad chefs would arrive to peel, dice, and mix the leftover potatoes with other ingredients to make the side order special of the day: Potato Salad. This had been a standard practice for years. The finished product was containerized and chilled before serving at noon.

One day, the potato salad was made and served as usual. Customers came in for lunch and some ate potato salad as usual. The next day, 34 customers were hospitalized for botulism; two died. Before this incident, the Food and Drug Administration (FDA) defined Potentially Hazardous Foods (PHF) as any moist, high protein food capable of supporting rapid germ growth. After this deadly incident, the FDA included cooked potatoes in the list of PHFs!

Just how did those people get botulism from potato salad? The germ, Clostridium botulinum, comes from the soil and can be found on just about any food. However, it is usually in its spore, or dormant form to protect itself from the deadly oxygen in the air. Although the potatoes were washed and scrubbed before baking, some botulinum spores still remained on the skins. (You can never totally get rid of microscopic bacterial spores by washing!) The cooking process heat- activated the spores. This means that when the potatoes had been given enough time to cool off, the spores turned into their vegetative, or non-dormant, forms and started reproducing.

To test for doneness, the cooks poked forks into the potatoes. That action carried some of the botulinum spores from the skins into the moist *oxygen-free insides of the potatoes. When you cook food, you drive out the oxygen from the food mass. Also, the heat of cooking cannot kill bacterial spores. The spores could then turn vegetative, start reproducing, and release toxin as the germs grew.*

In all the years that Restaurant A saved leftover potatoes to make salad, C. botulinum had not turned vegetative. That night in 1976, it did. All it took to destroy the reputation of the food establishment was that one incident. This tragedy did not have to happen—if they had only known how to handle the leftover potatoes...,

Learning Objectives

After reading this chapter, you should be able to:

▲ Identify the three main types of foodborne hazards and give examples of each

▲ Discuss how the three classes of foodborne illness cause disease

▲ List the factors that promote bacterial growth in foods

▲ Identify the food temperature danger zone

▲ Explain how temperatures in the danger zone affect bacterial growth

▲ Identify the major types of potentially hazardous foods and the characteristics that are common to this group of foods

Essential Terms

At risk	Mesophilic
	Psychrophilic
Acidic	Thermophilic
	Parasite
Alkaline	Pathogenic
	Virus
Bacteria	Spore
Aerobic	Vegetative state
Anaerobic	
Binary fission	Biological hazards
Facultative anaerobic	
Inherent	Chemical hazards
FATTOM	Toxin-mediated infection

Infection

Ingestion

Intoxication

Onset time

pH

Physical hazards

Potable water

Potentially Hazardous Foods

Ready-to-eat foods

Spoilage

Spore

Temperature abused

Temperature Danger Zone

Toxin

Vegetative cells

Water activity (A_w)

Types of bacteria:
Bacillus cereus
Campylobacter jejuni
    Clostridium perfringens
    Clostridium botulinum
    Escherichia coli
    Listeria monocytogenes
Salmonella spp.
Shigella spp.
Staphylococcus aureus
Vibrio spp.

Types of viruses:
Hepatitis A
Norwalk virus group
Rotavirus

Types of parasites:
Anisakis spp.
Cryptosporidium parvum
Giardia lamblia
Trichinella spiralis

Foodborne Illness

Have you ever had a foodborne illness? Many of us have, but it did not last long enough to be diagnosed. We think we have the "stomach flu" or a "24 hour bug" of some kind.

Did you become nauseated, feel abdominal pain and cramping, diarrhea, and even start vomiting? It could be foodborne illness. When this happens, do you think it is from eating or drinking too much? If you are far from home, do you blame the "strange water"?

What you experience is often a foodborne illness. The symptoms are often similar to those associated with the flu. The type of organism, how much contamination is in the food, and the general condition of the affected person determine the severity of symptoms.

General symptoms of foodborne illness usually include one or more of the following:

▲ Headache	▲ Abdominal pain
▲ Nausea	▲ Diarrhea
▲ Vomiting	▲ Fatigue
▲ Dehydration	▲ Fever

Foodborne illness is generally classified as a foodborne infection, intoxication, or toxin-mediated infection (Figure 2.1). Your awareness of how different microbes cause foodborne illness will help you understand how they contaminate food.

Infection	caused by eating food that contains living disease-causing microorganisms.
Intoxication	caused by eating food that contains a harmful chemical or toxin produced by bacteria or other source.
Toxin-Mediated Infection	caused by eating a food that contains harmful microorganisms that will produce a toxin once inside the human gut.

Figure 2.1—Classification of Foodborne Illness

When a living, disease-causing microorganism is eaten along with a food, it can cause a **foodborne infection**. After ingestion, the organism burrows into the lining of the victim's digestive tract and begins to grow in number. This can lead to the common symptoms of foodborne illness like diarrhea. Sometimes, the organisms may spread to other parts of the body through the blood stream. Bacteria, viruses, and parasites are examples of microorganisms that can cause infection. The most common type of foodborne infection is *Salmonellosis.* This disease is caused by *Salmonella* bacteria frequently found in poultry and eggs.

An **intoxication** is caused when a living organism multiplies in or on a food and produces a chemical waste or toxin. If the food containing the toxin is eaten, the toxin causes an illness. Typically called food poisoning, common examples of food intoxications are *Clostridium botulinum* and *Staphylococcus aureus*. An intoxication may also occur when an individual consumes food that contains toxic chemicals such as cleaning agents or pesticides.

A **toxin-mediated infection** is caused when a living organism is consumed with food (as in the case of an infection). Once the organism is inside the human body (usually in the large intestine) it produces a toxin that causes the illness. A toxin-mediated infection is different from an intoxication because the toxin is produced inside the human body. An example of an organism that causes this type of illness is *Clostridium perfringens*.

Foodborne illnesses have different onset times. The **onset time** is the number of hours between the time a person eats contaminated food and when they first show symptoms of the disease. This is usually expressed in a range of hours since individual onsets vary depending on factors such as age, health status, body weight, and the amount of contaminant they ingested with the food. However, for some foodborne diseases, such as trichinosis and Hepatitis A, the onset time can be several days.

Under the right circumstances, anyone can become ill from eating contaminated foods. In most cases, healthy adults will have flu-like symptoms and recover in a few days.

However, the risks and dangers associated with foodborne illness are much greater for certain members of the population. Those at risk include infants and young children, the elderly, pregnant women, those with suppressed immune systems as occurs with acquired immune deficiency syndrome (AIDS), cancer, diabetes, and people taking certain medications. For these individuals, the symptoms and duration of foodborne illness can be much more severe, even life threatening.

Foodborne Hazards

A **foodborne hazard** refers to a biological, chemical, or physical hazard that can grow in, or be carried by, food and causes illness or injury when consumed along with the food.

Biological hazards include bacteria, viruses, and parasites. These organisms are very small and can only be seen with the aid of a microscope. Biological hazards are commonly associated with humans and with raw products entering the food establishment. **Bacteria** are single-celled microorganisms that require food, moisture and warmth to reproduce. Bacteria can cause foodborne infections, intoxications, and toxin-mediated infections. Many of these organisms occur naturally in the environment where foods are grown. Most are destroyed by adequate cooking and numbers are kept to a minimum by adequate cooling during product distribution and storage.

Biological hazards are by far the most important foodborne hazard in any type of food establishment. They cause most foodborne illnesses and are the primary target of a food safety program.

Chemical hazards are toxic substances that may occur naturally or may be added during the processing of food. Examples of chemical contaminants include agricultural chemicals (i.e., pesticides, fertilizers, antibiotics), cleaning compounds, heavy metals (lead and mercury), and food additives. Harmful chemicals at very high levels have been associated with severe poisonings. Chemicals and other non-food items should never be placed near food items.

Physical hazards are hard or soft foreign objects in food that can cause illness and injury. They include items such as fragments of glass, metal, unfrilled toothpicks, jewelry, adhesive bandages, and human hair. These hazards result from accidental contamination and poor food handling practices that can occur at many points in the food chain from the source to the consumer.

Bacteria

Bacteria are the most important biological foodborne hazard for any food establishment. They are responsible for more cases of foodborne illness than any other hazard.

All bacteria exist in a vegetative state. **Vegetative cells** grow, reproduce, and produce wastes just like other living organisms.

Some bacteria have the ability to form spores. **Spores** help bacteria survive when their environment is too hot, cold, dry, acidic, or when there is not enough food. Spores are not able to grow or reproduce.

However, when conditions become ideal for growth, the spore will germinate much like a seed. The bacterial spore can then return to the vegetative state and begin to grow again. Bacteria can survive for many months as spores. Also, it is much harder to destroy bacteria when they are in a spore form (Figure 2.2).

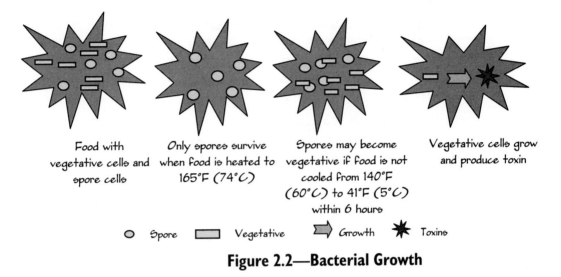

Food with vegetative cells and spore cells

Only spores survive when food is heated to 165°F (74°C)

Spores may become vegetative if food is not cooled from 140°F (60°C) to 41°F (5°C) within 6 hours

Vegetative cells grow and produce toxin

○ Spore   ▭ Vegetative   ⇨ Growth   ✳ Toxins

Figure 2.2—Bacterial Growth

Stress Conditions for Bacteria

Bacteria experience stress when they do not have the right environment. Bacteria are classified as either spoilage or pathogenic (disease-causing) microorganisms (Figure 2.3).

Spoilage bacteria degrade (break down) foods so that they look, taste, and smell bad. They reduce the quality of food to unacceptable levels which cause waste.

Pathogenic bacteria are disease-causing microorganisms that can make people ill if they or their toxins are consumed with food.

Both spoilage and pathogenic bacteria must be controlled in food establishments. The steps you take to keep foods safe from disease-causing bacteria will also improve the culinary quality and shelf life of the food.

	Vegetative State (Under Optimal Conditions)	**Spore State** (Under Stress Conditions)
Reproduce	Yes	No
Grow	Yes	No
Produce Toxin	Yes	No
Resistant to Stress	No	Yes
Harmful if Eaten	Yes	No

Figure 2.3—The Vegetative and Spore States of Bacteria Cells

Bacterial Growth

Bacteria reproduce when one bacterial cell divides to form two new cells. This process is called **binary fission**. The reproduction of bacteria and an increase in the number of organisms, is referred to as bacterial growth (Fig.2.4).

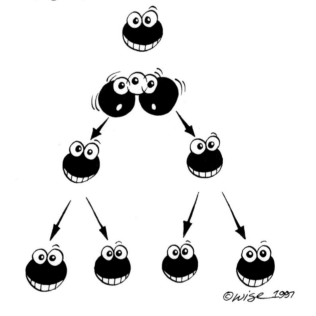

©wise 1997

Figure 2.4—Division of Bacterial Cells

What Bacteria Need for Growth

Bacteria need six conditions for growth. They need a source of food, a mildly acid environment (pH of 4.6 - 7.0), temperature between 41°F and 140°F (5° and 60°C), time, different oxygen requiring environments, and enough moisture. These requirements can be remembered using the acronym **F-A-T-T-O-M** (Figure 2.5). Since many foods naturally contain microorganisms, we need to be sure to control these six conditions as much as possible to prevent bacterial growth.

Food	Foods high in protein
Acid	Foods with pH 4.6 or higher
Temperature	41°F to 140°F (5° to 60°C)
Time	At least four hours cumulative time to allow bacteria to grow to high enough numbers to cause illness
Oxygen	Aerobic, anaerobic, facultative anaerobic, microaerophilic
Moisture	Water activity (A_w) of 0.85 or higher

Figure 2.5—Six Conditions for Bacterial Growth (FATTOM)

Bacterial growth follows a regular pattern that consists of four phases (Figure 2.6). The first phase is the *lag phase* in which the bacteria exhibit little or no growth. The bacteria adjust to their surroundings during the lag phase. The lag phase lasts only a few hours at room temperature. However, the duration of this phase can be increased by keeping foods at 41°F (5°C) or below.

The second phase of bacterial growth is the *log phase*. Bacterial growth is very rapid during the log phase with bacteria doubling in numbers every few minutes. Keeping bacteria from reaching the log phase of growth is critical for food safety.

The third phase of bacterial growth is the *stationary phase*. The number of new bacteria being produced equals the number of organisms that are dying off during this phase. The bacteria have used up much of the space, nutrients, and moisture in the food by this phase of the growth curve.

The final phase in the growth curve is the *decline phase*. Here bacteria die off rapidly because they lack nutrients and are poisoned by their own toxic wastes

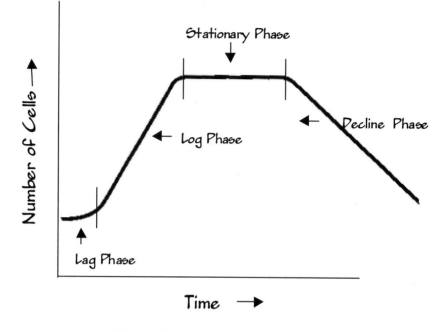

Figure 2.6—Bacterial Growth Curve

Source of Food

A suitable food supply is the most important condition needed for bacterial growth. Most bacteria prefer foods that are high in protein like meats, poultry, seafood, dairy products (Figure 2.7) and cooked rice, beans, and potatoes.

Figure 2.7—Foods that Support the Growth of Bacteria

Acidity

The **pH** symbol is used to designate the acidity or alkalinity of a food. The scale for measuring pH ranges from 0 to 14 (Figure 2.8).

A pH of less than 7.0 indicates the food is "**acidic.**" For example, lemons and limes are acidic. Very acid foods (pH of 4.5 or below) like citrus fruits and tomatoes, will not normally support the growth of disease-causing bacteria. Pickling fruits and vegetables preserves the food by adding enough vinegar to suppress bacterial growth.

A pH above 7.0 indicates the food is "**alkaline.**" Examples of alkaline foods are olives, egg whites, or soda crackers.

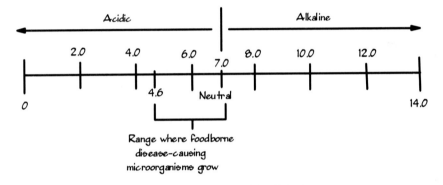

Figure 2.8—The pH Scale

Most bacteria prefer a neutral environment (pH of 7.0) but are capable of growing in foods that have a pH in the range of 4.6 to 9.0. Since most foods have a pH of less than 7.0, we have identified the range where harmful bacteria grow as from 4.6 to 7.0. Many of the foods offered for sale in food establishments have a pH in this range (Figure 2.9).

Disease-causing bacteria grow best when the food they live in and on has a pH of 4.6 to 7.0. Milk, meat, and fish are in this range.

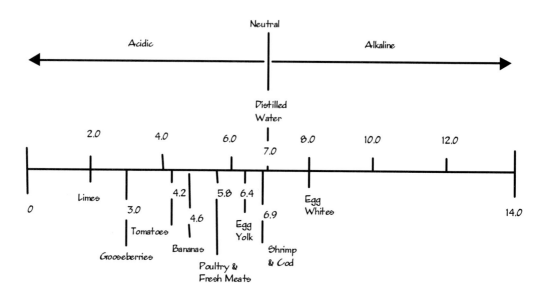

**Figure 2.9—Acidity Range of Common Foods Prepared
in Food Establishments**

Temperature

All bacteria do not have the same temperature requirements for
growth. **Psychrophilic** (cold loving) bacteria grow within a
temperature range of 32° to 70°F (0° to 21°C). These
microorganisms are especially troublesome because they are capable
of growing at both refrigerated and room temperatures. Most
psychrophilic bacteria are spoilage organisms, but some can cause
disease.

Mesophilic (middle range) bacteria grow at temperatures between
70° and 110°F (21° and 43°C) with most rapid growth at human
body temperature (98.6°F, 37°C).

Bacteria that grow best at temperatures above 110°F (43°C) are
called **thermophilic** organisms. Most thermophilic bacteria are
spoilage organisms.

**Time and temperature are the most critical factors affecting the
growth of bacteria in foods.** Most disease-causing bacteria can grow
within a temperature range of 41° to 140°F (5° to 60°C). This is
commonly referred to as the food **"Temperature Danger Zone"**
(Figure 2.10). Some disease-causing bacteria, such as *Listeria*

monocytogenes, can grow at temperatures below 41°F (5°C), but the rate of growth is very slow.

Careful monitoring of time and temperature is the most effective means a food establishment manager can take to control the growth of disease-causing and spoilage bacteria. A saying related to temperature control in the food industry is "Keep it hot, keep it cold, or don't keep it!" This means all cold foods must be stored at 41°F (5°C) or below and all hot foods held at 140°F (60°C) or above. **Temperature abused** is the term applied to foods that have not been heated to a safe temperature or kept at the proper temperatures and could, therefore, cause foodborne illness.

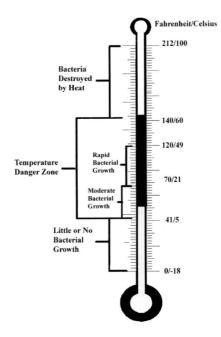

Figure 2.10—Temperature Control Guide

Time

Under ideal conditions, *bacterial cells can double in number every 15 to 30 minutes. Clostridium perfringens* bacteria can double every 10 minutes (Longrèe and Armbruster, 1996). For most bacteria, a single cell can generate over 1 million cells in just 5 hours (Figure 2.11). It is very important not to give bacteria an opportunity to grow. Proper storage and handling of foods helps to prevent bacterial growth.

Time	0	15 min.	30 min.	60 min.	3 hrs.	5 hrs.
# of cells	1	2	4	16	>1000	>1 million

Figure 2.II—Bacterial Growth Time

Because bacteria have the ability to multiply rapidly, it does not take long before many cells are produced. A rule of thumb in the foodservice industry is that **bacteria need about four hours to grow to high enough numbers to cause illness**. This includes total time that a food is between 41° and 140°F (5° and 60°C). Remember, a single bacterial cell can produce over one million cells in just five hours under ideal conditions.

Oxygen

Bacteria also differ in their requirements for oxygen. **Aerobic** bacteria *must* have oxygen in order to grow. **Anaerobic** bacteria, however, cannot survive when free oxygen is present because it is toxic to them. Anaerobic bacteria grow well in vacuum packaged foods or canned foods where oxygen is not available. Anaerobic conditions also exist in the middle of cooked food masses such as in large stock pots, baked potatoes, or in the middle of a roast or ham.

Facultative anaerobic forms of bacteria can grow *with* or *without* free oxygen but have a preference. Most foodborne disease-causing microorganisms are facultative anaerobes.

Microaerophilic organisms demand a very specific oxygen requirement usually in the range of three to six percent.

Controlling oxygen conditions may not be an effective way to prevent foodborne illness. Regardless of available oxygen, some disease-causing bacteria will find the conditions suitable for growth.

Moisture

Like most other forms of life, moisture is an important factor in bacterial growth. That is why man has dried foods for thousands of years as a way to preserve them.

Scientists have determined that it is not the percentage of moisture or "water by volume" in a food that most affects bacterial growth. Rather it is the amount of "available water" or water available for bacterial activity which is expressed as **water activity** and is designated with the symbol A_w. Water activity is a measure of the amount of water that is not bound to the food and is therefore available for bacterial growth (Figure 2.12).

For example, a fresh chicken has 60% water by volume and A_w is ~ .98. The same chicken, when frozen, still has 60% water by volume but Aw is now "0." Water activity is measured on a scale from 0-1.0. **Disease-causing bacteria can only grow in foods that have a water activity of .85 or higher**. Many foods are preserved by lowering their water activity to below .85. Drying foods or adding solids like salt or sugar reduces the amount of available water.

0		0.75	crisp cooked bacon
0.1		0.8	
0.2		0.82	dried beef
0.3		0.85	**Minimum required for bacterial growth**
0.4		0.9	
0.5	dried egg noodles	0.92	mayonnaise, raw bacon
0.59	honey	0.94	American cheese
0.6		0.98	steamed rice, chicken leg muscle, raw beef, halibut
0.67	flour	0.99	egg yolk/egg white
0.7		1.00	distilled water

Figure 2.12 Water Activity (A_w) of Common Foods Prepared in Food Establishments (Adapted from Applied Foodservice Sanitation, 1992)

Potentially Hazardous Foods (PHF)

Some types of foods have the ability to support the rapid and progressive growth of infectious and toxin-producing microorganisms. These foods are called "potentially hazardous." **Potentially hazardous foods (PHF)** are usually high in protein *and* have a pH of 4.6 or above *and* a water activity of .85 or higher.

Common examples of potentially hazardous foods are red meats, poultry and eggs, fish and shellfish, and dairy products. Other potentially hazardous foods are vegetables such as cooked rice or potatoes, refried beans, and fruits such as cut cantaloupe.

The Food Code classifies the following as Potentially Hazardous Foods:

▲ foods of animal-origin

▲ foods of plant origin that are heat-treated or consist of raw seed sprouts

▲ cut melons

▲ garlic and oil mixtures

Potentially hazardous foods always require special handling. If these foods are held at temperatures between 41° and 140°F (5° and 60°C) for four hours or more, harmful microorganisms can grow to dangerous levels. Potentially hazardous foods have been associated with most foodborne disease outbreaks. It is critical that you control the handling and storage of potentially hazardous foods to prevent bacterial growth.

Ready-to-Eat Foods

Ready-to-eat foods can also cause foodborne illness. These types of foods can become contaminated if not handled properly. They include raw or processed products that can be eaten immediately. Examples of ready-to-eat foods include:

▲ vegetables

▲ salad items

▲ hard-boiled eggs

▲ delicatessen items

Foodborne Illness Caused by Bacteria

In *Essentials of Food Safety and Sanitation*, bacteria are classified as *sporeforming* bacteria and *non-sporeforming* bacteria. In the following sections, each type of biological hazard is described, the common foods and route of transmission are identified, and preventive strategies are discussed. In Figure 2.13, common biological hazards are listed.

Bacillus cereus

Campylobacter jejuni

Clostridium perfringens

Clostridium botulinum

Escherichia coli

Listeria monocytogenes

Salmonella spp.

Shigella spp.

Staphylococcus aureus

Vibrio spp.

Hepatitis A

Norwalk virus group

Rotavirus

Anisakis spp.

Cryptosporidium parvum

Giardia lamblia

Trichinella spiralis

Figure 2.13—Common Biological Hazards in Food Establishments

Foodborne Illness Caused by Sporeforming Bacteria

The following group of bacteria are all capable of forming spores. A **spore** structure enables a cell to survive environmental stress such as cooking, freezing, high-salt conditions, drying, and high-acid conditions (Figure 2.14).

Spores are not harmful if ingested, except in a baby's digestive system, where *Clostridium botulinum* spores can cause infant botulism. However, if conditions of the food are changed and the spore turns into a vegetative cell, the vegetative cell can grow in the food and cause illness if eaten.

Sporeforming bacteria are generally found with foods that are grown in soil, like vegetables and spices. They may also be found in animal products. They can be particularly troublesome in food establishments. When environmental conditions improve, spores can become vegetative cells.

For example, a 10-gallon pot of chili was prepared for the next day's lunch. All the ingredients (beans, meat, spices, tomato base) were mixed together and cooked to a rapid boil. Vegetative cells die, but spores may survive.

Figure 2.14 Well-Protected Spores

The chili was stored in the 10-gallon pot and allowed to cool overnight in a walk-in refrigerator. It can take the core temperature of the chili 2 to 3 days to cool from 140° to 41°F (60°C to 5°C). If given enough time at the right temperature during the cooling process, sporeforming bacteria that survived the cooking process may change into vegetative cells and begin to grow.

Spores are most likely to turn vegetative when:

▲ **heat-shocked** (cooked)

▲ optimum conditions exist for growth (**high protein, high moisture**)

▲ temperatures are in the **food temperature danger zone** (between 41° to 140°F; 5° to 60°C)

▲ when the amount of time food is in the **danger zone is 4 hours or more**

To prevent sporeforming bacteria from changing to the dangerous vegetative state, it is critical that hot food temperatures

be maintained at 140°F (60°C) or above and cold foods should be held at 41°F (5°C) or below. Always cook and cool foods as rapidly as possible to limit bacterial growth.

Bacillus cereus

CAUSATIVE AGENT (* sporeforming bacteria)	TYPE OF ILLNESS	SYMPTOMS ONSET	COMMON FOODS	PREVENTION
Bacillus cereus	Bacterial intoxication or toxin-mediated infection	1) Diarrhea, abdominal cramps (8-16 hrs) 2) Vomiting type- vomiting, diarrhea, abdominal cramps (30 min.-6 hrs)	1) Diarrhea type - meats, milk, vegetables 2) Vomiting type- rice, starchy foods, grains and cereals	Properly heat, cool, and reheat foods

Description—*Bacillus cereus* is a sporeforming bacterium that can live with or without oxygen. It has been associated with two very different types of illnesses: one vomiting, the other diarrhea.

Symptoms and Onset Time—Depending on the type of toxin that is produced by the bacteria on the food, the illness will be either a vomiting type or diarrhea type problem. Nausea and abdominal cramps may also be associated with either type. The onset time for the vomiting type disease is 30 minutes to 6 hours, and it usually lasts a day or less. The onset time for the diarrhea type disease is 8 to 16 hours, and it lasts for 12 to 14 hours.

Common Foods—The vomiting type of illness is usually associated with grain products such as rice, potatoes, pasta, corn, cornstarch, soybeans, tofu, and flour. A wide variety of foods, including meats, milk, vegetables, and fish have been associated with the diarrheal type disease.

Transmission in Foods—Illness due to *Bacillus cereus* is most often attributed to foods that are improperly stored (cooled, hot-held), permitting the conversion of spores to vegetative cells. Vegetative cells then produce the toxin in the food that leads to illness.

Prevention—Foods must be cooked and, if not consumed immediately, held at 140°F (60°C) or above. Foods must also be cooled rapidly to below 41°F (5°C) prior to storage.

Clostridium perfringens

CAUSATIVE AGENT (* sporeforming bacteria)	TYPE OF ILLNESS	SYMPTOMS ONSET	COMMON FOODS	PREVENTION
Clostridium perfringens	Bacterial toxin-mediated infection	Intense abdominal pains and severe diarrhea, (8-22 hrs)	Spices, gravy, improperly cooled foods (especially meats and gravy dishes)	Properly cook, cool, and reheat foods

Description—*Clostridium perfringens* is an anaerobic (must not have oxygen), sporeforming bacterium that causes foodborne illness. Perishable foods that have been temperature abused (not kept hot-above 140°F, 60° C; or cold- below 41°F, 5°C) are frequently associated with this problem. *Clostridium perfringens* causes illness due to a toxin-mediated infection where the ingested cells colonize and then produce a toxin in the human intestinal tract.

Symptoms and Onset Time—*Clostridium perfringens* causes abdominal pain and diarrhea. The onset time is 8 to 22 hours and the illness usually lasts one day or less.

Common Foods—The organism is widely distributed and may be found in most foodstuffs. A common source of *Clostridium perfringens* is meat that has been boiled, steamed, braised, stewed, or insufficiently roasted, then allowed to cool slowly and served the next day either cold or improperly reheated.

Transmission in Foods—Illness due to *Clostridium perfringens* is most often attributed to foods that are temperature abused, especially those that have been improperly cooled and reheated.

Prevention—Foods must be cooked to 145°F (63°C) or above. Cooked foods must be cooled from 145° to 70°F (63° to 21°C) within 2 hours and from 70° to 41°F (21° to 5°C) in an additional four hours. Foods must also be reheated to 165°F (74°C) within 2 hours and held at 140°F (60°C) until served. Foods should be discarded after they have been reheated one time.

Clostridium botulinum

CAUSATIVE AGENT (* sporeforming bacteria)	TYPE OF ILLNESS	SYMPTOMS ONSET	COMMON FOODS	PREVENTION
Clostridium botulinum	Bacterial intoxication	Vertigo, double vision, difficulty in breathing and swallowing, headache (12-36 hrs)	Improperly canned foods, vacuum packed refrigerated foods; cooked foods in anaerobic mass.	Properly heat process anaerobically packed foods, DO NOT use home canned foods

Description—*Clostridium botulinum* is an anaerobic (must not have oxygen), sporeforming bacterium that causes foodborne intoxication due to improperly heat-processed foods (especially home-canning). The organism produces a **neurotoxin** which is one of the most deadly biological toxins known to man. This toxin is not heat stable and can be destroyed if the food is boiled for about 20 minutes. However, botulism still occurs because people do not want to boil food that has already been cooked.

Symptoms and Onset Time—Symptoms commonly associated with botulism are fatigue, headache, dizziness, visual disturbances, the inability to swallow, and respiratory paralysis. The onset time is 12 to 36 hours and the duration of the illness is several days to a year.

Common Foods—Low-acid foods (pH of 4.6 or above), that are inadequately heat-processed and then packaged anaerobically (can or vacuum pouch), and held in the food temperature danger zone. Examples would include home-canned green beans, meats, fish, and garlic or onions that are stored in oil and butter respectively. Botulinum toxin can be produced in 20 days at 41°F (5°C), 7 days at 50°F (10°C), and 3 days at 60°F (15°C). (See the *Food Code*.)

Transmission in Foods—Illness due to *Clostridium botulinum* is almost always attributed to ingestion of foods that were not heat processed correctly and packaged anaerobically.

Prevention—Do not use home-canned foods or buy foods from unapproved sources. Do not can or vacuum package foods in a food establishment. Discard damaged cans (see Chapter 4). The Food Code stipulates that a variance is required for any food establishment that prepares products in reduced-oxygen packaging.

Clostridium botulinum is not necessarily confined to foods canned or bottled at home. Anaerobic conditions created in hot-food masses which are not cooled properly can become contaminated. For example, a "perpetual" butter stockpot in the corner of the griddle, the advanced cooking of a mass of chopped onions in butter or oil and held on a griddle, or "baked" potatoes left to cool without refrigeration are all capable of producing *Clostridium botulinum* toxin. (Refer to the case study at the beginning of this chapter.)

Foodborne Illness Caused by Non-Sporeforming Bacteria

The following group of bacteria do not form spores. That is, they stay in the vegetative state all the time. Compared to bacterial spores, vegetative cells are easily destroyed by proper cooking. There are numerous examples of non-sporeforming foodborne bacteria that are important in the food industry.

Campylobacter jejuni

CAUSATIVE AGENT	TYPE OF ILLNESS	SYMPTOMS ONSET	COMMON FOODS	PREVENTION
Campylobacter jejuni	Bacterial infection	Watery, bloody diarrhea (2-5 days)	Raw chicken, raw milk, raw meat	Properly handle and cook foods, avoid cross contamination

Description—*Campylobacter jejuni* is a major cause of foodborne infection. The organism is unique compared to most other foodborne pathogens because it requires a very strict amount of air for growth. As a microaerophile, it can tolerate only 3 to 6 percent oxygen for growth.

Symptoms and Onset Time—*Campylobacter jejuni* commonly causes abdominal pain and slight to severe bloody diarrhea. The onset time is 2 to 5 days. Symptoms of this disease usually last from 2 to 7 days.

Common Foods—This organism is commonly found in raw milk, raw poultry, and raw meats. Some scientists estimate that *Campylobacter jejuni* may be present in nearly 100% of all retail chickens.

Transmission in Foods—*Campylobacter jejuni* is often transferred from raw meats to other foods by cross contamination. This is typically done by transfer from a food contact surface (such as a cutting board or knife) or a food worker's hands.

Prevention—Cook raw meats properly. Thoroughly clean food contact surfaces (cutting boards) and wash hands thoroughly after handling raw foods.

Escherichia coli 0157:H7

CAUSATIVE AGENT	TYPE OF ILLNESS	SYMPTOMS ONSET	COMMON FOODS	PREVENTION
Escherichia coli 0157:H7	Bacterial infection or toxin-mediated infection	Hemolytic uremic syndrome (HUS), bloody diarrhea, kidney failure, (12-72 hrs)	Undercooked hamburger, raw milk, unpasteurized apple cider, lettuce	Practice good food sanitation, handwashing, properly handle and cook foods

Description—The *Escherichia coli* (or *E. coli*) group of bacteria includes four foodborne pathogens; enterotoxigenic *E. coli*, enteropathogenic *E. coli*, enterohemorrhagic *E. coli*, and enteroinvasive *E. coli*. Of particular importance is enterohemorrhagic *E. coli* called *E. coli 0157:H7*. This facultative anaerobic bacteria can be found in the intestines of warm-blooded animals, especially cows, and causes an infraction or a toxin-mediated infection.

Symptoms and Onset Time—Illness due to *E. coli* 0157:H7 is a threat to children up to 16 years old and the elderly. It can cause severe abdominal pain, nausea, vomiting, bloody diarrhea, kidney failure, and death. The organism burrows into the intestine and produces a toxin which coagulates the blood (especially in the kidneys) causing Hemolytic Uremic Syndrome (HUS). The infection usually begins with flu-like symptoms and fever followed by bloody diarrhea. The onset time is 12 to 72 hours and the illness usually lasts from 1 to 3 days.

Common Foods—This organism has been isolated in raw milk and in raw and undercooked beef and other red meats, improperly pasteurized milk, raw finfish, and prepared foods. Recent outbreaks were linked to lettuce, and unpasteurized apple cider.

Transmission in Foods—*E. coli 0157:H7* is usually transferred to foods like beef through contact with the intestines of slaughter animals. Apples used for juice from orchards where cattle or deer grazed is also suspected. Transmission can occur if employees who are carriers do not wash their soiled hands properly after going to the toilet. Cross contamination by soiled equipment and utensils may also spread *E. coli 0157:H7*.

Prevention—Cook ground meats to at least 155°F (68°C) or until all the juices run clear (Chapter 4). Make sure that employees wash their hands thoroughly before starting to work with food, and after going to the toilet. Prevent cross contamination and keep hot foods above 140°F (60°C) and cold foods below 41°F (5°C). Wash lettuce in sinks used only for food preparation. Use only pasteurized apple cider and milk products.

Listeria monocytogenes

CAUSATIVE AGENT	TYPE OF ILLNESS	SYMPTOMS ONSET	COMMON FOODS	PREVENTION
Listeria monocytogenes	*Bacterial infection*	1) Healthy adult: flu-like symptoms 2) At-risk population: septicemia, meningitis, encephalitis, birth defects3) Still-birth (1 day- 3 weeks)	Raw milk, dairy items, raw meats, refrigerated ready-to-eat foods, raw vegetables, and seafood	Properly store and cook foods, avoid cross contamination; rotate processed refrigerated foods using FIFO to assure timely use

Description—*Listeria monocytogenes* is a facultative anaerobic (can grow with or without oxygen) bacterium that causes foodborne infection. This microbe is important to foodservice operations because it has the ability to survive under many conditions such as in high-salt foods and, unlike most other foodborne pathogens, can grow at refrigerated temperatures (below 41°F; 5°C).

Symptoms and Onset Time—Listeriosis, the illness caused by *Listeria monocytogenes*, usually causes a flu-like disease in healthy adults. Symptoms include nausea, vomiting, headache, fever, chills, and backache. Complications from listeriosis can be life threatening (septicemia, meningitis, encephalitis, birth defects) for pregnant women, or the at-risk population such as the young, elderly, and those with weakened immune systems. The onset time is 1 day to 3 weeks and the duration of the disease is indefinite depending on when treatment is administered to the patient.

Common Foods—This organism is everywhere and has been isolated in many foods. It is most common in raw meats, raw poultry, dairy products (cheeses, ice cream, raw milk), raw vegetables, and seafood.

Transmission in Foods—Transmission to foods can occur by cross contamination or if foods are not cooked properly.

Prevention—Cook foods thoroughly and practice good food handling techniques. Specific practices for control are timely use and rotation of refrigerated products, such as cooked turkey breasts, hot dogs, hams, and luncheon meats.

Salmonella spp.

CAUSATIVE AGENT	TYPE OF ILLNESS	SYMPTOMS ONSET	COMMON FOODS	PREVENTION
Salmonella spp.	Bacterial infection	Nausea, fever, vomiting, abdominal cramps, diarrhea (6-48 hrs)	Raw meats, raw poultry, eggs, milk, dairy products	Properly cook foods, avoid cross contamination

Description—*Salmonella* are facultative anaerobic (grow with or without oxygen) bacteria frequently implicated as a foodborne infection. Like *E. coli 0157:H7*, *Salmonella* is found in the intestinal tracts of humans and warm-blooded animals. They frequently get into foods as a result of fecal contamination.

Symptoms and Onset Time—*Salmonella* infection produces abdominal pain, headache, nausea, vomiting, fever, and diarrhea. The onset time is 6 to 48 hours and the disease generally lasts 2-3 days.

Common Foods—This organism is inherent to many foods, especially raw meat and poultry products, eggs, milk, dairy products, pork, chocolate, and cream-filled desserts.

Transmission in Foods—Transmission to foods is commonly through cross contamination where fecal material is transferred to food through contact with raw foods (especially poultry), contaminated food contact surfaces (i.e., cutting boards), or infected food handlers. The incidence of salmonellosis has risen more than twenty-fold since 1946. One reason may be the increased number of centrally processed foods along with bulk distribution (Longrèe and Armbruster, 1996).

Prevention—Cook foods thoroughly. Clean and sanitize food contact surfaces after use with raw foods; and make sure food handlers wash hands adequately before working with food, especially after going to the toilet.

Shigella spp.

CAUSATIVE AGENT	TYPE OF ILLNESS	SYMPTOMS ONSET	COMMON FOODS	PREVENTION
Shigella spp.	Bacterial infection	Bacillary dysentery, diarrhea, fever, abdominal cramps, dehydration, (1-7 days)	Foods that are prepared with human contact, salads, raw vegetables, milk, dairy products, raw poultry, non-potable water, ready to eat meat	Wash hands and practice good personal hygiene, properly cook foods

Description—*Shigella* are facultative anaerobic bacteria that account for about ten percent of foodborne illnesses in the United States. The organism is commonly found in the intestines and feces of humans and warm-blooded animals. These microorganisms cause shigellosis, a foodborne infection. The bacterium lodges in the outer layer of the gut of humans and multiplies. It produces a toxin that reverses the absorption of water back into the body. Water flows into the gut and feces to cause watery diarrhea. Ulcerations of the gut lining produce bloody diarrhea.

Symptoms and Onset Time—*Shigellosis* causes diarrhea, fever, abdominal cramps, chills, fatigue, and dehydration. The onset time is 1 to 7 days and the duration of the disease frequently depends on when treatment is administered to the patient.

Common Foods—This organism is common in ready-to-eat salads (i.e., potato, chicken), milk and dairy products, poultry, raw vegetables, and any food contaminated by feces that contain the microbe.

Transmission in Foods—Water that is contaminated by fecal material and food and utensils handled by workers who are carriers of the bacteria can cause this problem.

Prevention—Do not allow individuals who have been diagnosed with shigellosis to handle food. Make certain that food handlers wash their hands thoroughly after going to the toilet. Cook foods to proper temperature and do not allow cross contamination. Wash produce and other foods with potable water (water that is safe to drink).

Staphylococcus aureus

CAUSATIVE AGENT	TYPE OF ILLNESS	SYMPTOMS ONSET	COMMON FOODS	PREVENTION
Staphylococcus aureus	Bacterial intoxication	Nausea, vomiting, abdominal cramps, headaches;(2-6 hrs)	Foods that are prepared with human contact, cooked or processed foods	Wash hands and practice good personal hygiene. Cooking WILL NOT inactivate the toxin

Description—*Staphylococcus aureus* is a facultative anaerobic bacterium that produces a heat stable toxin as it grows on foods. This bacterium can also grow on cooked, and otherwise safe, foods that are re-contaminated by food handlers who mishandle the food. *Staphylococcus aureus* bacteria do not compete well when other types of microorganisms are present. However, they grow well when alone and without competition from other microbes. *Staphylococcus aureus* bacteria produce toxins that cause an intoxication. These bacteria are commonly found on human skin, hands, hair, and in the nose and throat. They may also be found in burns, infected cuts and wounds, pimples, and boils. At any given time, *Staphylococcus aureus* bacteria can be found living in and on 30 to 50% of people, including those who are otherwise healthy. These organisms can be transferred to foods easily, and they can grow in foods that contain high salt or high sugar, and a lower water activity.

Symptoms and Onset Time—*Staphylococcus aureus* intoxication produces severe nausea, acute abdominal pain, vomiting and diarrhea. The onset time is 1 to 6 hours, usually 2 to 4 hours. The illness lasts 1-2 days.

Common Foods—This organism has been found in cooked ready-to-eat foods such as luncheon meats, ready-to-eat meat, vegetable and egg salads (like taco, potato, and tuna salad), meat, poultry, custards, high-salt foods like ham, and milk and dairy products.

Transmission in Foods—Since humans are the primary reservoir, contamination from the worker's hands is the most common way the organism is introduced into foods. Foods requiring considerable food preparation and handling are especially susceptible. The bacteria are also spread by droplets of saliva from talking, coughing, and sneezing near food. Food handlers who improperly use tasting spoons and ladles can transfer bacteria from their mouth to food.

Prevention—Avoid contamination of food from bare hands. Do not allow individuals who have infected cuts, burns, or wounds to handle food unless the wound has been properly bandaged and a plastic glove or similar barrier is used to cover the bandaged area. Make certain that food handlers wash their hands thoroughly before starting to work, and whenever their hands become contaminated. Do not allow food handlers to re-use tasting spoons and ladles. Heat and cool foods properly, and keep ready-to-eat foods out of the temperature danger zone.

Vibrio spp.

CAUSATIVE AGENT	TYPE OF ILLNESS	SYMPTOMS ONSET	COMMON FOODS	PREVENTION
Vibrio spp.	Bacterial infection	Headache, fever, chills, diarrhea, vomiting, severe electrolyte loss, gastroenteritis, (2-48 hrs)	Raw or improperly cooked fish and shellfish	Practice good sanitation, properly cook foods, avoid serving raw seafood

Description—There are three organisms within the *Vibrio* group of bacteria that have been connected with foodborne infections. They include *Vibrio cholera*, *Vibrio parahaemolyticus*, and *Vibrio vulnificus*. All are important since they are very resistant to salt and are common in seafood.

Symptoms and Onset Time—Foodborne illness from *Vibrio spp.* is characterized by diarrhea, abdominal cramps, nausea, vomiting, headache, fever, and chills. The onset time is 2 to 48 hours, and the disease typically lasts 2 to 3 days, but can be longer.

Common Foods—*Vibrio spp.* are commonly found in raw, under-processed, improperly handled, and contaminated fish and shellfish. Common vehicles of the bacteria are clams, oysters, crabs, shrimp, and lobster. These bacteria are more common in summer months and in seafood harvested from warmer waters. *Vibrio cholera* is spread by fecal contamination, especially in seafood that is harvested from polluted waters; *Vibrio vulnificus* bacteria are natural to certain saltwater species and can kill individuals in the at-risk population who have damaged livers. *Vibrio parahoemolyticus* is natural in certain species of saltwater fish and seafood.

Transmission in Foods—Since the organism is inherent in many raw seafoods, transmission to other foods by cross contamination is a concern. Most illnesses are caused due to the consumption of raw or undercooked seafood.

Prevention—Buy seafood from approved sources only. Cook seafood to the proper temperature, and avoid eating raw or lightly-cooked seafood, especially if you are in the at-risk segment of the population. Food handlers must practice good personal hygiene and use correct handwashing procedures.

Foodborne Illness Caused by Viruses

The viruses that cause foodborne disease differ from foodborne bacteria in several ways. **Viruses** are much smaller than bacteria, and they require a living host (human, animal) to grow and reproduce. Viruses do not reproduce or grow (multiply) in foods. A susceptible person needs to consume only a few viral particles in order to experience an infection.

The viruses are usually transferred from one food to another, from a food handler to a food, or from a contaminated water supply to a food. **A potentially hazardous food is not needed to support survival of viruses. Ready-to-eat foods are most frequently associated with viral infections.** There are three viruses that are of primary importance to food establishments: Hepatitis A, Norwalk, and Rotavirus. **Proper handwashing, especially after using the toilet, is the key to controlling the spread of foodborne viruses.**

Hepatitis A

CAUSATIVE AGENT	TYPE OF ILLNESS	SYMPTOMS ONSET	COMMON FOODS	PREVENTION
Hepatitis A	Viral infection	Fever, nausea, vomiting, abdominal pain, fatigue, swelling of the liver, jaundice (15-50 days)	Foods that are prepared with human contact; contaminated water	Wash hands and practice good personal hygiene; avoid raw seafood

Description—Hepatitis A is a foodborne virus that has been associated with many foodborne infections. Hepatitis A causes a liver disease called infectious hepatitis. The hepatitis virus is a particularly important hazard to food establishments because food handlers can harbor it for up to 6 weeks and not show symptoms of illness. Food workers are infectious for one week before onset of symptoms and two weeks after the symptoms of the disease appear. During that time, infected workers can contaminate foods and other workers by spreading fecal material from unwashed hand and nails.

Symptoms and Onset Time—The symptoms of infectious hepatitis are fever, nausea, vomiting, abdominal pain, and fatigue. Advanced stages of the disease cause swelling of the liver and possibly jaundice—a yellowing of the skin. The onset time for infectious hepatitis is 15 to 50 days after eating the contaminated food. A mild case of infectious hepatitis typically lasts several weeks. More severe cases can last several months.

Common Foods—Hepatitis A virus can be found in raw and lightly-cooked oysters and clams that are harvested from polluted waters. Also, raw vegetables that have been irrigated or washed with polluted water can be contaminated. Most potentially hazardous foods, if they are mishandled by a food worker who is infected with the Hepatitis A virus, can carry the microbe. Examples of these foods include prepared salads, sliced luncheon meats, salad-bar items, sandwiches, and bakery products. Due to the onset time, it is very difficult to identify the food source of Hepatitis A infection.

Transmission in Foods—The virus is transmitted by ingestion of food and water that contain the Hepatitis A virus.

Prevention—Handle foods properly and cook them to recommended temperatures. Avoid eating raw seafood. Food handlers must practice good personal hygiene and wash hands and fingernails thoroughly before working with food and after going to the toilet.

Norwalk virus

CAUSATIVE AGENT	TYPE OF ILLNESS	SYMPTOMS ONSET	COMMON FOODS	PREVENTION
Norwalk virus	Viral infection	Vomiting, diarrhea, abdominal pain, headache, low grade fever; onset 24-48 hrs.	Sewage contaminated water; contaminated salad ingredient, raw clams, oysters, and infected food handlers	Use potable water; cook all shellfish; handle food properly meet time temperature guidelines for PHF

Description—The Norwalk virus is another common foodborne virus that has been associated with many foodborne infections.

Symptoms and Onset Time—Common symptoms caused by Norwalk and Norwalk-like viruses are nausea, vomiting, diarrhea, and abdominal pain. Headache and low-grade fever may occur. A mild, brief illness usually develops 24 to 48 hours after contaminated food or water is consumed and lasts about one to three days. Severe illness is very rare.

Common Foods—Sewage-contaminated water is the most common source of Norwalk outbreaks. Shellfish and salad ingredients are the foods most often associated with this illness. Ingestion of raw or insufficiently-steamed clams and oysters poses a high risk for infection with Norwalk virus. Foods other than shellfish are contaminated by ill food handlers.

Transmission in Foods—The virus is primarily transmitted by ingestion of food and water that has been contaminated with feces that contain the Norwalk virus.

Prevention—Use potable water (safe to drink) when preparing shellfish. Handle foods properly and cook foods to the correct temperature. Avoid consumption of raw seafood. Food handlers must practice good personal hygiene and wash hands and fingernails thoroughly before working with food and after going to the toilet.

Rotavirus

CAUSATIVE AGENT	TYPE OF ILLNESS	SYMPTOMS ONSET	COMMON FOODS	PREVENTION
Rotavirus	Viral infection	Diarrhea (especially in infants and children), vomiting, low grade fever; 1-3 days onset; lasts 4-8 days	Sewage, contaminated water, contaminated salad ingredients, raw seafood	Good personal hygiene and handwashing; proper food handling practices

Description—Group A rotaviruses cause several diseases known as rotavirus gastroenteritis. Group A rotavirus is the leading cause of severe diarrhea among infants and children. Over 3 million cases of rotavirus gastroenteritis occur annually in the United States.

Symptoms and Onset Time—Individuals infected with rotavirus may experience mild to severe symptoms. Common symptoms of rotavirus gastroenteritis are vomiting, watery diarrhea, and low-grade fever. The onset time ranges from 1-3 days. Symptoms often start with vomiting followed by 4-8 days of diarrhea.

Common Foods—Infected food handlers may contaminate foods that require handling and no further cooking, such as salads and fruits.

Transmission in Foods—Person-to-person spread through contaminated hands is probably the most common means by which rotaviruses are transmitted in day care centers and family homes. Contaminated hands may spread the virus to foods that will not be cooked before eating.

Prevention—Cook foods to the proper temperature and handle properly. Food handlers must practice good personal hygiene and wash hands and fingernails thoroughly before working with food and after going to the toilet.

Foodborne Illness Caused by Parasites

Foodborne parasites are another important foodborne biological hazard. **Parasites** are small or microscopic creatures that need to live on or inside a living host to survive. There are many examples of parasites that can enter the food system and cause foodborne illness. In this chapter, we list a few of the most troublesome ones that may appear in food establishments. Parasitic infection is far less common than bacterial or viral foodborne illnesses.

Anisakis spp.

CAUSATIVE AGENT	TYPE OF ILLNESS	SYMPTOMS ONSET	COMMON FOODS	PREVENTION
Anisakis spp.	Parasitic infection	Coughing, vomiting	Raw or undercooked seafood-especially bottom feeding fish	Cook fish to the proper temperature throughout. Freeze to meet Code specification.

Description—*Anisakis spp.* are nematodes (roundworms) associated with foodborne infection from fish. The worms are about 1 - 1-1/2 inches long and the diameter of a human hair. They are beige, ivory, white, gray, brown, or pink. Other names for this parasite are "cod worm" (not to be confused with common roundworms found in cod) and "herring worm."

Symptoms and Onset Time—If the worms attach themselves to the victim's stomach, the typical symptoms are vomiting and abdominal pain. Coughing is the most common symptom if the worms attach themselves in the throat. When the worms attach themselves in the large intestine they produce sharp pain and fever, symptoms similar to those produced by appendicitis.

Common Foods—*Anisakis spp.* have been implicated in foodborne disease after consumption of raw or undercooked seafood. This organism has been found in bottom-feeding fish such as cod, haddock, fluke, salmon, herring, flounder, monkfish, plus sea urchins, crab, shrimp, starfish, and tuna. Cerviche or fresh seafood salad are known to carry this parasite.

Transmission in Foods—The natural hosts of the parasite are walruses, and perhaps sea lions and otters. The worms are transferred to fish, their intermediate host, in the water in which the walruses live. Humans become the accidental host upon eating fish that are infested with the parasites. Humans do not make good hosts for the parasites. The worms will not complete their life cycles in humans, and eventually die.

Prevention—Inspect seafood and handle it carefully to expose worms. Cook seafood to proper temperature.

Cryptosporidium parvum, Giardia lamblia

CAUSATIVE AGENT	TYPE OF ILLNESS	SYMPTOMS ONSET	COMMON FOODS	PREVENTION
Cryptosporidium parvum	Parasitic infection	Severe watery diarrhea within 1 week of ingestion	Contaminated water; food contaminated by infected food handlers	Use potable water supply; practice good personal hygiene and handwashing
Giardia lamblia	Parasitic infection	Diarrhea within 1 week of contact;	Contaminated water	Potable water supply; good personal hygiene and handwashing

Description—*Crytosporidium parvum* and *Giardia lamblia* are single-cell microorganisms called protozoa. *Cryptosporidium* is found in water that has been contaminated with cow feces. *Giardia* is found in the feces of wild animals, domestic pets, and infected persons. Both types of organisms can cause foodborne infection. These organisms are important sources of non-bacterial diarrhea in the United States.

Symptoms and Onset Time—The most common symptom of intestinal cryptosporidiosis is severe watery diarrhea, which usually lasts 2 to 4 days. Human giardiasis may cause diarrhea within one week of ingestion of the cyst. The illness may last as much as a month. The disease is more severe among the at-risk population.

Common Foods—These parasites are most commonly found in water and raw foods that have been polluted with sewage containing the cysts of *Cryptosporidium* or *Giardia*. *Cryptosporidium* could occur, theoretically, on any food touched by a contaminated food handler. Incidence is higher in child care centers that serve food. Fertilizing salad vegetables with manure is another possible source of human infection. Five outbreaks of giardiasis have been traced to food contamination by infected food handlers. Infections from contaminated vegetables that are eaten raw cannot be ruled out. Cool moist conditions favor the survival of the organism.

Transmission in Foods—These parasites could occur, theoretically, on any food touched by a contaminated food handler. They are primarily transmitted by a water supply that is contaminated with feces and by fecal contamination of food and food contact surfaces.

Prevention—Provide a potable water supply in the food establishment, and handle foods carefully to prevent contamination and cross contamination. Food handlers must practice good personal hygiene and wash hands thoroughly before working with food, and after going to the toilet.

Trichinella spiralis

CAUSATIVE AGENT	TYPE OF ILLNESS	SYMPTOMS ONSET	COMMON FOODS	PREVENTION
Trichinella spiralis	Parasitic infection from a nematode worm	Nausea, vomiting, diarrhea, sweating, muscle soreness(2-28 days)	Primarily undercooked pork products and wild game meats (bear, walrus)	Cook foods, to the proper temperature throughout

Description—*Trichinella spiralis* is a foodborne roundworm that causes a parasitic infection. It must be eaten with the infected fleshy muscle of certain meat-eating animals to be transmitted to a new host. This parasite does not exit the body in vomitus or fecal discharge.

Symptoms and Onset Time—The first symptoms of trichinosis are nausea, vomiting, diarrhea, and abdominal pain. Later stages of the disease are characterized by fever, swelling of tissues around the eyes, and muscle stiffness. The onset time is 2 to 28 days after eating the contaminated meat. Death may occur in severe cases.

Common Foods—Pork is by far the most common vehicle for *Trichinella spiralis*. However, it can also be found in wild-game animals, such as bear, walruses, and wild boar.

Transmission in Foods—This parasite is frequently carried by meat-eating, scavenger animals. These animals are exposed to the parasite when they eat infected tissues from other animals, and garbage that contains contaminated raw-meat scraps.

Prevention—Cook pork and wild-game animals to the proper temperature. Make certain there are no signs of pink color in cooked pork.

Foodborne Illness Caused by Chemicals

Chemical hazards are usually classified as either naturally occurring or man-made chemicals. Naturally occurring chemicals include toxins that are produced by a biological organism. Man-made chemicals include substances that are added, intentionally or accidentally, to a food during processing. Figure 2.15 provides a summary of some of the more common naturally occurring and man-made chemicals.

Naturally Occurring:	Ciguatoxin
	Mycotoxin
	Scombrotoxin
	Shellfish toxins
Man-Made Chemicals:	Cleaning solutions
	Food additives
	Pesticides
	Heavy metals

Figure 2.15—Types of Chemical Hazards in a Food Establishment
(Source: the Food Code)

Naturally Occurring Chemicals

Ciguatoxin

CAUSATIVE AGENT	TYPE OF ILLNESS	SYMPTOMS ONSET	COMMON FOODS	PREVENTION
Ciguatoxin	Fish toxin originating from toxic algae of tropical waters	Vertigo, hot/cold flashes, diarrhea, vomiting (30 min - 30 hours)	Marine finfish including groupers, barracuda, snappers, jacks, mackerel, triggerfish, reef fish	Purchase fish from a reputable supplier; cooking WILL NOT inactivate the toxin

Description—Ciguatoxin poisoning is an example of an intoxication caused by eating contaminated tropical reef fish. The toxin is found in tiny, free-swimming sea creatures called algae which live among certain coral reefs. When the toxic algae are eaten by small reef fish, it is stored in the flesh, skin, and organs. When the small reef fish are eaten by bigger fish such as mackerel, mahi, bonito, jackfish, and snapper, the toxin accumulates in the flesh and skin of the consuming fish. The contaminated fish are not affected by the toxin. The toxin is heat stable and not destroyed by cooking. At the present time, there is no commercially known method to determine if ciguatoxin is present in a particular fish.

Symptoms and Onset Time—The symptoms of the disease ciguatera vary a lot but include nausea, vomiting, diarrhea, dizziness, and shortness of breath. The classic symptom of ciguatera is a reversal of hot and cold sensation. The first symptoms usually appear within 30 minutes after the contaminated fish is eaten. Most symptoms stop within a few days, but complete recovery may take several weeks or months. Death can occur from a concentrated dose of the toxin.

Common Foods—Marine finfish are most commonly implicated with ciguatoxin poisoning. Common marine species include barracudas, groupers, jacks, mackerel, snappers, and triggerfish.

Transmission in Foods—The toxin is transferred to finfish when they eat toxin-containing algae or other fish that contain the toxin.

Prevention—The toxin is not destroyed by cooking; therefore, prevention can be very difficult. Purchasing seafood from a reputable supplier is the best preventive measure.

Scombrotoxin

CAUSATIVE AGENT	TYPE OF ILLNESS	SYMPTOMS ONSET	COMMON FOODS	PREVENTION
Scombrotoxin	Seafood toxin originating from histamine producing bacteria	Dizziness, burning feeling in the mouth, facial rash or hives, peppery taste in mouth headache, itching, teary eyes, runny nose,(1 - 60 min)	Tuna, mahi-mahi, bluefish, sardines, mackerel, anchovies, amberjack, abalone	Purchase fish from a reputable supplier, store fish at low temperatures to prevent growth of histamine-producing bacteria, toxin IS NOT inactivated by cooking

Description—Scombrotoxin, also called histamine poisoning, is caused by eating foods high in a chemical compound called histamine. Histamine is usually produced by certain bacteria when they decompose foods containing the protein histidine. Dark meat of fish has more histidine than other fish meat. Histamine is not inactivated by cooking.

Symptoms and Onset Time—Symptoms of the illness include dizziness, a burning sensation, a facial rash or hives, shortness of breath, and a peppery taste in the mouth when contaminated fish is eaten. The symptoms of scombroid poisoning begin within a few minutes to one hour after the toxic fish is eaten. The illness lasts only a short period of time, and recovery usually occurs within 8 to 12 hours. In severe cases, loss of muscle control, inability to speak, swallow, or breathe can lead to death (Benenson et al., 1995).

Common Foods—The most common foods implicated in scombrotoxin include tuna, anchovies, blue fish, mackeral, amberjack, abalone, and mahi-mahi, the dark meat fishes. Swiss cheese has also been implicated.

Transmission in Foods—Over time, bacteria that are inherent to a particular food can break down histidine and cause the production of histamine. Leaving fish out at room temperature usually results in histamine production.

Prevention—Purchase seafood from a reputable supplier. Store "fresh" seafood at temperatures between 32° and 39°F (0° and 4°C), and do not accept seafood that is suspected of being thawed and refrozen or temperature abused in some way.

Shellfish Toxins—PSP, DSP, DAP, NSP

CAUSATIVE AGENT	TYPE OF ILLNESS	SYMPTOMS ONSET	COMMON FOODS	PREVENTION
Shellfish toxins: PSP, DSP, DAP, NSP	Intoxication	Numbness of lips, tongue, arms, legs, neck, lack of muscle coordination. 10 to 60 minutes	Contaminated mussels, clams, oysters, scallops	Purchase from a reputable supplier

Description—There are several shellfish toxins that have been associated with foodborne illness. The most common illnesses are Paralytic Shellfish Poisoning (PSP), Diarrhetic Shellfish Poisoning (DSP), Domoic Acid Poisoning (DAP), and Neurotoxic Shellfish Poisoning (NSP). The toxins are produced by certain algae called dinoflagellates. When filter-feeding shellfish such as mussels, clams, oysters, and scallops, feed on the toxic algae, they accumulate the toxins in their internal organs and become toxic to humans. The amount of toxin in the shellfish depends on the amount of toxic algae (dinoflagellates) in the water and the amount of water filtered by the shellfish.

Symptoms and Onset Time—The first symptoms of the disease are numbness in the lips, tongue, and tips of the fingers. As the disease progresses, symptoms include numbness in the arms, legs, and neck and a lack of muscle coordination. Severe respiratory distress and muscular paralysis accompanies advanced stages of the disease. The symptoms of shellfish poisoning usually occur within 30 to 60 minutes after eating the toxic shellfish. In the case of Domoic Acid poisoning, symptoms can begin as early as 10 minutes after ingestion.

Common Foods—PSP is more common with mussels, clams, oysters, and scallops. DSP is more common with mussels, oysters, and scallops. DAP is more common with mussels in cold waters. NSP is common for Gulf Coast marine (saltwater) animals.

Transmission in Foods—Most cases of seafood toxins are caused by contaminated shellfish that have been harvested by sport fishermen or poached from polluted waters. Commercially harvested shellfish are rarely involved in foodborne disease outbreaks because health agencies monitor the level of toxin in shellfish during high risk periods (May to October). Toxin levels in the shellfish are determined in public health laboratories. When the amount of toxin in the shellfish exceeds safe limits, sale of the shellfish from that harvesting area is prohibited.

Prevention—Purchase shellfish only from a reputable supplier. Avoid buying shellfish that have been harvested by sport fishermen or poached from polluted waters.

Mycotoxins

CAUSATIVE AGENT	TYPE OF ILLNESS	SYMPTOMS ONSET	COMMON FOODS	PREVENTION
Mycotoxins	Intoxication	1)Acute onset-hemorrhage, fluid buildup 2) Chronic cancer from small doses over time	Moldy grains, corn, corn products, peanuts, pecans, walnuts, and milk	Purchase food from a reputable supplier; keep grains and nuts dry; and protect products from humidity

Description—Mycotic organisms or fungi are molds, yeasts, and mushrooms, some of which are capable of causing foodborne illness. Fungi are larger than bacteria, and they usually prefer foods that are high in sugar or starches. Molds and yeasts withstand more extreme conditions (more acidic foods, lower A_w foods) than bacteria can. Most molds and yeasts are spoilage organisms which cause foods to deteriorate. However, some types of fungi produce toxic chemicals called mycotoxins. Many mycotoxins have been shown to cause cancer. An important foodborne mycotoxin, called aflatoxin, is produced by *Aspergillus spp.* molds. Many mycotoxins are not destroyed by cooking.

Symptoms and Onset Time—Acute aflatoxicosis is produced when moderate to high levels of aflatoxins are consumed. Acute episodes of the disease may include hemorrhage, acute liver damage, fluid buildup in the body, altered digestion and metabolism of nutrients, and possibly death. Chronic aflatoxicosis results from long term ingestion of low to moderate levels of the toxin. The main concern with mycotoxins is they can cause cancer if consumed over a long period of time.

Common Foods—Mycotoxins are commonly found in drier or more acidic foods that do not support the growth of bacteria. Common foods containing mycotoxins include corn and corn products, peanuts, pecans, walnuts, and milk.

Transmission in Foods—Foodborne fungi are important because they can produce chemical compounds called mycotoxins which have been linked to cancer. People, pets, and farm animals have died from eating moldy peanuts or grain.

Prevention—Purchase food from a reputable supplier. Keep grains and nuts dry and protected from humidity.

Added Man-Made Chemicals

There is an extensive list of chemicals added to foods that may pose a potential health risk. Intentionally added chemicals may include food additives, food preservatives, and pesticides. Pesticides leave residues on fruits and vegetables, and can usually be removed by a vigorous washing procedure. Non-intentionally added chemicals may include contamination by chemicals such as cleaning and sanitary supplies. Also, chemicals from containers or food contact surfaces of inferior metal that are misused may lead to heavy-metal or inferior-metal poisoning (cadmium, galvanized metals, etc.)

Foodborne Illness Caused by Physical Hazards

Physical hazards are foreign objects in food that can cause illness and injury (Figure 2.16). They include items such as fragments of glass from broken glasses, metal shavings from dull can openers, unfrilled toothpicks that may contaminate sandwiches, human hair and jewelry, or bandages that may accidentally be lost by a food handler and enter food. Stones, rocks, or wood particles may contaminate raw fruits and vegetables, rice, beans, and other grain products.

Figure 2.16 Common Physical Hazards in a Food Establishment
(Source: Food Code)

Physical hazards commonly result from accidental contamination and poor food handling practices that can occur at various points in the food chain from harvest to consumer. To prevent physical hazards, wash raw fruits and vegetables thoroughly and visually inspect foods that cannot be washed (such as ground beef). Food handlers must be taught to handle food safely to prevent contamination by glass fragments and metal shavings. Finally, discourage food handlers from wearing jewelry when involved in the production of food.

In this chapter you learned about the many agents that can cause foodborne illness. The following summary of disease causing agents (Figure 2.17) provides a quick reference to foodborne illnesses. In the busy work world of a food manager, this reference can save you time when searching for such information.

CAUSATIVE AGENT (* Sporeforming bacteria)	TYPE OF ILLNESS	SYMPTOMS ONSET	COMMON FOODS	PREVENTION
Anasakis spp,	Parasitic infection	Coughing, vomiting	Raw or undercooked seafood- especially bottom feeding fish	Cook fish to the proper temperature throughout, freeze to meet Food Code specification.
*Bacillus cereus	Bacterial intoxication or toxin-mediated infection	1) Diarrhea, abdominal cramps (8-16 hrs) 2) Vomiting type- vomiting, diarrhea, abdominal cramps (30 minutes - 6 hrs)	1) Diarrhea type - meats, milk, vegetables 2) Vomiting type- rice, starchy foods; grains and cereals	Properly heat, cool, and reheat foods
Campylobacter jejuni	Bacterial infection	Watery, bloody diarrhea (2-5 days)	Raw chicken, raw milk, raw meat	Properly handle and cook foods, avoid cross contamination
Ciguatoxin	Fish toxin originating from toxic algae of tropical waters	Vertigo, hot/cold flashes, diarrhea, vomiting (30 min - days)	Marine finfish including groupers, barracuda, snappers, jacks, mackerel, triggerfish, reef fish	Purchase fish from a reputable supplier; cooking WILL NOT inactivate the toxin
*Clostridium botulinum	Bacterial intoxication	Vertigo, double vision, difficulty in breathing and swallowing headache(12-36 hrs)	Improperly canned foods, vacuum packed refrigerated foods; cooked foods in anaerobic mass.	Properly heat process anaerobically packed foods, DO NOT use home canned foods

Figure 2.17—Summary of Agents That Cause Foodborne Illness

CAUSATIVE AGENT (* Sporeforming bacteria)	TYPE OF ILLNESS	SYMPTOMS ONSET	COMMON FOODS	PREVENTION
Clostridium perfringens	Bacterial toxin-mediated infection	Intense abdominal pains and severe diarrhea, (8-22 hrs)	Spices, gravy, improperly cooled foods (especially meats and gravy dishes)	Properly cook, cool, and reheat foods
Cryptosporidium parvum	Parasitic infection	Severe watery diarrhea within 1 week of ingestion;	Contaminated water; food contaminated by infected food handlers;	Use potable water supply; practice good personal hygiene and handwashing
Escherichia coli O157:H7	Bacterial infection or toxin-mediated infection	Hemolytic uremic syndrome (HUS), bloody diarrhea, kidney failure, (12-72 hrs)	Undercooked hamburger, raw milk, unpastuerized apple cider and lettuce	Practice good food sanitation, handwashing, properly handle and cook foods
Giardia lamblia	Parasitic infection	Diarrhea within 1 week of contact;	Contaminated water	Potable water supply; good personal hygiene and handwashing
Hepatitis A	Viral infection	Fever, nausea, vomiting, abdominal pain, fatigue, swelling of the liver, jaundice (15-50 days)	Foods that are prepared with human contact; contaminated water	Wash hands and practice good personal hygiene; avoid raw seafood
Listeria monocytogenes	Bacterial infection	1) Healthy adult: flu-like symptoms 2) At risk population: septicemia, meningitis, encephalitis birth defects (1 day-3 weeks)	Raw milk, dairy items, raw meats, refrigerated ready-to-eat foods, raw vegetables, and seafood	Properly store and cook foods, avoid cross contamination; rotate processed refrigerated foods using FIFO to assure timely use.

Figure 2.17—Summary of Agents That Cause Foodborne Illness (Cont.)

CAUSATIVE AGENT (* Sporeforming bacteria)	TYPE OF ILLNESS	SYMPTOMS ONSET	COMMON FOODS	PREVENTION
Mycotoxins	Intoxication	1)Acute onset-hemorrhage, fluid buildup, possible death. 2) Chronic cancer from small doses over time	Moldy grains-corn, corn products, peanuts, pecans, walnuts, and milk	Purchase food from a reputable supplier; keep grains and nuts dry; and protect products from humidity
Norwalk virus	Viral infection	Vomiting, diarrhea, abdominal pain, headache, and low grade fever; onset 24-48 hrs.	Sewage contaminated water; contaminated salad ingredients, raw clams, oysters	Use potable water; cook all shellfish; handle food properly; meet time temperature guidelines for PHF
Rotavirus	Viral infection	Diarrhea (especially in infants and children), vomiting, low grade fever; 1-3 days onset; lasts 4-8 days	Sewage contaminated water; contaminated salad ingredients, raw seafood	Good personal hygiene and handwashing; proper food handling practices
Salmonella spp.	Bacterial infection	Nausea, fever, vomiting, abdominal cramps, diarrhea (6-48 hrs)	Raw meats, raw poultry, eggs, milk, dairy products	Properly cook foods, avoid cross contamination
Scombrotoxin	Seafood toxin originating from histamine producing bacteria	Dizziness, burning feeling in the mouth, facial rash or hives, peppery taste in mouth headache, itching, teary eyes runny nose, (1 - 60 min)	Tuna, mahi-mahi, bluefish, sardines, mackerel, anchovies, amberjack, abalone	Purchase fish from a reputable supplier, store fish at low temperatures to prevent growth of histamine-producing bacteria, toxin IS NOT inactivated by cooking

Figure 2.17—Summary of Agents That Cause Foodborne Illness (Cont.)

CAUSATIVE AGENT (* Sporeforming bacteria)	TYPE OF ILLNESS	SYMPTOMS ONSET	COMMON FOODS	PREVENTION
Shellfish toxins: PSP, DSP, DAP, NSP	Intoxication	Numbness of lips, tongue, arms, legs, neck, lack of muscle coordination. (10 to 60 minutes	Contaminated mussels, clams, oysters, scallops	Purchase from a reputable supplier
Shigella spp.	Bacterial infection	Bacillary dysentery, diarrhea, fever, abdominal cramps, dehydration (1-7 days)	Foods that are prepared with human contact, salads, raw vegetables, milk, dairy products, raw poultry, non-potable water, ready to eat meat	Wash hands and practice good personal hygiene, properly cook foods
Staphylococcus aureus	Bacterial intoxication	Nausea, vomiting, abdominal cramps, headaches (2-6 hrs)	Foods that are prepared with human contact, cooked or processed foods	Wash hands and practice good personal hygiene. Cooking WILL NOT inactivate the toxin
Trichinella spiralis	Parasitic infection from a nematode worm	Nausea, vomiting, diarrhea, sweating, muscle soreness (2-28 days)	Primarily undercooked pork products and wild game meats (bear, walrus)	Cook foods, to the proper temperature throughout
Vibrio spp.	Bacterial infection	Headache, fever, chills, diarrhea, vomiting, severe electrolyte loss, gastroenteritis (2-48 hrs)	Raw or improperly cooked fish and shellfish	Practice good sanitation, properly cook foods, avoid serving raw seafood

Figure 2.17—Summary of Agents That Cause Foodborne Illness (Cont.)

Summary

Return to the incident about botulism in potato salad. It is so much easier to see what can happen when you have a few facts at your fingertips. Spores can become vegetative and grow. An oxygen-free environment is perfect for *C.botulinum* bacteria. The potatoes should have been cut and loosely covered then put into the refrigerator all night. Microbes do not always cause problems, but when conditions are ideal—it happens. Prevention of foodborne illness is a full-time exercise. You must maintain procedures that protect consumers from foodborne illness.

There are many foodborne hazards that a food establishment may encounter. These hazards differ depending on the type of food and method of preparation involved. Food establishments are typically toward the end of the food production chain because foods are prepared, served, and eaten or transported from there. Therefore, it is very important to control and prevent foodborne hazards that could lead to foodborne illness. Control and prevention of foodborne hazards in a food establishment start with understanding the different types of foodborne hazards. The next step is to understand how to control foodborne hazards with good personal hygiene, prevention of cross contamination, as well as proper storage, cooking, cooling, and reheating of foods. These items will be covered in the next chapter.

Case Study 2.1

Bruce, the morning prep cook at a local restaurant, was preparing shredded cheese to be used on pizza. His procedure included cutting the cheese into small blocks and then shredding the cheese by hand. He prepared several 4-gallon containers and left the containers out at room temperature (70°F, 21°C) until use. Three of the four containers were used on pizzas later that day. The next day, the fourth container of cheese was used. On both days, the pizzas were cooked in an oven set to 500°F (260°C).

Four days later, several people came back to the restaurant and said that they had become ill a few hours after eating pizza there. Only people who ate pizza on the second day appeared to be ill.

1. What foodborne hazard may have been associated with this foodborne illness?

2. How could this have been prevented?

Answers to the case study can be found in Appendix A.

Discussion Questions (Short Answer)

1. Briefly explain the difference between an infection, an intoxication, and a toxin-mediated infection. Give an example of each.

2. What groups of people have a greater risk of acquiring foodborne illness?

3. Identify the three categories of foodborne illness hazards and give an example of each.

4. What type of biological hazard should be of greatest concern to food establishment managers? Why?

5. What does FATTOM represent?

6. At what pH and water activity (A_w) levels do bacteria grow best?

7. What is the food temperature danger zone?

8. What is a bacterial spore?

9. What is a potentially hazardous food? What three characteristics do they share?

10. What are viruses? What are parasites?

Answers to the multiple choice questions are provided in Appendix A.

Quiz 2.1(Multiple Choice)

1. Bacteria are the most common cause of foodborne disease in a food establishment because

   a. under ideal conditions, they can grow very rapidly.

   b. bacteria are found naturally in many foods.

   c. bacteria can be easily transferred from one source to another.

   d. all of the above.

2. Most of the bacteria that cause foodborne illness grow

   a. with or without oxygen at an ideal temperature of 98.6°
      F (39°C).

   b. only without oxygen at an ideal temperature of 110°F
      (43°C).

   c. only with oxygen at an ideal temperature of 110°F
      (43°C).

   d. only without oxygen at an ideal temperature of 98.6°F
      (39°C).

3. Which of the following organisms are most likely to cause a
   foodborne disease outbreak in a food establishment?

   a. *Salmonella spp.* and *Staphylococcus aureus*

   b. *Crytosporidium parvum* and *Giardia lamblia*

   c. Hepatitis A and Norwalk virus group

   d. *Anisakis simplex.* and *Trichinella spiralis*

4. Bacteria grow within a narrow temperature range called the
   temperature danger zone. The temperature danger zone is
   between

   a. 0° and 220°F (-18°C and 104°C).

   b. 0° and 140°F (-18° and 60°C).

   c. 41° and 140°F (5° and 60°C).

   d. 41° and 220°F (5° and 104°C).

5. Bacteria that cause foodborne illness will only grow on foods
   that have a pH greater than _____ and a water activity (A_w)
   greater than _____.

   a. 3.2, .85

   b. 4.6, .85

   c. 6.5, .80

   d. 8.0, .70

6. Which of the following bacteria produce a toxin that is most
   likely to cause death if consumed?

   a. *Campylobacter jejuni*

   b. *Clostridium botulinum*

   c. Escherichia coli 0157:H7

   d. *Listeria monocytogenes*

7. Some bacteria form spores to help them

   a. reproduce.

   b. move more easily from one location to another.

   c. survive adverse environmental conditions.

   d. grow in high acid foods.

8. Which of the following is a toxin produced by molds?

   a. Ciguatoxin

   b. Mycotoxin

   c. Scombrotoxin

   d. Paralytic Shellfish Poisoning (PSP)

9. Which of the following is not considered a potentially hazardous food group?

   a. Red meats

   b. Fish and shellfish

   c. Poultry and eggs

   d. Dried grains and spices

10. The most effective way to control the growth of bacteria in a food establishment is by controlling

    a. time and temperature.

    b. pH and oxygen conditions.

    c. temperature and water activity.

    d. time and food availability.

References/Suggested Readings

Benenson, A. S. (Ed.) (1995) *Control Of Communicable Diseases In Man* (16th ed.). Washington, D.C.: American Public Health Association.

Cichy, R. F. (1994). *Quality Sanitation Management.* East Lansing, MI: Educational Institute of the American Hotel and Motel Association.

Educational Foundation (1992). *Applied Food Service Sanitation.* Chicago, IL: National Restaurant Association.

Kolchenar, L. H., and R. Donnelly, (1994). *Quantity Food Sanitation.* New York, NY: Macmillan.

Longrèe, K., and G. Armbruster, (1996). *Quantity Food Sanitation*. New York: Macmillan.

Rue, N., National Assessment Institute (1994). Handbook for safe food service management. Englewood Cliffs, NJ: Prentice Hall.

United States Department of Health and Human Services, (1995). 1995 Food Code, Washington, D.C.: Recommendation of the U.S. Department of Health and Human Service.

3 FACTORS THAT EFFECT FOODBORNE ILLNESS

Hepatitis A Outbreak Linked to Tainted Lettuce

An outbreak of foodborne Hepatitis A occurred in a small Missouri town. One hundred and thirty people became ill and four died as a result of their illness. Cases stemming from this outbreak were reported as far away as Oklahoma, Florida, Alabama, and Maine.

A foodborne disease investigation revealed that all of the victims had consumed lettuce, either in salad or as a garnish. Investigators ruled out the theory that the lettuce had been contaminated at the source, because other restaurants supplied by the same source experienced no illnesses. In the end, Missouri Department of Health Officials concluded that direct contamination of food by infected workers was the most likely cause of the outbreak. The initial source of the illness was believed to be a waiter who had been infected by his child in daycare. The waiter and four other food handlers who tested positive for the Hepatitis A virus handled lettuce and were involved in preparing and serving salads.

Violations detected when the restaurant was inspected after the outbreak included employees drinking and smoking in food preparation areas, failure to prevent cross contamination of foods and no soap at the hand-washing sink. It is likely the food handler's hands became contaminated with feces when they had a bowel movement. If the workers did not wash their hands properly before returning to work, the Hepatitis A virus could be transferred from their hands to lettuce and other foods. Lettuce is a ready-to-eat food which will not be heated to destroy the virus.

Learning Objectives

After reading this chapter, you should be able to:

▲ Identify potential problems related to temperature abuse of foods

▲ Describe how to properly measure and maintain food temperatures to assure that foods are safe for consumption

▲ Identify potential problems related to poor personal hygiene of a food handler

▲ Explain how to improve personal hygiene habits to reduce the risk of foodborne illness

▲ Identify potential problems related to cross contamination of food

▲ Discuss procedures and methods to prevent cross contamination

Essential Terms

Biofilm	Impermeable
Calibrate	Measuring device
Centers for Disease Control and Prevention (CDC)	Personal hygiene
Dial face bi-metal thermometer	Temperature abuse
Digital thermometer	Thermocouple
Food temperature	T-stick type melt devices

Factors That Contribute to Foodborne Illness

The **Centers for Disease Control and Prevention (CDC)** is an agency of the federal government. One of CDC's primary responsibilities is to collect statistics about diseases that affect people in America. The list includes foodborne illness. CDC statistics show that most foodborne disease outbreaks occur because *food is mishandled*. The most frequent factors that lead to foodborne illness, as identified by the CDC, are presented in Figure 3.1.

Almost all foodborne illnesses are linked to three general food handling errors:

▲ Time and temperature abuse

▲ Poor personal hygiene and improper handwashing

▲ Cross contamination

It is extremely important that you recognize these three major factors as they contribute to food contamination. This chapter describes prevention strategies necessary for safe food management.

4% Use of leftovers
7% Improper cleaning
7% Cross contamination
11% Contaminated raw food
12% Inadequate reheating
16% Improper hot storage
16% Inadequate cooking
20% Infected persons touching food
21% Time between preparing and serving
40% Improper cooling of foods

Figure 3.1—Factors Leading to Foodborne Illness (ranked by percentage of outbreaks)

Note: The total of the percentages is more than 100% because more than one factor may contribute to a foodborne disease outbreak.
(Source: Surveillance for Foodborne Disease Outbreaks—United States, 1988-1992)

What Is Temperature Abuse?

Controlling temperature is perhaps the most critical way to assure food safety. Most cases of foodborne illness can in some way be linked to **temperature abuse.** The term temperature abuse is used to describe situations when foods are:

▲ held at temperatures for enough time to allow growth of harmful microorganisms

▲ not cooked or reheated sufficiently to destroy harmful microorganisms

In Chapter 2, Hazards to Food Safety, you learned that harmful microbes can grow in potentially hazardous foods when temperatures are between 41° and 140° F (5° and 60°C).

Keep **food temperatures**, the temperature inside the core of a food item, above the temperature danger zone (140°F, 60°C) to prevent harmful microbes from growing (Figure 3.2). Higher temperatures destroy microbes. However, toxins produced by microbes may or may not be affected by heat.

Keep food temperatures below the temperature danger zone (41°F, 5°C) to prevent most microbes from growing. Bacteria that can grow in lower temperatures, do so very slowly.

Figure 3.2—Temperature Danger Zone

There are unavoidable situations during food production when foods must pass through the temperature danger zone such as:

▲ cooking

▲ cooling

▲ reheating

▲ food preparation (slicing, mixing, etc.)

During these activities, you must minimize the amount of time foods are in the temperature danger zone to control microbial growth. **Temperatures of food held in cold storage, should never be in the temperature danger zone.**

Cooking foods to make them more enjoyable to eat began with the discovery of fire. Heating improves texture and flavor and also affects harmful microorganisms. As you learned in Chapter 2, many raw foods naturally contain harmful microbes or can become contaminated during handling. When you cook and reheat foods properly, microbes are reduced to safe levels or destroyed. *Cooking and reheating are two very important processes* for safe food management.

How and When to Measure Food Temperatures

Maintaining safe food temperatures is an essential and effective part of food safety management. You must know *how* and *when* to correctly measure food temperatures to prevent temperature abuse. Thermometers, thermocouples, or other devices are used to measure the temperature of stored, cooked, hot-held, cold-held, and reheated foods.

Thermometers

The first item you will need is an approved **food temperature measuring device**. Four devices commonly used to measure food, water, and air temperatures are shown in Figure 3.3.

Figure 3.3 Temperature Measuring Devices

The most common type of thermometer is the *dial face, metal stem-type (bi-metallic) thermometer*. The metal-stemmed thermometer probe is at least five inches long with a one-inch diameter dial face. Use this type of thermometer to measure internal food temperatures at every stage of food preparation.

The *digital thermometer*, shows the temperature numerically on a digital display.

Thermocouple thermometers provide a digital readout of the temperature and have a variety of immersion, surface, and specialty probes that can be interchanged to suit most applications.

T-sticks are examples of *melt devices*. This single-use disposable thermometer measures only one temperature. The wax melts when the temperature reaches or exceeds the set point and the color changes (usually from white to black). Melt devices may be used to monitor product temperatures and the sanitizing temperature in dishwashing machines.

Maximum registering (holding) thermometers measure the temperature of hot water used to sanitize dishware and utensils in mechanical warewashing machines.

Thermometers used in food establishments should measure temperatures ranging from 0° to 220°F (-18° to 104°C) with 2°F (1°C) increments. Food temperature measuring devices scaled only in Celsius or dually scaled in Celsius and Fahrenheit must be accurate to +1.8°F (+1°C). Food temperature measuring devices scaled in Fahrenheit only must be accurate to +2°F.

Clean and sanitize thermometers properly to avoid contaminating food that is being tested. This is very important *when testing raw* and *then ready-to-eat food items.* To clean and sanitize a food thermometer, wipe off any food particles, place the stem or probe in sanitizing solution for at least 5 seconds, then air dry. When monitoring *only raw* foods, or *only cooked* foods being held at 140°F (60°C), wipe the stem of the thermometer with an alcohol swab between measurements.

When and How to Calibrate Thermometers

Calibrate dial face metal stem-type (bi-metal) thermometers:

▲ before their first use

▲ at regular intervals

▲ if dropped

▲ if used to measure extreme temperatures

▲ whenever accuracy is in question

Most dial face thermometers have a *calibration nut* just behind the dial (Figure 3.4). **Calibrate** dial face thermometers by the boiling point or ice point method. See specific directions for calibration as described in the following section. Use pliers or an open-ended wrench to adjust the indicator needle.

Boiling Point Method

Immerse at least the first two inches of the stem from the tip (the sensing part of the probe) into boiling water, and adjust the needle to 212°F (100°C). At higher altitudes, the temperature of the boiling point will vary. Consult your local health department if you have any questions.

Should deionized H₂O be used? [handwritten margin note]

Ice Point Method

Insert the probe into a cup of crushed ice. Add enough cold water to remove any air pockets that might remain. Let the probe and ice mixture stabilize and adjust the needle to 32°F (0°C).

Figure 3.4—Calibrating a Dial-faced Thermometer
(Source: Cooper Instrument Corporation)

Measuring Food Temperature

The sensing portion of a food thermometer is on the tip of the stem or probe. On the bi-metal stem thermometer, the sensing portion is located approximately 1 inch from the tip. The end of the sensing portion is marked by a "dimple" on the stem.

Before you calibrate or measure food temperature, locate the sensing portion of your thermometer. Then, insert the sensing element of the thermometer into the center of the thickest part of the food. *Always wait for the temperature reading to stabilize.* [See Figure 3.5(a).]

In some cases, the temperature of packaged foods can be measured accurately without opening the package. Place the stem or probe of the thermometer between two packages of food or fold the package around the stem or probe to make good contact with the packaging (Figure 3.5(b) and (c).]

(a)

(b)

(c)

Figure 3.5—Measuring Food Temperature

To accurately and safely measure food temperatures, be sure to:

▲ Use an approved temperature measuring device that measures temperature from 0° to 220°F(-18° to 104°C).

▲ Locate the sensing portion of the measuring device.

▲ Calibrate the measuring device using the ice or boiling point method.

▲ Clean and sanitize the probe of the temperature measuring device according to procedure.

▲ Measure the internal temperature of the food by inserting the probe into the center of the thickest part of the item.

Preventing Temperature Abuse

Controlling temperatures in potentially hazardous food is important in almost all stages of food handling. Thus, measuring temperatures of potentially hazardous food is an important duty for nearly all food workers. The following table (Figure 3.6) lists safe temperature guidelines with the rationale for each step. Each of these guidelines will be discussed throughout the remainder of this book.

Step in the Flow of Food	Safe Temperature Guidelines	Rationale for Temperature Guidelines
Receiving and Storing Frozen Potentially Hazardous Foods	Foods should be frozen solidly and maintained at a temperature of less than 0°F (-18°C) at all times.	Proper freezing of foods helps to maintain food quality and prevents the growth of spoilage and harmful microorganisms.
Receiving and Storing Refrigerated Potentially Hazardous Foods	Foods should be received and stored so that food is always below 41°F (5°C).	Receiving and storing foods below 41°F (5°C) prevents or slows the growth of harmful microorganisms.
Cooking Potentially Hazardous Foods	Different foods, and the method by which it is cooked, require different end point temperatures to be safe. The range of safe cooking temperatures can vary from 145° to 190°F (63° to 88°C).	Proper cooking destroys harmful microorganisms that may be present in the food.
Cooling Potentially Hazardous Foods	During cooling, food must be cooled from 140° to 70°F (60° to 21°C) within 2 hours and from 70° to 41°F (21° to 5°C) in less than an additional 4 hours.	Proper cooling prevents the conversion of sporeforming bacterial cells to vegetative bacterial cells, and the growth of vegetative bacterial cells.

Figure 3.6—Safe Temperature Guidelines for Various Steps in the Flow of Food

Step in the Flow of Food	Safe Temperature Guidelines	Rationale for Temperature Guidelines
Reheating Potentially Hazardous Foods	All reheated foods must be reheated to at least 165°F (74°C) within 2 hours.	Proper reheating destroys harmful bacteria (especially sporeforming bacteria) that may be present in foods.
Hot-holding Potentially Hazardous Foods	All foods must be cooked to a safe temperature and then held at greater than 140°F (60°C).	Proper holding of food prevents the growth of harmful bacteria.
Cold-Holding Potentially Hazardous Foods	All foods that are held and served cold must be held at less than 41°F (5°C).	Holding cold foods below 41°F (5°C) prevents or slows the growth of harmful microorganisms.
Thawing Potentially Hazardous Foods	Thawing may be done in a refrigerator at 41°F (5°C) or less, in a microwave oven & then immediately cooked, or under cold running water 70°F(21°C) in two hours or less.	Proper thawing prevents or reduces the growth or harmful bacteria.
Food Preparation	During food preparation, food should only be in the temperature danger zone (between 41° and 140° F, 5° and 60°C) for a maximum total time of 4 hours.	Maintaining foods between 41° and 140°F (5° and 60°C) for no more than 4 hours limits the number of microorganisms that can grow.

Figure 3.6—Safe Temperature Guidelines for Various Steps in the Flow of Food (Cont.)

Keep Cold Foods Cold and Hot Foods Hot!

Frozen foods should be solidly frozen and held at 0°F (-18°C) or below until used. Ice cream products should be stored at 10°F (-12°C) or colder. Freezing helps to retain product quality. Proper frozen food temperatures do not permit disease-causing and spoilage microorganisms to grow. Cold temperatures also help to preserve the color and flavor characteristics. Frozen foods can be stored for long periods of time without losing their wholesomeness and quality.

Refrigerated foods are held cold, not frozen. Cold foods should be maintained at 41°F (5°C) or below. Do not forget that some harmful bacteria and many spoilage bacteria can grow at temperatures below 41°F (5°C), although their growth is very slow (Longrèe & Armbruster, 1996). By keeping cold foods at 41°F (5°C) or below, you can reduce the growth of most harmful microorganisms and extend the shelf-life of the product. For maximum quality and freshness, hold cold foods for the shortest amount of time possible.

Applying heat is another method used to preserve food. To destroy harmful bacteria, heat food to proper temperatures. Established safe cooking temperatures are based on the type of food and the method used to heat the product. Cooked foods that have been cooled and then reheated must be maintained at 140°F (60°C) or above until used. You must keep foods hot to stop growth of harmful bacteria.

There are times during food production when foods must be in the temperature danger zone. Recognize that the time spent in the temperature danger zone should be minimal for potentially hazardous items.

Improper cooling of foods is the number one contributing factor that leads to foodborne illness. Spores of certain bacteria like *Clostridium botulinum, Clostridium perfringens,* and *Bacillus cereus* can survive cooking temperatures. Remember, if spores survive and are exposed to ideal conditions, they can again become vegetative cells (Figure 2.2).

The *Food Code* contains cooling guidelines that permit foods to be in the temperature danger zone for a total of 6 hours. The Food Code specifically states that foods must be cooled from 140° to 70°F (21° to 5°C) in 2 hours, and 70° to 41°F (60° to 21°C) in an additional 4 hours.

The industry standard for cooling requires food temperatures to go from 140°F (60°C) to 40°F (5°C) in 4 hours.

To destroy many of the bacteria that may have grown during the cooling process, reheat foods to 165°F (74°C) within two hours.

Fahrenheit/Celsius

Botulism Toxin is Inactivated by Boiling, but Staphylococcus Toxin is Not — 212/100

165/74

Poultry, Poultry Stuffing, Stuffed Meats, and Stuffing Containing Meat Must Be Internally Cooked to This Temperature

Pork, Ground Beef, and Other Ground Meat Products Cooked to This Temperature — 155/68

145/68

All Other Potentially Hazardous Foods Cooked to This Temperature

Heated Foods Maintained at This Temperature — 140/60

120/49

Foods Must Be Rapidly Refrigerated Through This Entire Temperature Range to Minimize Bacterial Growth

70/21

0/-18

Frozen Foods Kept in This Range

-20/-29

Figure 3.7—Improper Cooling: The #1 Cause of Foodborne Illness

The preferred method for thawing foods is in the refrigerator at 41°F (5°C) or below. This prevents the food from entering the food temperature danger zone.

Other acceptable methods for thawing include using a microwave oven, as a part of the cooking process, or under cold running water. Proper thawing reduces the chances for bacterial growth, especially on the outer surfaces of food.

More detailed strategies for minimizing the amount of time a food is in the temperature danger zone during cooling, thawing, and food preparation will be presented in the next chapter.

The Importance of Handwashing and Good Personal Hygiene

The cleanliness and personal hygiene of food handlers are extremely important. If a food handler is not clean, the food can become **contaminated**.

As you know, even healthy humans can be a source of harmful microorganisms. Therefore, **good personal hygiene is essential for those who handle foods. Desirable behaviors include:**

▲ Knowing when and how to properly wash hands

▲ Wearing clean clothing

▲ Maintaining good personal habits (bathing, clean and restrained hair, short fingernails, washing hands after using toilet, etc.)

▲ Maintaining good health and reporting when sick to avoid spreading possible infections

Just think of all the things your hands touch during a typical work day. You may take out the trash, cover a sneeze, scratch an itch, or mop up a spill. When you touch your face or skin, run your fingers through your hair or a beard, use the toilet, or blow your nose, you transfer potentially harmful germs to your hands. *Staphylococcus aureus*, Hepatitis A, and *Shigella* spp. are examples of pathogens that may be found in and on the human body and can be transferred to foods by hand contact.

Personnel involved in food preparation and service must know how and when to wash their hands. Figure 3.8 provides **a list of situations when handwashing is required.**

Using approved cleaning compounds (soap or detergent), vigorously rub surfaces of hands, wrists, and arms for at least 20 seconds and remember, soap, water, and friction are needed to adequately clean skin. **A significant number of germs are removed by friction alone.**

Always wash hands:

▲before food preparation

▲after touching human body parts

▲after using the toilet

▲after coughing, sneezing, using a handkerchief or tissue, using tobacco, eating, or drinking

▲during food preparation when switching between raw foods and ready-to-eat products

▲after engaging in any activities that may contaminate hands (taking out the garbage, wiping counters or tables, handling cleaning chemicals, picking up dropped items, etc.)

▲after caring for or touching animals

Figure 3.8—Handwashing Guidelines (Food Code)

Thoroughly rinse under clean running water; and clean under and around fingernails and between fingers.

Dry hands using a single service paper towel, an electric hand dryer, or clean section of continuous rolled cloth towel (if allowed in your jurisdiction). *Do not dry hands on your apron or a dish towel.* (See the handwashing procedure in Figure 3.9.)

In addition to proper handwashing, fingernails should be trimmed, filed, and maintained so that handwashing will effectively remove soil from under and around them.

According to the *Food Code,* hands shall be washed in a separate sink specified as a handwashing sink (Figure 3.10).

Each handwashing sink must be provided with hand cleanser (soap or detergent) in a dispenser and a suitable hand-drying device.

Figure 3.9—Proper Handwashing Technique

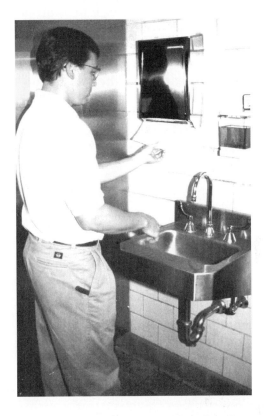

Figure 3.10—Handwashing Station

Hand sanitizing lotions and chemical hand sanitizing solutions may be used by food employees *in addition to handwashing*. Proper washing helps to remove visible hand dirt and the microorganisms it contains. **Hand sanitizing lotions must never be used as a replacement for handwashing**.

After washing, the sanitizing chemical remains on the hands after application because the hands do not receive additional washing or rinsing. It is critical that hand sanitizers be formulated with safe ingredients because it is likely that a food employee's hands will touch food, food contact surfaces, or equipment and utensils after using the product.

Except when washing fruits and vegetables, food handlers should not contact exposed ready-to-eat foods with their hands. Instead, they should use suitable utensils such as deli-tissue, spatulas, and tongs. Also, minimize bare hand and arm contact with exposed food that is not in ready-to-eat form.

Food establishments sometimes allow their food handlers to use disposable gloves to help prevent contamination of foods. Gloves protect food from direct contact by human hands. Gloves must be impermeable, therefore not allowing anything to penetrate the porous texture of the glove. **You must treat disposable gloves as a second skin. Whatever can contaminate a human hand can also contaminate a disposable glove. Therefore, whenever hands should be washed, a new pair of disposable gloves should be worn (Figure 3.11).**

Figure 3.II—Example of Disposable Gloves

For example, if you are wearing disposable gloves and handling raw food, you must discard those gloves, wash your hands, and put on a fresh pair of gloves before you handle ready-to-eat foods.

Never handle money with gloved hands unless you immediately remove and discard the gloves. Money is highly contaminated from handling. If you take latex gloves off by rolling them inside out, the inner surface of the glove is very contaminated from your skin. Again, if you take disposable gloves off, throw them away. **Never reuse or wash disposable gloves—always throw them away.**

Outer Clothing and Apparel

Work clothes and other apparel should always be clean. The appearance of a clean uniform is more appealing to your guests.

During food preparation and service, it is easy for a food handler's clothing to become contaminated. If you feel that you have contaminated your outer clothing, change into a new set of work clothes.

For example, if you normally wear an apron and work with raw foods, put on a fresh, clean apron before working with ready-to-eat foods. Also, never dry or wipe your hands on the apron. As soon as you do that, the apron is contaminated. Smocks and aprons help to reduce transfer of microbes to exposed food.

Keep in mind, however, that **protective apparel is similar to a disposable glove. They no longer protect food when contaminated.**

Caps and hair or beard restraints discourage workers from touching their hair or beard. These restraints also prevent hair from falling into food or onto food contact surfaces. Most state and local jurisdictions require some type of hair restraint.

Personal Habits

Personal hygiene is good health habits including bathing, washing hair, wearing clean clothing and frequent hand washing. Poor personal habits are serious hazards in food establishments (Figure 3.12). Smoking or eating on the job can contaminate food. Body fluids, such as sweat or perspiration, can also contaminate food.

Figure 3.12—A Bad Example: How Many Errors Can You Find?

Supervisors should enforce rules against eating, chewing gum, and smoking in food preparation, service, and warewashing areas. The *Food Code* permits food workers to drink water to prevent dehydration. The water must be in a covered container with a straw. The container must be handled in a way that prevents contamination of the employee's hands, the container, exposed food, equipment, and single-use articles.

Jewelry has no place in food production and warewashing areas. Rings, bracelets, necklaces, earrings, watches, and other body part ornaments can harbor germs that can cause foodborne illness. Jewelry can also fall into food causing a physical hazard. A plain wedding band is the only piece of jewelry that should be worn in food production and warewashing areas.

Personal Health

In an attempt to reduce the risk caused by sick food workers, **the *Food Code* requires employees to report to the person in charge when they have been diagnosed with:**

▲ *Salmonella typhi*

▲ *Shigella spp.*

▲ *E. coli 0157:H7*

▲ Hepatitis A

▲ symptoms of intestinal illness (such as vomiting, diarrhea, fever, sore throat, or jaundice)

If a food handler is directly or indirectly exposed to *Salmonella typhi, Shigella spp., E. coli 0157:H7,* or Hepatitis A, it must be reported to the supervisor. All of these diseases are easily transferred to foods and are considered severe health hazards.

If you have been exposed to any of these agents, you may be excluded from work or be assigned to restricted activities having no food contact. Employees and workers diagnosed with one of these diseases should not handle exposed food, have contact with clean equipment, utensils, linens, or unwrapped single-service utensils.

Infected wounds, cuts, pimples, and lesions on the hands, face, or arms that may be draining blood, fluid, or pus must be reported to the supervisor. *Staphylococcus aureus* bacteria are often found in these sites. Exposed areas of arms, wrists, and forearms that contain infected wounds should be completely covered by a dry, tight-fitting, impermeable bandage. Cuts or burns on the food worker's hands must be thoroughly bandaged, and covered with a clean disposable glove.

When a foodborne illness outbreak occurs and an employee is suspected of carrying the disease, they should not work until certified as safe by a licensed physician. Exclusions and restrictions for those exposed to or experiencing symptoms of a foodborne illness are specified in the *Food Code*. *The health of food workers is extremely important in safe food management.*

Why Is Cross Contamination Such a Problem?

Contaminated food contains germs or harmful substances that can cause foodborne illness. The transfer of germs from one food item to another is called cross contamination. This commonly happens when germs from a raw food are transferred to a cooked or ready-to-eat food via contaminated hands, equipment, or utensils.

For example, bacteria from raw chicken can be transferred to a ready-to-eat food such as lettuce or tomato when a single cutting board is used without being washed and sanitized in between (Figure 3.13).

Figure 3.13—Cross Contamination of a Cutting Board

Cross contamination also happens when raw foods are stored above ready-to-eat foods. Juices from the raw product can drip or splash onto a ready-to-eat food as in Figure 3.14.

Figure 3.14—Never Put Raw Food Over Cooked or Ready-to-Eat Food

In a food establishment, germs can be transferred by a food handler, equipment and utensils, or another food. Remember to keep things **clean**—removal of the soil, and **sanitary**—reduce the disease causing microorganisms to a safe level. Therefore, it is extremely important to:

▲ always store cooked and ready-to-eat foods over raw products

▲ keep raw and ready-to-eat foods separate during storage

▲ use good personal hygiene and handwashing

▲ keep all food contact surfaces clean and sanitary

Avoiding Cross Contamination

There are many things you can do to avoid, or at least reduce, opportunities for cross contamination during food preparation and service. An important part of food safety is to impress upon your employees the importance of clean hands and clothing. *Stress the importance of when and how to properly wash hands.* Provide ongoing supervision to ensure that employees remain clean and apply safe food handling practices when working with food.

To avoid cross contamination by way of food contact surfaces (i.e., cutting boards, knife blades, slicers, and preparation tables) **an effective in-house cleaning and sanitation program is important**. You will learn more on this subject in Chapter 7, Cleaning and Sanitizing Operations.

If a food contact surface is not properly cleaned and sanitized, bacteria can accumulate and grow on the surface. This is called a **biofilm** (Figure 3.15). Once a biofilm is formed, it is difficult to remove. To avoid such buildup, *always* clean and sanitize food contact surfaces thoroughly before working with ready-to-eat foods and foods that will not be heat processed.

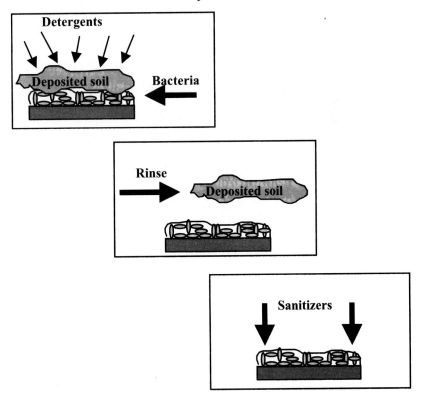

Figure 3.15—Biofilm Formation on Improperly Cleaned and Sanitized Surfaces (Adapted from: Food Technology, 1994)

Preventive measures eliminate the possibility of cross contamination between products and may include the following:

▲ use of separate equipment, such as cutting boards, for raw foods and ready-to-eat foods (color coding may be helpful for this task)

▲ use of clean, sanitized equipment and utensils for food production

▲ preparation of ready-to-eat foods first—then raw foods

▲ preparation of raw and ready-to-eat foods in separate areas of the kitchen

Always keep raw foods separate from ready-to-eat foods. In the refrigerator, ready-to-eat foods must be stored above raw foods. Display cases, such as those used to display seafood items, should be designed to keep raw and cooked food items separate. In addition, separate buckets and wiping cloths should be used for cleaning food contact surfaces in raw and ready-to-eat food production areas.

What Are Other Sources of Contamination?

Raw foods, such as fruits and vegetables, should be treated like ready-to-eat foods. Always wash these foods before use. Washing removes soil and other contaminants. Chemicals may be used to wash or peel raw, whole fruits and vegetables. These chemicals must be non-toxic and meet the requirements set forth in the Code of Federal Regulations uder title 21CFR173.315.

Animals are not allowed in food establishments unless they are being used for support or special service. It is very important that you not touch animals during food preparation and service. If you should touch an animal for any reason, wash your hands before returning to work.

Animals, rodents, and pests are important sources for food contamination. Rodents and pests usually enter food establishments during delivery or when garbage facilities are not properly maintained. A good integrated pest management (IPM) program should be established and maintained in any food establishment. You will learn about IPM programs in Chapter 8, Environmental Sanitation and Maintenance.

Summary

At the beginning of this chapter, we looked at an outbreak of foodborne illness related to lettuce contaminated by a foodhandler. What was the first thing that went wrong? How can you prevent this type of problem in a food establishment?

Almost all foodborne illness can be prevented with proper food handling practices. Most foodborne illnesses are due to temperature abuse, poor personal hygiene and handwashing practices, and cross contamination.

Temperature abuse can occur during receiving, storing, cooking, cooling, reheating, hot-holding, and cold-holding of foods. Depending on the type of food, there are specific temperature requirements to assure food safety. These requirements will be discussed in the next chapter. **A good rule to follow in any food establishment is, "Keep It Clean! Keep It Hot! Keep It Cold! Or Don't Keep It!"**

Food workers should always use good health and hygiene practices. Clean clothing, hair restraints, and proper handwashing practices are fundamental in safe food management. Effective supervision and enforcement of proper procedures form the foundation of a successful food operation.

Control cross contamination with proper cleaning and sanitizing. Avoid cross contamination from one food to another. Keep foods separate and store raw foods below cooked and ready-to-eat foods. Always use proper food handling techniques.

Keep foods at proper temperature, use good personal hygiene, and control cross contamination. These are the essentials of safe food management.

Case Study 3.1

Michelle is in charge of all the cold salad preparation at a local hotel restaurant. The main responsibilities of her job are to prepare green salads for the evening meals. When she arrived at work one day, the food manager on duty noticed that she was coughing and sneezing frequently. Michelle also indicated that she was battling a case of the flu. How should the food manager handle this situation?

Case Study 3.2

Cameron just received his new food thermometer. He checked to see that it was approved for use in food and it could measure 0° to 220° F (-18° to 104°C). He found the sensing area and then calibrated it properly. He was excited by his new purchase and wanted to see how well the thermometer performed. He first measured raw meats in the cold room. They all checked out well and measured between 35° and 41° F (2° and 5°C). As he exited the cold room, he immediately went to the customer self-service bar and measured the temperature of the cooked scrambled eggs. They measured 145° F (63°C). Cameron was satisfied because the cold foods were less than 41°F (5°C) and the hot foods measured higher than 140°F (60°C). What error did Cameron make when measuring food temperature?

Answers to the case studies are provided in Appendix A.

Discussion Questions (Short Answer)

1. When purchasing and using a food thermometer, what are the six important things that you need to remember?

2. How frequently should thermometers be calibrated? Describe the two methods for calibrating food thermometers.

3. Under what conditions are foods "temperature abused"?

4. What is meant by *poor personal hygiene* and how can this lead to foodborne illness?

5. What does the term *cross contamination* mean?

Answers to the multiple choice questions are provided in Appendix A.

Quiz 3.1 (Multiple Choice)

1. The number one contributing factor leading to foodborne illness in food establishments is:

    a. improper cooling of foods.

    b. cross contamination.

    c. poor personal hygiene.

    d. inadequate cooking of foods.

2. Foodborne illness can be caused by:

    a.   poor personal hygiene.

    b.   cross-contamination.

    c.   temperature abuse.

    d.   all of the above.

3. Regarding food thermometers, which statement is **false**? They should

    a.   be calibrated.

    b.   measure temperatures between 41° and 140°F (5° and 60°C).

    c.   measure temperatures between 0°and 220°F (-18° and 104°C).

    d.   be approved for use in foods.

4. Good personal hygiene includes

    a.   wearing latex gloves.

    b.   keeping hands and clothes clean and sanitary.

    c.   wearing attractive uniforms.

    d.   cleaning and sanitizing food contact surfaces.

5. Food handlers should wash their hands after which of the following?

    a.   Taking out the trash

    b.   Touching their face

    c.   Handling raw food

    d.   All of the above

6. Cross contamination is a term used to describe the transfer of a foodborne hazard from one food to another

    a.   by a food handler's hands.

    b.   from a cutting board.

    c.   from a meat grinder.

    d.   all of the above.

7. A good method to prevent cross contamination of foods is to

    a.   keep raw and cooked foods separate.

    b.   properly clean and sanitize food contact surfaces.

    c.   properly wash hands.

    d.   all of the above.

8. Which is the preferred method for thawing potentially hazardous foods?

   a. In the microwave oven

   b. At room temperature

   c. In the refrigerator

   d. Under 70°F (21°C) running water

9. After proper cooking, all foods that are to be held **cold** should be

   a. cooled quickly and held at 41°F (5°C) or below.

   b. cooled quickly and held at 140°F (60°C) or above.

   c. stored at room temperature until serving.

   d. cooled slowly and held at 140°F (60°C) until serving.

10. After proper cooking of foods, all foods that are to be held **hot** should be

   a. cooled quickly and held at 41°F (5°C) or below.

   b. cooled quickly and held at 140°F (60°C) or above.

   c. stored at room temperature until serving.

   d. cooled slowly and held at 140°F (60°C) or above until serving.

References/Suggested Readings

Council for Agricultural Sciences and Technology (1995). Prevention of Food-borne Illness. Dairy. *Food and Environmental Sanitation.* Vol. 15(6), 357-367.

Food and Drug Administration(1995). *1995 Food Code.* Washington, D.C.: United States Public Health Service.

Hecht, A. (1991) Preventing foodborne illness. *FDA Consumer.* Jan./Feb. (pp. 19-25)

Zottola, E. A. (1994). Microbial attachment and biofilm formation: a new problem for the food industry?. *Food Technology.* 8(1), 107-144.

Centers for Disease Control and Prevention (1996). *Surveillance for Foodborne Disease Outbreaks—United States, 1988-1992.* Atlanta, GA; U.S. Department of Health and Human Services.

4 FOLLOWING THE FOOD PRODUCT FLOW

How Would You Like It Cooked?

*In the mid 1990's, health departments in Washington, California, Idaho, and Nevada identified nearly 600 people with culture-confirmed **E. coli 0157:H7** infection. Many of the victims reported eating at Chain A restaurants during the days preceding onset of symptoms. Of the patients who recalled what they ate in a Chain A restaurant, a large percentage reported eating regular-sized hamburger patties. Chain A issued a multi-state recall of unused hamburger patties.*

*The **E. coli 0157:H7** bacteria were isolated from 11 batches of patties from Chain A. These patties had been distributed to restaurants in all states where the illness occurred. Approximately 20% of the patties connected with the outbreak were recovered during a recall.*

A team of investigators from the Centers for Disease Control and Prevention identified five slaughter plants in the United States and one in Canada as the likely sources of carcasses used in the contaminated meat. The animals slaughtered in domestic slaughter plants were traced to farms and auctions in six western states. No one slaughter plant or farm was identified as the source of contamination.

***E. coli 0157:H7** lives in the intestines of healthy cattle, and can contaminate meat during slaughter. Slaughtering practices can result in contamination of raw meat with these bacteria. In addition, the process of grinding beef can transfer the disease-causing agents from the surface of the meat to the interior. Therefore ground beef can be internally contaminated. In this outbreak, undercooked hamburger patties played an important role. As a result of this outbreak, the Food and Drug Administration now recommends that ground beef be cooked thoroughly until the center is no longer pink, and the juices are clear. The internal temperature of the ground beef should reach 155°F (69°C).*

Learning Objectives

After reading this chapter, you should be able to:

▲ Recognize codes and symbols used to designate food products that have been inspected by governmental agencies; therefore coming from approved sources

▲ Apply purchasing and receiving procedures that enhance the protection of food products

▲ Evaluate equipment used to transport food products to food establishments

▲ Display the ability to use approved devices to measure temperatures in food products, safely and accurately

▲ Recognize product defects and refuse acceptance of products that do not meet established food safety criteria

▲ Discuss safe methods to thaw frozen foods

▲ Identify internal temperature requirements for cooking foods

▲ Explain the proper methods used to cool foods

▲ Discuss the importance of employee health and hygiene related to the food flow

Essential Terms

Additives	Inspection for wholesomeness
Aseptic packaging	Leftovers
Cold-holding	Modified Atmosphere Packaging (MAP)
Cooking	Pasteurization
Cooling	Reheating
First in, first out (FIFO)	Sensory evaluation
Grade standards	Sous-vide
Hermetic packaging	Wholesome
Hot-holding	

A Sound Food Supply

Effective purchasing paves the way for a successful food service operation. Purchasing is a highly skilled activity requiring knowledge of products and market conditions.

The basic objectives of an effective purchasing program are to:

▲ Buy the product that is best suited for the job

▲ Buy the proper quantity of the item

▲ Pay the right price for the item

▲ Deal with only reputable and dependable suppliers

Purchasing techniques include comparative shopping, evaluation of new products, wise judgment in timing large purchases of seasonal items, and selection of the most efficient supplier. In addition, a buyer must understand foods, specifications, formulations, and be able to evaluate these in terms of price and quality.

Purchase specifications are important to both buyer and management. They are the guidelines that detail the characteristics of a product, including such properties as:

▲ quality grade

▲ weight

▲ count

▲ contents

▲ packaging

Specifications make the task of comparison shopping easier, since the characteristics of a product are expressed in a common language and can be used as a basis for evaluation.

Buying from Approved Sources

You should always purchase food that is safe and **wholesome.** Something is wholesome if it is favorable to or promotes health. Food must come from an approved source that complies with all applicable local, state, and federal food laws.

Reputable suppliers deliver food products in vehicles that are clean and in good repair. These vehicles will also keep perishable foods at safe temperatures during transport. Reputable suppliers keep food products separate from general supplies (such as sanitizers or cleaning agents) during shipping. They also protect food packages from becoming damaged or torn. Receiving clerks should be instructed to inspect delivery vehicles from time to time. During these inspections, the clerk should check for:

▲ cleanliness of the cargo area

▲ temperature of refrigerated and frozen storage areas (if applicable)

▲ proper separation of food and nonfood items

▲ signs of insect, rodent, or bird infestation

Foods prepared in a private home are not considered to be from an approved source. They must not be used or offered for sale in a retail food establishment. Aunt Lou may make the best brownies in town, but unless the health department inspects and approves her kitchen, her homemade products may not be used, or offered for sale, in a food establishment. The use of "home-canned" food is prohibited because of the risk of such food causing illness.

In the United States, government agencies closely monitor and regulate food supplies to protect the public from foodborne illness. These agencies at the federal, state, and local levels are concerned with the protection of the food supply available to consumers. The fundamental concern of all these agencies is the wholesomeness of the food supply as it reaches the customers. These agencies work in close cooperation with each other and the food industry. Additional information about these governmental agencies will be provided in Chapter 11, Food Safety Regulations.

Strategies for Determining Food Quality

Sensory evaluation is a commonly used method for making routine quality determinations on foods received at retail food establishments. This type of evaluation involves using the senses of smell, touch, sight, and sometimes taste.

As a first step, foods should be observed for color, texture, and visual evidence of spoilage. Quite often, spoilage is easily seen as in the case of slime formation, mold growth, and discoloration. Product containers should also be checked for tears, punctures, dents, or other signs of damage.

Flavor is a combination of smell and taste. Spoiled foods frequently give off foul odors indicative of compounds such as ammonia and hydrogen sulfide (the smell of rotten eggs). These odors, caused by the breakdown of proteins through bacterial action, are usually very easy to smell.

The flavor of spoiled foods can range from loss of good characteristic taste to the development of objectionable tastes. Spoilage due to yeasts produces bubbles and an alcoholic flavor or smell. Milk develops an acidic taste and is often bitter when it spoils.

The feel of spoiled foods is frequently determined by the type of food and the spoilage organism involved. Some foods feel slimy, while others may feel mushy.

Spoilage organisms alter food in many ways. **However, harmful bacteria and other disease-causing organisms can multiply to high numbers in food without altering the food's appearance, flavor, and odor.**

Measuring Temperatures at Receiving and Storage

Maintaining safe product temperature is a critical part of your food safety system. According to foodborne disease investigations, improper temperature control during food preparation and service is one of the leading contributors to foodborne illness. Temperature measuring devices are used in food establishments to measure temperatures of food, water, and the air of food storage areas (refrigerators, ovens, etc.).

You can measure the temperature of packaged foods accurately without opening the package. Place the probe of the thermometer or thermocouple between two packages of food or fold the package around the stem or probe to make good contact with the packaging. The photographs in Chapter 3, Figure 3.5, illustrate ways to measure the temperature of packaged and prepared foods.

To measure the temperature of an unpackaged food, insert the sensing element of the thermometer or thermocouple into the thickest part of the food. To avoid cross contamination of food items, be sure to wash, sanitize, and air dry the probe of the thermometer before going from a raw food to a cooked food.

Cold- or hot- holding equipment used for potentially hazardous foods must be equipped with an indicating or recording thermometer to measure the temperature of the storage environment. Equipment thermometers are either built into a piece of equipment or are fastened onto shelving or other apparatus. Position them where they can be easily read. **Place the sensor portion of the thermometer in the warmest part of a refrigeration unit, or in the coolest part of a hot food storage unit.**

Following the Flow of Food

The flow of food on-site begins with receiving and storage. From storage, food products move into the preparation and service phases, which can involve one or more steps. A simple diagram showing the flow of food is presented in Figure 4.1.

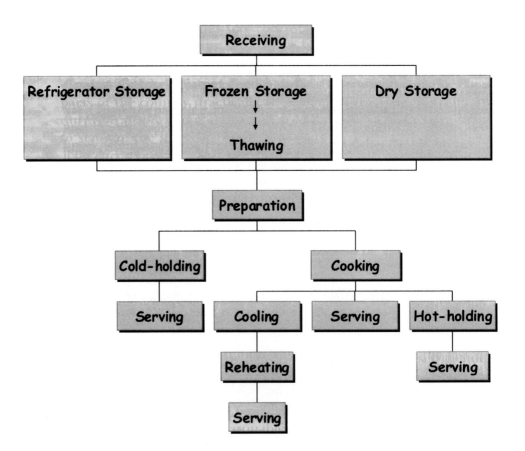

Figure 4.1—Food Flow Diagram

Receiving

Employees responsible for receiving products must carefully inspect all incoming food supplies to make sure they are in sound condition, free from filth or spoilage, and at the proper temperatures.

As a first step, observe foods for color, texture, and visual evidence of spoilage. Quite often, spoilage is easily visible as in the case of slime formation, mold growth, and discoloration. Check the product containers for tears, punctures, dents, or other signs of damage.

Proper receiving requires a knowledgeable person who follows specific guidelines. Poor receiving procedures increase the chance of:

▲ theft

▲ acceptance of underweight merchandise

▲ contamination

▲ waste

▲ acceptance of products that do not meet specifications

Anticipate the arrival of deliveries and make sure enough space is available to receive them. These are two critical elements of receiving. Schedule deliveries to avoid peak periods of the day. Employees need to receive and store incoming shipments as soon as they arrive. Always make certain that food products are delivered in clean, well-maintained vehicles that protect the food from contamination and maintain proper product temperature.

Whatever the size of the food establishment, receiving requires:

▲ prompt handling

▲ exacting quality control procedures

▲ trained staff who have good judgment and experience in interpreting:

  ▼ product specifications

  ▼ coding

  ▼ temperature measurement

Packaged Foods

The term **hermetic** refers to a container sealed completely to prevent the entry of gases and vapors. Such a container, since it remains intact, also stops the entry of bacteria, yeasts, molds, and other types of contamination. The most common hermetic containers are rigid metal cans and glass bottles.

Always check cans for:

▲ leaks

▲ bulges

▲ dents

▲ broken seals

▲ damage along seams

▲ rust

▲ missing labels

Do not accept cans if they leak or bulge at either end. Swollen ends on a can indicate that gas is being produced inside. This gas may be caused by a chemical reaction between the food and the metal in the container, or it may be caused by microbial activity inside the can.

Dents in cans do not harm the contents unless they have actually penetrated the can or sprung the seam. Shipments with many dented cans or torn labels indicate poor handling and storage procedures by the supplier. Figure 4.2 shows some common defects found in cans.

Figure 4.2—Defective Cans

Modified Atmosphere Packaging (MAP) is a process whereby foods are placed in flexible containers, and air is removed from the package (Figure 4.3). Different gases, such as nitrogen and carbon dioxide, are then added to the packaged food to preserve it. This technique allows centralized processing and packaging of retail cuts of meat and poultry, thus eliminating entirely the need for processing in the food establishment.

Figure 4.3—Examples of MAP Foods

Sous-vide is the French term for "under vacuum." Processors of sous-vide foods seal raw ingredients, often entire recipes, in plastic pouches, then vacuum out the air. They then minimally cook the pouch under precise conditions and immediately refrigerate it. Some processors replace some of the air in the pouches with nitrogen or carbon dioxide. Processing food in this manner eliminates the need for the extreme cold of freezing and the intense heat of canning, thus better preserving taste. Many foods, including pasta, vegetables, fish, chicken, and beef are packaged using the sous-vide method.

Potentially hazardous foods processed using the sous-vide technique must be kept out of the food temperature danger zone. The lack of oxygen inside the package provides a suitable environment for the growth of *C. botulinum*. **The sous-vide process may not destroy these harmful bacteria or their spores**. If the food is not refrigerated and kept out of the temperature danger zone, the spores may germinate and form vegetative bacterial cells. The botulism bacteria can produce toxins that may be fatal if eaten. The FDA recommends that sous-vide foods be:

▲ used by the expiration date printed on the package

▲ be refrigerated constantly

▲ be heated according to the time and temperature provided on the package directions

Red Meat Products

The main sources of red meat and meat products are cattle (beef), calves (veal), hogs (ham, pork, and bacon), sheep (mutton), and young sheep (lamb). These products are inspected for wholesomeness by officials of the United States Department of Agriculture (USDA) or state agencies. Animals must be inspected prior to and after slaughter to make certain they are free of disease and contamination. *The USDA also offers voluntary meat grading services. Grades for meat represent the quality or palatability of the meat and are not measures of product safety.* Figure 4.4 contains examples of inspections and grading stamps applied to products approved for use.

Inspection   **Grade**

Figure 4.4—USDA Inspection and Grade Stamps for Beef, Veal, and Lamb

Meat and meat products are obtained in several forms such as fresh, frozen, cured, smoked, dried, and canned. **Since meats are potentially hazardous foods, never accept them if there is any sign of contamination, temperature abuse, or spoilage.**

Never accept fresh meat if the product temperature exceeds 41°F (5°C) at delivery. Fresh meat should be firm and elastic to the touch and have characteristic aromas. Off odors are frequently an indicator of spoilage. Sliminess is another characteristic of spoilage and is caused by bacterial growth on the surface of meat. Control of factors that cause spoilage and sliminess also extends the shelf life of meat products.

Frozen meats should arrive frozen solid at an air temperature of 0°F (-18°C) or below. Look for signs of freezing and thawing and refreezing such as frozen blood juices in the bottom of the container or the presence of large ice crystals on the surface of the product. Frozen meats should be packaged to prevent freezer burn. Move these products quickly from the delivery truck to the freezer for storage.

Game Animals

Game animals are not allowed for sale or service in retail food establishments unless they meet federal code regulations. This ban does not apply to commercially raised game animals approved by regulatory agencies, field dressed game allowed by state codes, or exotic species of animals that must meet the same standards as that of other game animals.

Game animals that are commercially raised for food must be raised, slaughtered, and processed according to standards used for meat and poultry. Common examples of animals raised away from the wild and used for food are farm-raised buffalo, ostrich, and alligator. The USDA inspects the slaughter and processing of this meat in the usual manner.

Some states permit game animals, such as deer, bear, and elk, that have been killed and dressed in the field, to be used in food establishments. Game meat must be dressed soon after the kill to prevent rapid growth of bacteria already present in the meat. Next, the meat must be chilled rapidly, transported in a sanitary manner, and processed in an approved facility. Veterinarians are frequently appointed to inspect meat for contamination that would harm humans.

Some people consider exotic species of animals a delicacy. A distributor providing this type of product (elephant, tiger, monkey, etc.) must meet the same standards as those for domestic wild game. Endangered species may be prohibited by law from being used for food.

Poultry

Poultry is a very popular food item in America. Chicken, turkey, ducks, geese, and other types of poultry are used all year long for roasting, frying, broiling, grilling, and stewing.

All poultry products must be inspected for wholesomeness by USDA or state inspectors. Inspection for wholesomeness involves an examination of the poultry to make certain it is wholesome and not adulterated. The poultry is examined live before slaughter, during evisceration (removal of the internal organs), and during or after packaging. Inspected poultry products carry a USDA seal for wholesomeness on the individual package or on bulk cartons. Examples of inspection and grade stamps for poultry are shown in figure 4.5.

Most poultry are also graded for quality. Top quality birds receive a Grade A rating. To earn a Grade A rating, the poultry must have good overall shape and appearance, be meaty, practically free from defects, and have a well-developed layer of fat in the skin.

Inspection   Grade

Figure 4.5—USDA Inspection and Grade Stamps for Poultry

Poultry products support the growth of disease-causing and spoilage microorganisms. The intestinal tract and skin of poultry may contain a variety of foodborne disease bacteria, including *Salmonella spp.* and *Escherichia coli.* The near neutral pH, high moisture, and high protein content of poultry make it an ideal material for bacteria to grow in and on.

Poultry products are also vulnerable to spoilage caused by enzymes and spoilage bacteria.

Most spoilage bacteria come from the live bird's skin or intestinal tract. The bacteria grow on the skin of slaughtered birds and inside the birds' carcasses. Spoilage is indicated by meat tissue that is soft, slimy, and has an objectionable odor. Stickiness under the wings is another sign of poultry spoilage. Darkened wing tips on poultry are caused by drying or exposure to freezing temperatures. Poultry that is discolored or has darkened wing tips or sticky skin should be rejected. At the time of delivery, poultry should be packaged on a bed of ice that drains away from the meat as it melts and held at or below 41°F (5°C).

Eggs

Many food establishments, regardless of their size or menu, use eggs in one form or another. Eggs are usually purchased by federal grades, the most common being AA, A, and B (Figure 4.6). Grades for eggs are based on exterior and interior conditions of the egg. Eggs cannot receive a grade when they are dirty, cracked, or broken.

Inspection   **Grade**

Figure 4.6—USDA Inspection and Grade Stamps for Eggs

The USDA reports that approximately 50 billion eggs are sold in the U.S. each year. *Salmonella enteritidis* bacteria are present in about one percent (approximately 500 million) of the eggs sold. These bacteria enter the yolk of the egg as it is formed inside the hen. The eggshell surface also contains *Salmonella spp.* bacteria, especially if the shell is soiled with chicken droppings. Even if the shell is not cracked, bacteria can enter through the pores in the egg's shell. Whole shell eggs should be clean, fresh, free of cracks or checks, and properly refrigerated when delivered. The egg, when opened, should have no noticeable odor, the yolk firm, and the white should cling to the yolk. Reject eggs that are dirty or cracked, and remember that washing eggs only increases the possibility of contamination.

An egg product is defined as an egg without its shell. As a safeguard against *Salmonella spp.*, the FDA requires that all egg products, such as liquid, frozen, and dry eggs, be pasteurized to render them *Salmonella*-free. Pasteurized egg product should be in a sealed container and kept at 41° F (5°C). Egg containers should carry labels that verify the contents have been pasteurized.

The shelf life of eggs is limited. Only buy the quantity of eggs the establishment will use in a one- or two-week period.

Fluid Milk and Milk Products

This group of foods includes milk, cheese, butter, ice cream, and other types of milk products. When receiving milk and milk products, make certain they have been pasteurized. **Pasteurization** destroys all disease-causing microorganisms in the milk and reduces the total number of bacteria to increase storage time. All market milk must be Grade A quality. Pasteurization also destroys natural milk enzymes that might shorten the shelf-life of the products.

Milk that is marked "UHT" is pasteurized using ultra-high temperatures and is packaged aseptically. UHT products do not require refrigeration, if used within a few weeks. Individual creamers are sometimes processed in this manner.

Fluid Milk

Fluid milk is a potentially hazardous food that must be refrigerated immediately upon delivery. Keep containers of fluid milk and dairy creamers at 41°F (5°C) or below. Individual containers of milk should be clearly marked with an expiration date and the name of the dairy plant that produced it. Check the expiration date of all dairy products before using them.

Cheese

Cheese should be received at 5°C (41°F). It should be inspected to make certain it possesses the proper color, flavor, and moisture content. Cheese should be rejected if it contains mold that is *not* a normal part of the cheese or if the rind or package is damaged.

Butter

Butter is made from pasteurized cream. Since disease-causing and spoilage bacteria and mold may grow in butter, handle the product as a perishable item. The most common type of deterioration in butter is the development of a strong odor and flavor. Check to see that butter has a firm texture, even color, and is free of mold. The package should be intact and provide protection for the contents.

Staphylococcus aureus toxin has been the cause of foodborne disease outbreaks where butter and cheese were involved. *Staphylococcus aureus* does not require as much moisture as other pathogens and can thrive in salty foods which would inhibit other pathogens. Therefore, cheese and butter must be handled carefully and kept out of the temperature danger zone except as required during production.

Fish

Fish includes finfish that are harvested from saltwater and freshwater, and seafood that comes mainly from saltwater. Catfish and trout are two of the most popular types of freshwater finfish. Tuna, snapper, and flounder are saltwater finfish that are very popular with American consumers. Seafood consists of molluscan shellfish and crustaceans. Molluscan shellfish include oysters, clams, mussels, and scallops. Crustaceans include shrimp, lobster, and crab. Oysters, shrimp, catfish, salmon, and a few other types of finfish and seafood are being raised on fish farms using a technique called aquaculture.

Fish and seafood are generally more perishable than red meat tissue, even when stored in a refrigerator or freezer. The slime covering fish and shellfish contains a variety of bacteria that make them highly susceptible to contamination and microbial spoilage. Fish are also rich in unsaturated fatty acids which are susceptible to oxidation and the development of off-flavors and rancidity.

The quality of fish and seafood is measured by smell and appearance. Fresh finfish should have a mild, pleasant odor and bright, shiny skin with the scales tightly attached. Fish with the head intact should have clear, bulging eyes and bright red, moist gills. The flesh of fresh fish should be firm and elastic to the touch.

Fish must be commercially and legally caught or harvested, except when caught recreationally and approved for sale by the regulatory authority. Ready-to-eat raw, marinated, or partially cooked fish, other than molluscan shellfish, must be frozen throughout to a temperature of -4°F (-20°C) or below for 7 days in a freezer, or -31°F (-35°C) or below for 15 hours in a blast freezer, before service or sale. Records must be retained that show how the product was handled.

Shellfish must be purchased from sources approved by the Food and Drug Administration and the health departments of states located along the coastline where the shellfish is harvested. Shellfish transported from one state to another must come from sources listed in the *Interstate Certified Shellfish Shippers List*. The reason for requiring tight control over molluscan shellfish is the risk of Hepatitis A and other foodborne illnesses that may result from eating raw or insufficiently cooked forms of this product.

When received by a food establishment, molluscan shellfish must be reasonably free of mud, dead shellfish, and shellfish with broken shells. Dead shellfish and shellstock with badly broken shells must be discarded.

Molluscan shellfish must be purchased in containers that bear legible source-identification tags or labels (Figure 4.7) that have been fastened to the container by the harvester and each dealer that depurates, ships, or reships the shellstock. Molluscan shellfish tags must contain the following information:

▲ The harvester's identification number

▲ The date of harvesting

▲ The harvesting site

▲ The shellfish type and quantity

▲ A statement about leaving the tag on the container until shellfish is used

▲ Instructions to keep the tag on file for ninety (90) days

Figure 4.7—Example of Shellfish Tag

Hold the tags that come with shellstock for at least 90 days after the container is emptied. If that seafood is suspected of being the source of foodborne illness, the investigating team can use the tags to determine where and when the product was harvested and processed.

Do not remove shellstock from the shipping container until right before sale or preparation for service, unless it is held on drained ice or in a display case that protects it from contamination. When it is necessary to remove the shellfish from the original, tagged container, only one container of shellfish should be used at a time. Molluscan shellfish caught recreationally *may not* be used or sold in food establishments.

Vegetables and Fruits

Most fruits and vegetables spoil very rapidly. They continue to ripen even after they are picked. Therefore, they may become too ripe if not properly handled. Microorganisms found in water and soil can also cause fruits and vegetables to spoil. Fruits and vegetables hold their top quality for only a few days. Always purchase vegetables and fruits from a reputable supplier.

Some products, like wild mushrooms, may only be used if they have been inspected and approved by a mushroom-identification expert who is approved by the regulatory authority. Beware of fresh mushrooms that are packaged in styrofoam trays and covered with plastic shrink wrap. Mushrooms have a high rate of respiration which will quickly use up the oxygen inside the package. Unless holes are poked in the plastic wrap that covers the package to permit oxygen inside, oxygen-free conditions may occur that are favorable for the growth of *C. botulinum* bacteria.

Frozen Foods

Frozen products must be at or below 0°F (-18° C) when delivered. The temperature of frozen foods can be checked by inserting the sensing portion of a thermometer between two packages. Receiving personnel should also look for signs that the product has been thawed and refrozen. Common signs of thawing and refreezing are large ice crystals on the surface of a frozen food and frozen liquids or juices inside the package. Reject frozen foods that are not solidly frozen or show signs of temperature abuse.

Proper Storage of Food

Merely assigning someone to check incoming shipments is not enough. Besides knowing what to look for upon delivery, employees must also know how and why to safely handle the food products that are left at the establishment. They must move the materials to the desired storage areas quickly, using clean carts and dollies to transport the food.

Stock rotation is a very important part of effective food storage. A **first in, first out (FIFO) method** of stock rotation helps insure that older foods are used first. Product containers should be marked with a date or other readily identifiable code to help food workers know which product has been in storage longest. When expecting food shipments, always make certain the older stock is moved to the front of the storage area to make room for the newly arriving products.

Types of Storage

The three most common types of food storage areas are the:

▲ refrigerator

▲ freezer

▲ dry storage

Refrigerated storage is used to hold potentially hazardous and perishable foods for relatively short periods of time, usually a few days. Freezer storage is used to hold foods for longer periods of time, usually a few weeks to several months. Dry storage is typically used to store less perishable items and foods that are not potentially hazardous foods.

Refrigerated storage slows down microbial growth and preserves the quality of foods. Some common types of refrigerated storage equipment are walk-in, reach-in, and pass-through refrigerators. This equipment usually maintains the air temperature in the storage compartment at about 38°F (3° C). Potentially hazardous foods must be stored at 4107°F (5°C) or below. Fish and shellfish that are especially vulnerable to spoilage should be stored at colder temperatures ranging from 30° to 34°F (-1.1° to 1.1°C). Some fruits and vegetables, such as bananas and potatoes, undergo undesirable chemical changes when they are refrigerated. Therefore, although fruits and vegetables are perishable products, not all types of them should be refrigerated. Fresh fruits and vegetables requiring refrigeration should be stored at temperatures between 41° and

45°F (5° to 7°C). Refrigerators must be equipped with either indicating or recording thermometers to monitor the temperature of the air inside the storage unit.

Freezers are designed to keep foods at 0°F (-18°C) or below. Freezer equipment must also be equipped with indicating or recording thermometers to monitor the temperature of the ambient air inside the unit. If your freezer is not frost free, defrost it regularly to assure proper operation. Wrap frozen foods and transfer them to the refrigerated storage area until the defrosting process is complete.

Some important procedures for cold storage are listed below:

▲ Rotate refrigerated and frozen foods on a *first in, first out* (FIFO) basis. Store foods in covered containers that are properly labeled and dated.

▲ Store foods in refrigerated and freezer storage areas at least six inches off the floor. Space products to allow the cold air to circulate around them.

▲ Store raw products under cooked or ready-to-eat foods to prevent cross contamination (Figure 4.8).

Figure 4.8—Contamination of Ready-to-Eat Food

Use a *dry storage* area to store foods that are usually packaged in cans, bottles, jars, and bags (see Figure 4.9). These products must be labeled according to federal regulation and come packaged from approved commercial facilities.

The dry storage area should have moderate room temperature of 50° to 70°F (10° to 21°C) and a relative humidity of 50 to 60% to maximize the shelf life of the foods stored there. The quality of some foods is reduced by sunlight. Therefore, windows are not recommended in dry storage areas. If windows are present, they should be blocked out or shaded.

Figure 4.9—Dry Storage Areas

Stored foods in the dry storage area should be on slatted shelves, at least six inches off the floor and away from the wall. The six inch clearance permits thorough cleaning under and behind the shelving. It also discourages insects and rodents from harboring there. Products should be spaced on the shelves so that air can circulate around them.

If it is necessary to transfer bulk items, such as flour, sugar, and grain foods, into other containers, these containers must be constructed of food-grade materials and equipped with tight fitting lids. Make certain the containers are properly coded, or dated, and labeled.

Do not use toilet rooms, locker areas, mechanical rooms, and similar spaces for storage of food, single-service items, paper goods, or equipment and utensils. Do not store products under overhead water and sewer lines that might be sources of contamination.

Figure 4.10—Do Not Store Chemicals Such as Cleaning Agents and Sanitizing Agents Near Food

Do not store chemicals, such as cleaning and sanitizing agents, near foods. If space permits, store these products in a completely separate area away from the dry storage area. If a separate storage space is not available, store these chemicals in a locked and labeled cabinet. Pesticides must be stored in an area away from food and materials used for cleaning and sanitizing. Always discourage employees from storing their clothing, handbags, and other personal items in dry storage areas.

Storage Conditions for Foods

Meat and meat products come in a variety of forms including fresh, frozen, cured and smoked, dried and canned. Fresh meat can be stored for up to three weeks at temperatures between 32° and 41°F

(0° and 5°C) and a relative humidity between 85 and 90%. Cold temperatures extend the shelf life of red meats by slowing down the growth of bacteria that cause spoilage. The high relative humidity prevents excessive drying and shrinkage.

Frozen meats can be stored for several months when held at 0°F (-18°C) or below. Frozen meats must be wrapped in moisture-proof paper to prevent them from drying out. Packaging for frozen foods should also be strong, flexible, and protect against light.

Poultry can be safely stored at temperatures between 30° and 36°F (-1.1° to 2°C) for short periods of time. A relative humidity of 75 to 85% is recommended, as excessive humidity causes sliminess due to excessive bacterial growth. Poultry should be wrapped carefully to prevent dehydration, contamination, and loss of quality. Frozen poultry and poultry products can be stored for four to six months when held at 0°F (-18°C) or below.

Whole shell eggs will keep fresh for eight to nine months when stored at 29° to 31°F (-2° to -1°C) and 85 to 90% relative humidity. Egg quality deteriorates rapidly at room temperature. Egg shells are porous and odors can be absorbed very easily. Keep eggs covered and store them away from onions and other foods that have a strong odor. Discard eggs that are dirty or cracked. Always make sure to wash your hands after handling whole shell eggs.

Egg products such as whole eggs, egg whites, and yolks are pasteurized to destroy *Salmonella* bacteria. Fresh egg products should be stored at 41°F (5°C) or below. Store frozen eggs at 0°F (-18°C) or below and keep them frozen until time for defrosting. Refrigerate dried egg products or keep them in a cool, dry place. Once dried eggs have been reconstituted, they are considered potentially hazardous and must be stored out of the temperature danger zone.

Milk is one of the most perishable foods handled in a food establishment. However, properly pasteurized milk that has not been recontaminated and is held at 41°F (5°C) will keep up to ten days or longer. The optimal storage temperature for fluid milk is 33° to 41°F (1° to 5°C), and the shelf life of milk is shortened significantly at higher storage temperatures. For example, milk held at 60°F (16°C) will stay fresh less than one day. Milk also picks up odors from other foods. Therefore, store milk in an area away from onions and other foods that give off odors.

Fish and shellfish are more perishable than red meats, even when refrigerated or frozen. There are many bacteria in the surface slime and digestive tracts of living fish. When a fish is killed, bacteria attack the tissue of the fish. These bacteria are used to living on cold-blooded fish at low water temperatures. Therefore, they adapt well to cold and continue to grow even under refrigerated conditions. The shelf life of fresh fish depends on many factors including: species, season of the year, physical condition (whether filleted or dressed), and manner of handling.

Most shellfish are even more perishable than finfish. The shells of live clams and oysters should be closed or close when tapped. Lobsters and crabs should be kept alive until they are cooked or frozen. Otherwise, they lose quality in a day or less.

Fish and shellfish should be used within 24 hours unless they are stored in crushed ice that will drain away from the product as it melts. Products that are stored in ice should be placed under cooked or ready-to-eat foods to prevent cross contamination.

The ideal storage conditions for fresh fruits are temperatures between 41° and 45°F (5° and 7°C), a relative humidity of about 80%, and shaded from light. During respiration and ripening, fresh fruits give off carbon dioxide and water. Because of this, they may become wilted and lose flavor. Proper air circulation in the refrigerated storage area is necessary to maintain freshness and firmness. Inadequate ventilation leads to spoilage and deterioration. Regularly inspect stored fruits. Discard any that begin to spoil.

Vegetable storage, requires low temperatures and high humidity to preserve texture, tenderness, flavor, color, and nutritive content. To retain top quality, vegetables should be stored between 41° and 45°F (5° and 7°C) with a relative humidity of 85 to 95%. If fresh fruits and vegetables come packed with an airtight film, poke holes in it to allow the contents to breathe. Otherwise, off-flavors and odors may develop.

Preparation and Service

The preparation and service of foods can involve one or more steps. In small food establishments, such as convenience stores, food products are commonly purchased in ready-to-eat forms which are stored until sold to the consumer. Large operations, such as restaurants, supermarkets, and institutional feeding facilities, prepare and serve food in vast quantities. Food production in these larger establishments may span several hours or days. These operations are more complex and may involve many steps.

Regardless of how many steps may be involved in food production and service, foodborne illness prevention requires effective food safety measures that assure good personal hygiene and avoid cross-contamination and temperature abuse. Food safety strategies aimed at addressing these practices will be discussed in the remainder of this chapter.

Handwashing

Hands are known to be significant sources of contamination and cross contamination of foods. This is especially true during the steps of preparation and service. Prevention of foodborne illness begins with good personal hygiene and includes proper handwashing (Figure 4.11). The importance of scrubbing forearms, hands, and nails using soap, running water, and friction cannot be overstated. With the vigorous removal of visible soil, harmful microbes can be washed down the drain.

Figure 4.11—Which Hand Do You Want to Handle Your Food?

Avoiding Temperature Abuse

In Chapter 5, the Hazard Analysis Critical Control Point System is presented, and you will identify areas of risk. If you work in a food establishment, you must *know how and when to use a thermometer*. **Temperature and time are the most common critical control points as identified in the HACCP flow charts in preparation and service.** *Monitoring and controlling food temperatures* are extremely effective ways to *minimize the risks of foodborne illness*. Thermometers are used for stored, cooked, hot-held, cold-held, and reheated foods. Various types of thermometers are used throughout the food establishment. Some of these instruments were described and shown earlier in Chapter 3, Figure 3.3. Before using a thermometer, make sure that it is clean, sanitary, and properly calibrated. The "sensor" portion or probe stem of the thermometer must be inserted into the thickest part of the food.

Freezing

Most harmful bacteria and other microorganisms do not grow at temperatures below 41°F (5°C). However, many spoilage microorganisms grow at much colder temperatures. Therefore, frozen foods must be kept *solidly* frozen and *stored* at 0°F (-18°C) or below.

Sometimes freezing foods can make them safer. Although bacteria are generally not destroyed by freezing, parasites can be killed if frozen at the proper temperature for the proper length of time. Figure 4.12 presents the parasitic destruction guidelines that have been established for fish.

Food should be frozen throughout to -4°F (-20°C) and held for 7 days in a freezer.

Food should be frozen throughout to -31°F (-35°C) using a blast chiller, and held at that temperature for 15 hours.

Figure 4.12—Guidelines for Parasitic Destruction (Source: *Food Code*)

It is difficult to measure the *internal* temperature of packaged frozen foods. However, it is acceptable to place a thermometer between two fully-frozen packaged foods to gain a reading. Be sure to monitor the temperature of your freezer unit from time to time to make sure it is working properly. However, you must understand that measuring the temperature of the freezer is never the same as measuring the actual food temperature.

Thawing

Thawing frozen foods is a common activity in food establishments. The most common and acceptable methods for thawing foods include: in a refrigerator, in a microwave oven followed by immediate cooking, under cool running water, and as part of the cooking process (Figure 4.13).

▲ Under refrigeration that maintains a food temperature at 41°F (5°C) or below

▲ Completely submerged under running water

  ▼ at a water temperature of 70°F (21°C) or below

  ▼ with sufficient water velocity to agitate and float loose particles in an overflow

  ▼ for a period of time that does not allow thawed portions of ready-to-eat foods to rise above 41°F (5°C)

  ▼ for a period of time that does not allow thawed portions of a raw animal food requiring cooking to be in the temperature danger zone for more than a total time of 4 hours

▲ As a part of the cooking process

Use any procedure (e.g., microwave oven) that thaws a portion of frozen ready-to-eat food that is prepared for immediate service in response to an individual consumer's order.

Figure 4.13—Recommended Methods for Thawing Food
(Source: 1997 *Food Code*)

The preferred method of thawing is in the refrigerator, since foods thawed in this manner would not have the opportunity to be in the temperature danger zone. This method requires good planning and adequate refrigeration space. It can take 2 or 3 days and sometimes longer to thaw large food masses such as turkeys, roasts, and hams. When using this method to thaw foods, you must plan ahead.

Foods thawed in the microwave must be cooked immediately after thawing. Cooking can be done in the microwave oven or with conventional cooking equipment. Do not thaw foods in a microwave oven and *then* store them in a refrigerator before they are cooked. The thawing process may initiate microbial activity that could reach dangerous levels during refrigerated storage.

Some foods, like turkey and roasts, can be thawed under cool (less than 70°F, 21° C) running water. The thawing time, when using the running water method, should be less than four hours including the time it takes for preparation for cooking. As soon as the temperature reaches 41°F (5°C), the meat should be prepared and cooked.

Under no circumstances should foods be thawed at room temperature. Room temperature thawing puts foods in the temperature danger zone—the very thing you don't want to happen. When foods are thawed at room temperature, the outer surface of the food thaws first and will soon reach room temperature. Microbial growth occurs very quickly at room temperature.

Cold Storage

Harmful microorganisms grow best at temperatures above 41°F (5°C). Therefore, it only makes sense to store potentially hazardous and perishable foods in cold storage at 41°F (5°C) or below. Microbial growth slows down significantly at temperatures of 41°F (5°C) and below. Some cold-loving bacteria can grow at temperatures below 41°F (5°C), but their growth is very slow. You should monitor the temperature of cold held foods routinely throughout the day to ensure that safe temperature requirements are being met.

Refrigerators and cold service bars differ in their capacity to keep foods cool. In all instances, the air inside the refrigerated compartment will need to be a few degrees colder than 41°F (5°C) to assure that cold foods are held at 41°F (5°C) or below.

Cooking

You must expect raw foods, especially those of animal origin, to contain harmful microorganisms. Foods such as meat, poultry, fish, seafood, eggs, and unpasteurized milk should not be prepared and served raw or rare. Establishments that choose to serve raw foods increase their risk of having a foodborne illness. Practices such as using raw eggs to make a Caesar salad, or serving raw oysters on the half shell, increase the risk of a foodborne illness. Raw animal foods need to be cooked to the proper temperatures to be safe.

The purpose of **cooking** is to make food more palatable by changing its appearance, texture, and aroma. Cooking also heats the food and destroys harmful microorganisms that may be found in and on the product. The destruction of disease-causing microorganisms is a phenomenon involving a direct relationship between time and temperature. For example, requirements for cooking a particular food item should include a final internal temperature as well as a prescribed length of time at that temperature.

Most foods are cooked using stoves, conventional ovens, and microwave ovens. Because heat transfer can be different depending on the heating source, final temperature requirements have been set for conventional oven cooking and microwave cooking. Cooking guidelines for various kinds of potentially hazardous foods are presented in Figure 4.14.

Food Type	Internal Temperature	Time Held at Internal Temperature Before Serving
Beef Roast (rare)	130°F (54°C)	121 min.
Eggs, Beef (other than roasts), Fish	145°F (63°C)	15 sec.
Pork products, ground beef and pork, game animals	155°F (69°C)	15 sec.
Beef Roast	145°F (63°C)	3 min.
Poultry, stuffed meats	165°F (74°C)	15 sec.

* Microwave cooking: Add 25°F (14°C) to the temperature shown above

Figure 4.14—Cooking Guidelines for Various Retail Foods
(Source: 1997 Food Code)

Rare beef roasts require the least internal temperature requirements. This is because the contamination is on the surface of the large roast. When an internal temperature of 130°F (54°C) for 121 minutes or 145°F (63°C) for 3 minutes is reached, the surface temperature of the food is much higher. This heat will destroy any pathogens that may have been on the surface of the roast. Animal foods such as eggs, fish, and beef (other than roasts) should be cooked to an internal temperature of at least 145°F (63°C) and held at that temperature for at least 15 seconds before serving.

Cook ground beef and pork and game animal products to 155°F (68°C) and hold for at least 15 seconds before serving. Pork and game animals need a higher cooking temperature due to the possible presence of the trichinosis worm and other parasites.

Poultry and stuffed meats should be cooked to an internal temperature of 165°F (74°C) and held for at least 15 seconds before serving.

When cooking foods in the microwave oven, the distribution of heat is often uneven. To distribute the heat more evenly you must stir frequently and rotate the food. The temperature requirements for microwave heated foods are typically 25°F (14°C) higher than for foods cooked using conventional equipment. This helps to provide an extra margin of safety. For example, chicken breasts cooked in a conventional oven should reach an internal temperature of 165°F (74°C), while poultry cooked in a microwave should reach 165°F + 25°F (74°C + 14°C) or 190°F (88°C). Allow microwave foods to sit for 5 to 10 minutes before serving to allow heat to disperse more evenly.

Measure the *internal temperature* of foods while they are *being cooked*. Ideally, the internal temperature should be measured in the geometric center of the food. A commonly used practice in the food industry is inserting the appropriate thermometer or thermocouple probe into the thickest part of the food mass. This will give you an accurate reading of the internal temperature of the product.

Proper cooking of products is extremely important for the preparation of safe food. If a potentially hazardous food is cooked to a safe temperature, bacteria and other harmful organisms will be destroyed. Bacterial spores and some toxins may not be destroyed by normal cooking temperatures. Therefore, proper handling of these foods is required at every stage of the food flow.

Cooling

Improper cooling is the number one cause of foodborne illness in food establishments. Foods are in the temperature danger zone during **cooling** and there is no way to avoid it. After proper cooking, potentially hazardous foods need to be cooled from 140° to 41°F (60° to 5°C) as rapidly as possible. The *Food Code* recommends that hot foods, not used for immediate service or hot display, be cooled from 140° to 70°F (60° to 21°C) within two hours, and from 70° to 41°F (21° to 5°C) within an additional four hours. Industry standards commonly recommend that hot foods be cooled from 140° to 41°F (60° to 5°C) in four hours. Industry often chooses a more stringent time guide than those suggested in the *Food Code*.

Large quantities of food and foods that have a thick consistency take a long time to cool. For instance, it can take 72 hours or more for the center of a 5-gallon stockpot of steamed rice to cool down to 41°F (5°C) when taken hot from the stove and placed in a refrigerator.

Foods must pass through the temperature danger zone as quickly as possible. Figure 4.15 lists some of the more commonly used methods for reducing cooling time.

▲ Use containers that facilitate heat transfer (stainless steel)

▲ Transfer food into shallow pans (less than 4 inches high)

▲ Transfer food into smaller containers

▲ Stir food while cooling

▲ Place containerized food in an ice water bath

▲ Stir food in a container placed in an ice water bath

▲ Add ice directly to a condensed food

Figure 4.15—Methods to Reduce Cooling Time for Food

Photographs of the three most commonly used methods of cooling are presented in Figure 4.16. As it was with cooking, you must monitor times and temperatures for foods that are cooling. When large masses of food are broken down into smaller portions, cooling is much more rapid.

For example, a large turkey can be sliced into smaller pieces, or creamed corn can be transferred into shallow pans to facilitate cooling. Foods cool faster in food-grade metal containers than in food-grade plastic containers.

When using shallow pans to cool liquid food, the pan should be only 4 inches high. Foods cooled in a shallow pan should be less than 3 inches deep for liquids (soup) and less than 2 inches for viscous products (chili).

Always use a thermometer to verify that foods are cooling properly. Never assume that any one method is working without checking the temperature and time that foods take to cool. Always depend on the thermometer reading with any of the methods you use to cool food.

A. Ice bath   B. Place food in shallow   C. Use smaller
                        pans 2-3" deep   containers to
                                                            reduce food mass

Figure 4.16—Approved Cooling Methods

Cooling time is greatly reduced when foods are stirred. Foods stirred every 10-15 minutes cool far more rapidly than unstirred foods. An ice water bath also helps to remove heat from foods.

An ice water bath involves putting the container of hot food inside a larger container and surrounding it with ice to promote cooling. It is sometimes desirable to combine cooling methods, such as stirring a food after putting the container into an ice water bath.

You may also fill a large pot with ice and water. Then, insert the container of hot food into the ice water and stir the product. Keep the water level below the rim of the food container. In some instances, ice from a potable water supply can be added as a "final ingredient" in preparing hot items from condensed foods. Large quantities of soup or broth can be prepared in this way.

Hot-holding, Cold-holding, Reheating

All potentially hazardous foods, except rare roast beef, that have been cooked, cooled, and then reheated must be held hot at temperatures of 140°F (60°C) or above. **Cold-holding** is holding potentially hazardous foods which are to be consumed cold at 41°F (5°C) or below. **Hot-holding** is holding potentially hazardous foods above 140°F (60°C) during transportation and delivery to any site away from the primary preparation and service areas.

Proper holding temperatures slow down or prevent the growth of harmful microorganisms. The key is to keep foods out of the temperature danger zone (140° to 41°F, 60° to 5°C). All potentially hazardous foods, meant to be eaten hot, that have been cooked and then cooled must be reheated to at least 165°F (74°C) within two hours. Foods can be heated more quickly when heated in smaller quantities or by using pre-heated ingredients. Stir food frequently during reheating to reduce the time needed to reheat. Foods should only be reheated once, and uneaten portions of a reheated food should be discarded.

Serving Safe Food

When you serve food, always practice good personal hygiene. Start by wearing a clean uniform and hair restraint. Food, or surfaces that may come in contact with food, should not be touched with hands,. Hold utensils only by the handles and do not touch beverage glasses by the outside or inside rim; handle plates and bowls by the bottom or outer rim. Finally, wash your hands after handling dirty tableware and utensils. Never dry your hands on your apron. Always use a single-service towel.

Self-Service Bar

Self-service bars are very popular. They offer convenience and a wide range of selections for consumers. A properly installed sneeze guard protects the food from contamination by your customers and is required in most jurisdictions (Figure 4.17).

Figure 4.17—Self-Service Bar with Sneeze Guard

Keep potentially hazardous foods on self-service bars hot at 140°F (60°C) or above and cold at 41°F (5°C) or below. Monitor food holding temperatures frequently in these operations. Never serve raw animal products at a self-service bar.

Always use clean sanitized utensils in a self-service bar. Monitor the bar and replace any utensils that become contaminated. Hold utensils by the handle. Do not allow hand contact with foods in containers.

Keep utensils in the food between use. Resting utensils on saucers beside containers is not an acceptable practice. Only one utensil should be used for each food item.

Self-service bars tend to get messy because of spills. *Clean the station* frequently throughout the day, to reduce the potential for cross contamination. Assign a properly trained food worker to monitor and maintain a self-service bar or buffet bar.

Self-service plates and bowls should only be used once to avoid contaminating food on the buffet or salad bar. Give your customers a clean plate or bowl each time they return to the salad bar. Beverage cups and glasses maybe reused to get refills.

Temporary and Mobile Food Facilities

The popularity of temporary and mobile food facilities such as street fairs, festivals, and mobile carts increased rapidly during the past decade (Figure 4.18). The public patronizes these events in increasing numbers. In addition to the opportunity for community involvement, commercial and non-commercial organizations are finding it profitable to sell food at temporary food facilities.

Mobile   Temporary

Figure 4.18—Examples of Temporary and Mobile Food Facilities

In the beginning, temporary facilities served food items such as hamburgers and hot dogs. These foods required minimal preparation. They were taken from a cooler, placed on a grill, and cooked to order.

Depending on where you are, the food served by temporary facilities in the 1990s might consist of anything from BBQ ribs, calamari, gyros, and pizza to sushi and shish kebabs. Today's sophisticated appetites demand foods which frequently involve risky preparation methods, such as heating, cooling, and reheating.

Consumers also insist on freshly prepared food, prompting vendors to transport raw ingredients to their make-shift booths to chop, shred, and assemble without access to the sanitary facilities that would be standard in a permanent food establishment.

The more extensive the menu or more complex the preparation, the higher the risk, and the more demanding public health requirements become to reduce these dangers. Vendors should contact the local regulatory agency in their jurisdiction to obtain a copy of the rules that govern temporary and mobile operations.

Protecting the food and food preparation equipment from contamination is the function of the structure. A temporary food stand should have:

▲ an overhead covering

▲ an enclosed area except for the serving windows and an entry door

▲ a source of hot and cold potable running water for handwashing, cleaning, and sanitizing

Your menu and method of food preparation will determine your selection of equipment and utensils. Food contact surfaces must be designed for effective cleaning and sanitizing. They must also be constructed of materials that are non-toxic. Cooking equipment must be capable of heating potentially hazardous foods to the required internal temperature. For example, hamburgers and other ground beef should be cooked to an internal temperature of 155°F (68°C); poultry to 165°F (74°C); and fish and other meats to 145°F (63°C). Foods to be reheated must reach an internal temperature of 165°F (74°C) within two hours. Do not use slow cooking devices such as crockpots, steam tables, and sterno to heat foods. These devices may never reach temperatures high enough to kill harmful bacteria.

Foods that require refrigeration must be cooled to 41°F (5°C) as quickly as possible and held at that temperature until served. Cold foods should be at 41°F (5°C) or below when delivered to the temporary facility. If for some reason it is necessary to cool foods down, use an ice water bath or place the food in shallow pans and refrigerate. Do not forget that proper food temperatures are your most important control measure against foodborne illness. Minimizing the time between preparation and service is another good practice to use to keep food safe.

An adequate handwashing facility must be provided, and strict handwashing procedures must be observed to keep food safe. Disposable gloves can provide an additional barrier to contamination. However, gloves are no substitute for handwashing.

Good food handling practices are an important line of defense in temporary food facilities. Raw foods must be kept and handled separate from ready-to-eat foods. It is best to use tongs, napkins, disposable gloves, or other tools to handle food.

Temporary food facilities should use disposable utensils for food service. If it is necessary to use multi-use utensils, they must be washed and sanitized using a four-step process:

1. washing in hot, soapy water

2. rinsing in clean water

3. chemical sanitizing

4. air drying

A detailed explanation of this process is presented in Chapter 7, Cleaning and Sanitizing Operations. It is a good idea to have additional clean and sanitized utensils on hand to accommodate peak periods when there is not adequate time to perform the dishwashing process. Rinse and store the wiping cloths used in the operation in a pail of sanitizer solution. The concentration of the sanitizer must be checked regularly to make certain it remains at the required strength. The strengh of the sanitizer can be measured using either a chemical test kit or test strips. Always replace the solution whenever it falls below the required minimum concentration.

Garbage and paper wastes should be placed in containers that are lined with plastic liners and equipped with tight-fitting lids. Keep foods and wastes covered to avoid attracting insects, rodents, and other pests. Always store pesticides away from food, and be sure to follow the manufacturer's instructions if you apply them. Clean and sanitize all food contact surfaces that may have been contaminated when the pesticides are applied.

Along with the fun and potential profit, food vendors should be aware of the potential public health problems with food served by temporary or mobile food service operations. *Improvised facilities, large volumes of food, severe weather conditions, and untrained food workers can make keeping foods safe and sanitary a real challenge.* Temporary events frequently serve large numbers of people which makes it necessary to prepare large quantities of food in advance. This increases the risk of contamination and makes proper cooking, cooling, and holding even more critical. Always consult your local food protection program on the specifics of your operation.

Summary

The outbreak of *E. coli 0157:H7* that you read about at the beginning of this chapter influenced consumer awareness in the United States. Remember the people who are "at risk". Children and older adults died from *E. coli 0157.H7* infection during this outbreak. Foodborne illness can kill, and you can prevent that.

Not all food managers or supervisors will actually select or purchase products. However, knowledge of the rules, regulations, and procedures of receiving and storage is expected of all who are responsible for food safety.

To assure that all foods are safe for human consumption, purchase your food supplies from approved sources and suppliers who comply with all laws concerning food processing and labeling. Schedule deliveries for the off peak times when someone is available to inspect incoming food supplies. Make sure that food is free from filth or spoilage, in sound condition, and is the proper temperature. If the product has been damaged or does not meet standards, reject the delivery. The supplier should be responsible for replacing or giving credit for rejected material.

Move delivered materials into designated storage areas quickly. Storage serves as a temporary link between receiving and preparation. Storage facilities must be capable of preserving the sanitary quality of the food stored there.

Store foods in their original containers or packages whenever possible. When food is removed from the package or container in which it was delivered, it must then be stored in a clean, covered container that is properly labeled and dated. Proper stock rotation using the FIFO system is necessary to assure that stocked items will be used within a reasonable period of time.

Provide adequate "dry storage" for dry items such as canned goods. For highly perishable items, refrigerator or freezer storage is necessary. Chilled storage is required for perishable and potentially hazardous foods such as dairy products, meat, poultry, eggs, fish, seafood, fruits, and vegetables. Store these products out of the temperature danger zone. Freezer storage, capable of holding products in a frozen condition, must be provided for all frozen foods.

To assure the maintenance of all potentially hazardous food at required cold temperatures during storage, refrigerators and freezers must be equipped with a numerically scaled thermometer. The thermometer should measure temperature in increments no greater than 2°F (1°C). The sensor of the temperature-measuring device must be located to measure the air temperature in the warmest part of a mechanically refrigerated unit. The temperature-sensing device should also be located to allow easy viewing of the device's temperature display. The temperature of food should be measured to verify that holding temperatures are correct.

To prevent the possibility of cross contamination, always store raw or unwashed foods below ready-to-eat foods and foods that will not receive any additional cooking. Do not store food containers on the floor or under any exposed or unprotected sewer or water lines.

Keep the storage areas, including the floors, walls, and ceilings, clean. Make sure that the shelving units in these areas are clean and in good repair. Spilled foods should be cleaned up immediately and removed from the area.

Errors that occur during the preparation and service of food are the leading causes of foodborne illness in food establishments. To assure safe food, proper food handling is essential.

Safe food preparation and service include good personnel hygiene and taking measures to avoid cross contamination. It is critical to know when and how frequently hands and other food contact surfaces should be cleaned and sanitized. Monitoring and controlling food temperatures during preparation are important for destroying microorganisms and/or preventing them from growing in the food. Keeping foods out of the temperature danger zone as much as possible and cooking them properly are both very important considerations. Foods should only be allowed in the temperature danger zone for a short time during thawing, heating and cooling activities. The three main problems in foodservice, time and temperature abuse, cross contamination, and poor personal health and hygiene practices of food handlers must be prevented during the flow of food. Preparation and service are critical processes in your food establishment because they are the last steps you take before the consumer eats your food.

Case Study 4.1

David Jones is manager of the Great American Cafe. As part of a newly implemented self-inspection program, David performs an inspection of the walk-in refrigerator. During the inspection, David notices that turkeys for tomorrow's dinner are not covered during thawing, and they are stored directly above several washed heads of lettuce. Other food items are stored in covered containers that are not labeled or dated. David also notices that boxes of produce have been stacked closely together on the floor of the walk-in cooler, and the thermometer is hanging from the condensing unit.

1. What sanitation hazards exist in the walk-in refrigeration unit at the Great American Cafe?

2. Which of these hazards might result in food contamination and spoilage?

3. What should be done to correct the problems that Mr. Jones observed during his inspection?

Case Study 4.2

Metro Market is a combination convenience store and delicatessen. Deliveries are received between 9:00 a.m. and 3:00 p.m., Monday through Friday. Store employees are frequently too busy to check the deliveries in and transfer products to approved storage facilities during the noon rush. Therefore, food and nonfood items are held in a secured area off the receiving dock until someone is available to process them.

1. What sanitation hazards exist at Metro Market?

2. If you were manager of Metro Market, what would you do to improve receiving and storage activities?

The answers to the case studies are provided in Appendix A.

Discussion Questions (Short Answer)

1. Purchase specifications are important to a food establishment's operation. Why?

2. Why should buyers purchase foods only from approved sources that comply with all applicable food laws?

3. What is the role of FDA and USDA, in regulating the nation's food supply?

4. What range of temperatures should food temperature measuring devices be able to measure?

5. Why should cans with swollen ends be rejected and sent back to the supplier?

6. What are typical signs of spoilage for red meats, poultry, and fish?

7. What is the meaning of FIFO?

8. Why should raw products be stored below cooked or ready-to-eat foods during storage?

9. Describe safe procedures for storing cleaning and sanitizing agents and pesticides.

10. Why should products be located at least 6 inches off the floor during storage?

11. Why is it important for a food handler to wash his/her hands?

12. Why is it important to not serve raw animal foods?

13. Why do safe temperature requirements differ when using a conventional oven as opposed to the microwave oven?

14. Suggest some ways to decrease the cooling time for a 5-gallon container of rice.

Answers to all multiple choice questions are provided in Appendix A.

Quiz 4.1 (Multiple Choice)

1. Which of the following is not a rule that should be closely followed when purchasing food?

   a. Foods prepared in a private home may not be used or offered for human consumption in a retail food establishment.

   b. Buyers should only purchase food that is safe, wholesome, and from an approved source.

   c. Avoid the use of commercially raised game animals for meat and poultry.

   d. Only buy meat and poultry that has been inspected by USDA or state agency officials.

2. The best method for measuring the temperature of frozen food products is by

   a. inserting the sensing probe into the center of a frozen food package until the recorded temperature stabilizes.

   b. inserting the sensing probe between two packages of frozen foods until the recorded temperature stabilizes.

   c. measuring the ambient temperature of the frozen food compartment of the delivery vehicle.

   d. looking for signs of freezing and thawing, such as large ice crystals and frozen juices in the bottom of the box.

3. Frozen foods should not be accepted at a food establishment if they are above what temperature at delivery?

   a. -10°F (-23°C)

   b. 0°F (-18°C)

   c. 10°F (-12°C)

   d. 32°F (0°C)

4. Which of the following foods should not be rejected upon delivery?

   a. Fresh fish that has dull, sunken eyes, and soft flesh.

   b. Poultry with darkened wing tips and soft flesh.

   c. Canned fruit with small amounts of surface rust on the lid of the can.

   d. Fresh beef products that are delivered at 45°F.

5. Which of the following statements about fish and seafood is false?

   a. Fish and shellfish are less likely to spoil than red meat and poultry.

   b. Quality in fish and shellfish is measured by their smell and appearance.

   c. Fish that may be eaten raw must be commercially frozen prior to consumption.

   d. Molluscan shellfish tags must be kept for 90 days from the date the container is emptied.

6. Which of the following storage practices should prompt a manager to take corrective action?

   a. Products in the dry storage area are being rotated on a first-in, first-out stock basis.

   b. Foods stored in the walk-in freezer are stored on slatted shelves that are 6 inches above the floor.

   c. Raw poultry is stored above potato salad in the walk-in refrigerator.

   d. Cleaning and sanitizing agents and pesticides are stored in a locked and labeled cabinet in the dry food storage area.

7. The regulatory agencies that have the greatest impact on food establishments are

   a. USDA and FDA.

   b. EPA and FDA.

   c. FDA and state health agencies.

   d. State and local health agencies.

8. Which of the following is the preferred method for thawing potentially hazardous foods?

   a. In the microwave oven

   b. At room temperature

   c. In the refrigerator

   d. Under 70°F (21°C) running water

9. Hot foods should be held at _____ or above and cold foods should be held at _____ or below.

   a. 165° and 41°F (74° and 5°C)

   b. 165° and 32°F (74° and 0°C)

   c. 140° and 41°F (60° and 5°C)

   d. 140° and 32°F (60° and 0°C)

10. Poultry and stuffed meats should be cooked to an internal temperature of _____ for 15 seconds to be considered safe.

    a. 140°F (60°C)

    b. 145°F (63°C)

    c. 155°F (68°C)

    d. 165°F (74°C)

11. Ground beef meats should be cooked to an internal temperature of _____ for 15 seconds to be considered safe.

    a. 140°F (60°C)

    b. 145°F (63°C)

    c. 155°F (68°C)

    d. 165°F (74°C)

12. Regardless of the type of food, all potentially hazardous foods that have been cooked and cooled need to be reheated to an internal temperature of _____ within two hours to be considered safe.

    a. 140°F (5°C)

    b. 145°F (63°C)

    c. 155°F (68°C)

    d. 165°F (74°C)

13. According to the FDA *Food Code*, foods that are cooked and then cooled must be cooled in which of the following ways:

    a. From 140° to 41°F (60° to 5°C) in 12 hours

    b. From 140° to 41°F (50° to 5°C)in 4 hours

    c. From 140° to 70°F (60° to 21°C) in 2 hours, and from 70° to 41°F (21° to 5°C) in an additional 4 hours

    d. From 140° to 70°F (60° to 21°C) in 4 hours, and from 7°F to 41°F (21° to 5°C) in an additional 2 hours

14. After proper cooking of foods, all foods that are to be held cold should be:

    a. cooled quickly and held below 41°F (5°C).

    b. cooled quickly and held below 140°F (60°C).

    c. stored at room temperature until serving.

    d. held at 140°F (60°C) until serving.

15. After proper cooking of foods, all foods that are to be held hot should be

    a. cooled quickly and held 41°F (5°C).

    b. cooled quickly and held 140°F (60°C).

    c. stored at room temperature until serving.

    d. held at 140°F (60°C) until serving.

References/Suggested Readings

Cichy, R. F. (1994). *Quality Sanitation Management*, East Lansing, MI: Educational Institute of the American Hotel and Motel Association.

Educational Foundation of the National Restaurant Association (1992). *Applied Food Service Sanitation*,: Chicago, IL: National Restaurant Association.

Kotchevar, L. H., and R. Donnelly, (1994). *Quantity Food Purchasing*, New York, NY: Macmillan Publishers.

Longrèe, Karla and G. Armbruster, (1996) *Quantity Food Sanitation*, New York, NY: John Wiley and Sons, Inc.

Rue, N., and National Assessment Institute, (1994) *Handbook For Safe Food Service Management*, Englewood Cliffs, NJ: Prentice Hall.

United States Department of Health and Human Services, (1997). *1997 Food Code.* Recommendations of the U.S. Department of Health and Human Service. Washington, D.C.: Food and Drug Administration.

5 THE HAZARD ANALYSIS CRITICAL CONTROL POINT (HACCP) SYSTEM: A SAFETY ASSURANCE PROCESS

E. coli 0157:H7 in Salad

*An **E. coli 0157:H7** outbreak at a restaurant in Boise, Idaho, was traced to romaine lettuce used in salad. Thirteen confirmed and eight probable cases of the illness were reported during the outbreak. While one of the ill required hospitalization, none experienced serious complications from their illness.*

All of the victims had eaten at the same restaurant and 95% of them had eaten the same meal - a chicken Caesar salad. Any suspicions that the outbreak may have been caused by cross-contamination between beef and chicken were ruled out when it was learned that beef products were prepared on one side of the kitchen and chicken on the other. In addition, food workers were responsible for working with either beef or chicken but not both.

Romaine lettuce turned out to be the cause of the outbreak. Investigators tracked the lettuce back to its source and determined that contamination had occurred at the restaurant.

*Sophisticated blood analysis showed that some food handlers at the restaurant had been previously infected by **E. coli 0157:H7** bacteria. It was learned that one food handler had been shedding **E. coli 0157:H7** bacteria for several days. It is suspected that the food handler did not wash his hands properly after having a bowel movement. The lettuce was contaminated by **E. coli 0157:H7** bacteria that were left on his hands.*

Learning Objectives

After reading this chapter, you should be able to:

▲ Recognize the usefulness of the HACCP system as a food protection tool

▲ Recognize the types of potentially hazardous foods that commonly require a HACCP system to insure product safety

▲ Identify the steps involved in implementing a HACCP system

▲ Define:

1. Hazard

2. Analysis

3. Critical Control Point

▲ List hazards (risk factors) related to each product analyzed

▲ Assess hazards (risk factors) in order of severity

▲ Identify points to be monitored

▲ Describe evaluation of the process

▲ State measures used to correct potential problems

▲ Identify data required to provide documentation for review and problem solving

▲ Apply the HACCP system to analyze and protect food items from contamination during processing, preparation, and service

Essential Terms

Critical Control Point (CCP)	Hazard analysis
Critical limit	Monitoring
HACCP plan	Risk
Hazard	Verification
Hazard Analysis Critical Control Point (HACCP) system	

The Problem

Our inability to reduce the number of reported cases of foodborne illness has made it necessary to reevaluate our nation's current food safety system. The food industry and food regulatory agencies are being confronted with:

▲ serious challenges from new microbes that cause foodborne illness

▲ the changing nature of our food supply

▲ new techniques for processing and serving food

▲ changing eating habits among consumers

▲ a growing number of people who are at increased risk of experiencing foodborne illness

The number of foods imported into the U.S. increases every year. In addition, the number of new methods used to process and prepare foods continues to grow. As appetites change, different foods are grown or imported, and more items are produced. This challenges the government's ability to effectively monitor food safety. In addition, governmental agencies at all levels are having to cut back their staff and services due to increased costs and taxpayer mandates to decrease spending. This makes it necessary to shift more of the responsibility for food safety to food establishments. At the same time, those individuals who are engaged in food production and service will be required to assume greater responsibility for assuring the safety of the food they produce.

The size and scope of the food industry exert great pressures on FDA, USDA, and state and local food safety assurance programs. The FDA has identified more than 30,000 food manufacturers and 20,000 food warehouses that process and store products. In addition, the retail portion of the food industry consists of more than one million establishments and employs a work force of over 12 million people. For these reasons, the HACCP system, which has been used effectively by food manufacturers, is recommended by regulatory agencies as a useful method for monitoring and protecting food from contamination in food establishments.

The Solution

As experts searched for more effective methods to protect food, the HACCP system emerged as the logical choice. This system turns the focus of inspections away from floors, ceilings, and walls to the food itself and the conditions of storage, preparation, and service. A sanitary environment is important to safe food production, but food can still be contaminated by employees if they do not use proper food handling techniques, practice good personal hygiene, or control food temperature properly.

The HACCP system helps food managers identify and control potential problems before they happen. Whether the HACCP system is employed in restaurants, retail food stores, institutions, health care facilities, or other food service operations, the primary goal is always the same—production of safe and wholesome food.

The HACCP System

Traditional food safety inspection programs react to problems and correct hazardous conditions *after* they occur. **The HACCP system, on the other hand, is designed to anticipate problems *before* they happen**. The FDA recommends the HACCP system "because it is a system of preventive controls that is the most effective and efficient way to assure that food products are safe" (*Food Code*). The HACCP system offers two additional benefits over conventional inspection methods.

First, **the HACCP system enables food managers to identify the foods and processes that are most likely to cause foodborne illness**. When a potential problem is identified, the food establishment can initiate procedures to reduce or eliminate the risk of foodborne illness and then monitor to make sure the procedures are being followed.

Secondly, the HACCP system more accurately describes the overall condition of the establishment. Traditional inspections may provide only an account of the establishment's condition at the time of the inspection. Those violations present at the time of the inspection are noted, but they may not relate directly to food, time, and temperature. The HACCP system enables food managers and health department personnel to track food handling practices over a period of time.

Unlike inspections that sometimes focus on aesthetic or non-critical items, the HACCP approach is based on *controlling time, temperature, and specific factors* that are known to contribute to foodborne disease outbreaks. Records produced in conjunction with the HACCP system provide a comprehensive source of information about the events that occurred during all stages of food production.

The first priority of the HACCP system is to assure the safety of the potentially hazardous foods on the menu. You will begin by developing HACCP flowcharts for recipes which allow you to follow the flow of food (see Chapter 4) from start to finish. In the course of developing HACCP flowcharts, you will identify "high risk" activities that occur during food production and might contribute to a foodborne illness.

You then ask, "What can be done to control these high-risk activities to reduce the risk of foodborne illness?"

HACCP recipes are guides for food workers during production.

Food managers and supervisors can use the flow charts and production logs to double check for product safety.

HACCP records also assist health department personnel as they perform routine inspections of your establishment.

If a foodborne disease outbreak occurs, HACCP logs are very useful to the investigators as they attempt to determine the cause of the illness.

Food managers and supervisors must learn how to effectively develop, implement, and maintain a HACCP system. This begins with knowing about and understanding the factors that affect food safety. There are several publications available, including an excellent guide in the *Food Code*, that can help you learn more about the HACCP system. Consult the suggested readings at the end of this chapter for a partial list of these publications.

The Seven Steps in a HACCP System

The basic structure of a HACCP system consists of seven steps as listed in Figure 5.1. While each step is unique, they all work together to form the basic structure of an effective food safety program. A more detailed description of each step will be presented in the remainder of this chapter.

"Hello! I'm Inspector Harry Hassup"

1. Hazard Analysis

2. Identify the Critical Control Points (CCP) in food preparation

3. Establish Critical Limits (thresholds) which must be met at each identified Critical Control Point

4. Establish procedures to monitor CCPs

5. Establish the corrective action to be taken when monitoring shows that a Critical Limit has been exceeded

6. Establish effective record keeping systems that document the HACCP system

7. Establish procedures to verify that the HACCP system is working

Figure 5.1—Seven Steps in a Hazard Analysis Critical Control Point System (Source: Food Code)

"First we have to analyze the food"

Step 1—Hazard Analysis

The first step in a HACCP system is hazard analysis. This involves identifying *hazards* that might be introduced to food by certain food production practices or the intended use of the product. Hazard analysis starts with a thorough review of your menu or product list to identify all of the potentially hazardous foods you serve. As you learned in Chapter 2, Hazards to Food Safety, potentially hazardous foods have properties that support rapid bacterial growth and can cause the food to be unsafe. Potentially hazardous foods include:

▲ meats

▲ dairy products

▲ poultry, eggs

▲ cooked foods such as beans, pasta, rice, potatoes

▲ cut cantaloupe and raw seed sprouts

All of these foods can be found in most food establishments.

Hazards may be biological, chemical, or physical in nature. These hazards are frequently introduced into the food by people, poor food-handling practices, and/or contaminated equipment. Some foods may be naturally contaminated as in the case of raw meats, poultry, fish, and unwashed fruits and vegetables.

Biological Hazards

Food is not produced in a *sterile (microorganism free)* environment. Therefore, it can easily be contaminated by biological hazards such as bacteria, viruses, fungi, and parasites. During the hazard analysis step, look for steps in food production where foods may be contaminated, microorganisms may survive, and then multiply. Knowledge of the sources of biological hazards and the foods they most frequently contaminate is essential to an effective HACCP plan. Refer to Chapter 2, Hazards to Food Safety, to review biological hazards and the conditions they need for growth and survival.

Do not forget, moderate hazards can become severe if contracted by high-risk individuals such as the very young, frail elderly, or those with weakened immune systems.

Chemical Hazards

Chemical hazards are substances that are either naturally present or are added to a food during production. When constructing a HACCP flowchart, consider the possibility of chemical contamination. Train food workers in the proper handling and storage of chemicals. This is essential to your overall food safety program. Reduce the chance of chemical contamination by purchasing food items and additives from approved sources. For more information about chemical contamination refer to Chapter 2 of this book.

Physical Hazards

Physical contaminants in food can cause injury to the consumer. Glass, metal shavings, a food handler's personal property (jewelry, false fingernails, and hair pins), toothpicks, and pieces of worn equipment are examples of physical agents that may accidentally enter food during production and service. A HACCP plan helps foodservice managers and supervisors to identify potential sources of physical hazards and provide safeguards to protect foods from this form of contamination.

During the hazard analysis step, you should also estimate risk. **Risk is the probability that a condition or conditions will lead to a hazard.** Some of the factors that influence risk are the:

▲ type of customers served

▲ types of foods on the menu

▲ nature of the organism

▲ past outbreaks

▲ size and type of food production operations

▲ extent of employee training

Each type of operation and each food establishment poses different levels of risk, to the consumer. **Hazards that pose little or no risk, or are unlikely to occur need not be addressed by your HACCP system**.

Focus on the most hazardous foods on your menu first. Once your HACCP system has been developed, implemented, and evaluated for these foods, move on to the next most hazardous foods. Within several months, you should be able to include all of the potentially hazardous foods on your menu under the HACCP system.

Review the menu items in Figure 5.2 and pick out the potentially hazardous foods.

Breakfast

Orange Juice	Apple Juice	Grapefruit Half	Strawberries
Oatmeal	*Cream of Wheat*	Shredded Wheat	Raisin Bran
Scrambled Eggs	*Bacon*	*Sausage Links*	Hash Browns
French Toast	*Sausage Gravy*	*Cheese Omelet*	Pancakes
Belgian Waffle	*Breakfast Burrito*	White/Wheat Toast	*Egg Beaters*

Lunch

Apple Sauce	*Pasta Salad*	*Potato Salad*	Spinach Salad
Chili	*Navy Bean Soup*	*Clam Chowder*	*Vegetable Soup*
French Fries	*Hamburgers*	*Pork Tenderloin*	*Fish Fillet*
Chicken Fillet	*Ham & Cheese*	*Chicken Wings*	*Corned Beef & Swiss*

Dinner

Tossed Salad	Cobb Salad	*Cottage Cheese*	*Tuna Salad in Tomato*
Baked Potato	*Broccoli & Cheese*	*Wild Rice*	*Melon Balls*
Country Fried Steak	*Turkey/Dressing*	*Liver & Onions*	*Meat Loaf*
Frozen Yogurt	Chocolate Brownie	Cherry Pie	Angel Food Cake
Coffee	Iced Tea	*Milk*	Soft Drinks

Potentially hazardous foods are in *italic*

Figure 5.2—Sample Menu

Foods that are not potentially hazardous in the sample menu above, do not support the growth of harmful bacteria. Fruits, such as orange juice, grapefruit half, and strawberries, all have a pH less than 4.6. Disease-causing bacteria will not grow in these acidic conditions. Melons, such as watermelon and cantaloupe, that have a pH greater than 4.6, are potentially hazardous.

Products such as shredded wheat, toast, and angel food cake will not support the growth of disease-causing bacteria due to their low water activity.

Tossed salad is generally not considered a potentially hazardous food. However, it is a ready-to-eat food that is not cooked. It must be handled carefully to prevent contamination and control microbial growth. For example, salad ingredients and other ready-to-eat foods may be contaminated by a virus from the food workers hands. In the case of viral infections, it takes a very small dose of harmful virus to cause an illness. When handling this type of food, handwashing and temperature control are important safeguards. The hazard identification phase of hazard analysis is made easier by asking a series of questions which are appropriate to each step in the flow of the food. The questions presented in Figure 5.3 help you identify potentially hazardous foods and possible problems. Select preventive measures that will protect foods based on the hazards and risks you have identified

---

Ingredients

▲ Does the food contain any sensitive ingredients (e.g., raw meat, poultry, fish, shellfish, eggs, or milk) that are likely to introduce microbiological, chemical, or physical hazards?

▲ Has this food been implicated in previous outbreaks? How frequently?

Intrinsic Factors of Food

▲ Which physical characteristics and composition of the food (e.g., pH, water activity, and preservatives) must be controlled in order to assure food safety?

▲ Does the food permit survival or multiplication of infectious and/or toxin-producing microorganisms in the food before or during preparation?

▲ Will the food permit survival or multiplication of infectious and/or toxin-producing microorganisms during later stages of preparation, storage, or consumer possession?

▲ Are there other similar products in the market place? What has been the safety record for these products?

Procedures Used for Preparation and Processing

▲ Does the process used to prepare or process the food include a manageable step that will destroy infectious microorganisms or prevent toxin formation?

▲ Is the product subject to recontamination between preparation and service or packaging?

Figure 5.3—Questions Included in a Hazard Analysis Checklist

Microbial Content of the Food

▲ Is the food commercially sterile? Is it a low acid (pH of 4.6 or above) canned item that has been heat treated to destroy both vegetative cells and spores of foodborne disease-causing microorganisms?

▲ Is it likely that the food will contain living microorganisms that are capable of causing foodborne illness?

▲ What is the normal microbial content of the food stored under proper conditions?

▲ Does the microbial population alter the safety of the food?

Facility Design

▲ Does the layout of the kitchen adequately separate raw foods from ready-to-eat foods to prevent cross contamination?

▲ Do the traffic patterns of workers and food flows present a potential source of contamination?

Equipment Design

▲ Will the kitchen equipment provide the time and temperature needed to assure safe food?

▲ Is the size of the kitchen equipment adequate for the volume of food that will be prepared?

▲ Is the kitchen equipment reliable or does it break down frequently?

▲ Is there a chance for product contamination with hazardous substances?

▲ Is kitchen equipment equipped with product safety devices, such as time/temperature controls, to boost food safety?

Packaging

▲ Does the type of food package support the growth of disease-causing germs and/or the formation of toxins?

▲ Is the food's packaging material resistant to damage, thereby preventing the entrance of microbial contamination?

Figure 5.3—Questions Included in a Hazard Analysis Checklist (Cont.)

▲ Is the package clearly labeled "Keep Refrigerated" if this is required to preserve and protect the food?

▲ Does the package include adequate instructions for the safe handling and preparation of the food by the consumer?

▲ Are tamper-evident packaging features used?

▲ Is each package legibly and accurately coded to indicate production lot?

▲ Does each package have a label that contains the required information?

Sanitation

▲ Can the sanitation practices that are employed in the food establishment impact upon the safety of the food that is being prepared?

▲ Can the facility be properly cleaned and sanitized to permit the safe handling of food?

▲ Is it possible to consistently provide sanitary conditions in the kitchen to assure production of safe foods?

Employee Health, Hygiene, and Education

▲ Can employee health or personal hygiene practices affect the safety of the food being prepared?

▲ Do food workers understand the food preparation process and the factors that they must control to assure safe foods?

▲ Will food workers inform managers of possible problems which could affect food safety when they suspect them?

Conditions of Storage Between Packaging and the Consumer

▲ Is it likely that food will be improperly stored at the wrong temperature?

▲ Would storage at improper temperatures lead to unsafe food?

Figure 5.3—Questions Included in a Hazard Analysis Checklist (Cont.)

Intended Use

▲ Is the food intended for consumption by people who do not have an increased risk of becoming ill?

▲ Is the food intended for consumption by high risk populations such as very young children, frail elderly, and those with suppressed immune systems?

Figure 5.3—Questions Included in a Hazard Analysis Checklist (Cont.)

Hazard identification and risk estimation provide a logical basis for determining which hazards are significant and must be addressed in the HACCP plan. **The severity of a hazard is defined as the degree of seriousness of the consequences of a hazard if it becomes a reality**. Hazards that involve low risk and are not likely to occur need not be addressed in the HACCP plan.

Personal experience, facts generated by foodborne illness investigations, and information from scientific articles can be useful when estimating the approximate risk of a hazard. When estimating risk, it is important to separate *safety* concerns from *quality* issues. For instance as a quality issue, perishable foods *spoil* quickly when stored at temperatures in the food temperature danger zone. It is a *safety concern* because foodborne disease investigations show that potentially hazardous foods left in the temperature danger zone too long can cause foodborne illness.

The last phase of the hazard analysis step involves establishing preventive measures. After the hazards have been identified, you must consider what preventive measures, if any, can be employed for each hazard.

Preventive measures include:

▲ heating

▲ cooling

▲ cross contamination control

▲ good personal hygiene practices

▲ other procedures that can:

     ▼ prevent

     ▼ minimize

     ▼ eliminate an identified health hazard

More than one preventive measure may be required to control certain types of hazards. For example, the transfer of *Salmonella* bacteria from raw chicken to a ready-to-eat food, such as lettuce or carrots, can be controlled by proper cleaning and sanitizing of equipment and utensils and handwashing practices. In other situations, more than one hazard may be controlled by a specific preventive measure. Just cook a food to 165°F (74°C) and many different types of microbes are eliminated, thus making the food safe.

Step 2—Identify Critical Control Points (CCPs)

The next step in creating a **HACCP** system is to identify the **critical control points (CCPs)** in food production. **A critical control point is an operation (practice, preparation, step or procedure) in the flow of food which will prevent, eliminate, or reduce hazards to acceptable levels.** A critical control point provides a *kill step* that will destroy bacteria or a *control step* that prevents or slows down the rate of bacterial growth.

Some examples of CCPs are:

▲ Cooking, reheating, and hot-holding

▲ Chilling, chilled storage, and chilled display

▲ Receiving, thawing, mixing ingredients, and other food handling stages

▲ Product formulation (e.g., reducing the pH of a food to below 4.6)

▲ Purchasing seafood, MAP foods, and ready-to-eat foods where further processing would not prevent a hazard, from approved sources

The most commonly used CCPs are cooking, cooling, reheating, and hot/cold holding. Cooking and reheating to proper temperatures will destroy bacteria, while proper cooling, hot-holding and cold-holding will prevent or slow down the rate of bacterial growth.

The *Food Code* also recognizes specific food handling and sanitation practices (such as proper thawing methods), prevention of cross contamination and certain aspects of employee and environmental hygiene as CCPs. These latter types of practices are more difficult to measure, monitor, and document. Therefore, many food establishment operators prefer to think of them as "standard operating procedures" (SOPs) or "house policies" rather than CCPs.

For the purpose of this textbook, **CCPs** are considered to be operations that involve:

▲ **time**

▲ **temperature**

▲ **acidity**

▲ **receiving procedures related to:**

  ▼ **seafood**

  ▼ **modified atmosphere packaged foods**

  ▼ **ready-to-eat foods where a later processing step in the food flow would not prevent a hazard**

SOPs include:

▲ **good employee hygiene practices (i.e. handwashing)**

▲ **cross contamination control (i.e. keeping raw products separate from cooked and ready-to-eat foods)**

▲ **environmental hygiene practices (i.e. effective cleaning and sanitizing of equipment and utensils)**

Figure 5.4—CCPs and SOPs

There must be at least one critical control point in the production process to qualify as a HACCP food safety system, and the *critical control point must be monitored and controlled to guarantee the safety of the food.*

Identification of critical control points *begins with a review of the recipe for the potentially hazardous ingredients* and the *development of a flow chart* for the recipe. The flow chart will track the steps in the food flow from receiving to serving. The specific path that a food follows will be slightly different for each product. However, some of the more common elements in the flow of food include:

1. Purchase of products and ingredients from inspected and approved sources

2. Receiving products and ingredients

3. Storage of products and ingredients

4. Preparation steps which may involve thawing, cooking, and other processing activities

5. Holding or display of food

6. Service of food

7. Cooling food

8. Storing cooled food

9. Reheating food for service

Consider conditions unique to your establishment when developing a HACCP plan for your facility. The decision tree for determining critical control points presented in Figure 5.5 may prove helpful in verifying which of the steps in your food flow are CCPs. .

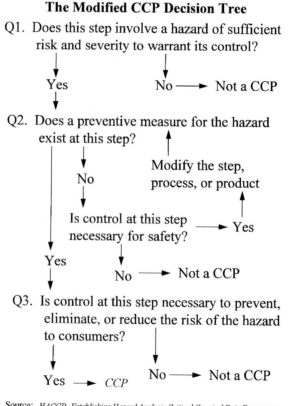

The Modified CCP Decision Tree

Q1. Does this step involve a hazard of sufficient risk and severity to warrant its control?

Yes   No ⟶ Not a CCP

Q2. Does a preventive measure for the hazard exist at this step?

No

Modify the step, process, or product

Is control at this step necessary for safety? ⟶ Yes

Yes

No ⟶ Not a CCP

Q3. Is control at this step necessary to prevent, eliminate, or reduce the risk of the hazard to consumers?

Yes ⟶ *CCP*   No ⟶ Not a CCP

Source: *HACCP- Establishing Hazard Analysis Critical Ccontrol Poin Programs: A Workshop Manula. The Food Processors Institute, Washington, D.C. 1995.*

Figure 5.5—Critical Control Point Decision Tree

By answering each of these questions as the food flow is reviewed, critical control points that could influence product safety are found. Apply the decision tree at each step in the food production process where a hazard has been identified.

Step 3—Establish the Critical Limits (Thresholds) Which Must Be Met at Each Critical Control Point

At this step of the process, consider what should be done to reduce the risk of hazards to safe levels. Set critical limits to make sure that each critical control point effectively blocks a biological, chemical, or physical hazard. **Critical limits** should be thought of as the upper and lower boundaries of food safety. When these boundaries are exceeded, a hazard may exist or could develop. The critical limit should be as specific as possible, such as "ground beef or pork must be heated to an internal temperature of 155°F (68°C) or greater for 15 seconds." A well-defined critical limit makes it easier to determine when the limit has not been met.

Each CCP has one or more critical limit to monitor to assure that hazards are:

▲ prevented

▲ eliminated

▲ reduced to acceptable levels

Each limit relates to a process that will keep food in a range of safety by controlling:

▲ temperature

▲ time

▲ the ability of the food to support the growth of infectious and toxin-producing microorganisms

(See Figure 5.6)

"This is Critical!"

Critical Limit	Boundaries of Food Safety
Time	Limit the amount of time food is in the temperature danger zone during the cooking and cooling processes to 4 hours or less.
Temperature	Keep potentially hazardous foods at 41°F (5°C) or below or 140°F (60°C) or above. Maintain specific cooking, cooling, reheating and hot-holding temperatures.
Water Activity	Foods with a water activity (A_w) of .85 or less do ***not*** support growth of disease causing bacteria.
pH (acidity level)	Disease-causing bacteria do not grow in foods that have a pH of 4.6 or below.

Figure 5.6—Criteria Most Frequently Used for Critical Limits

To be effective, each critical limit should be based on information from food regulatory codes, scientific literature, experimental studies, and food safety experts. **You must be able to easily measure or observe a critical limit.**

"Now what do I see?"

Recipes and sample flow charts for three foods served in food establishments are presented in Figures 5.7, 5.8, 5.9, 5.10, 5.11, and 5.12. Review these carefully paying particular attention to the steps from source through the preparation process to service.

Ingredients	Amount	Servings		
		25	**50**	**100**
Fresh broccoli	Heads	2.0	4.0	8.0
Red onions	Lbs.	0.5	1.0	2.0
Fresh mushrooms	Lbs.	1.0	2.0	4.0
Spiral pasta	Lbs.	1.0	2.0	4.0
Black olives, sliced	Cups	0.5	1.0	2.0
Italian salad dressing	Cups	0.5	1.0	2.0
Ranch style dressing	Cups	0.5	1.0	2.0

Figure 5.7—Sample Recipe and HACCP Flow Chart for Pasta Salad

Pre-preparation

SOP-1   1. Wash your hands prior to beginning food preparation.

SOP-2   2. Clean and wash broccoli, onions, and mushrooms under cool running water. Use immediately in the pasta salad or cover and refrigerate at 41°F (5°C) until needed.

         3. Pre-chill the salad dressings by storing them at 41°F (5°C) until ready for use in the pasta salad.

Preparation

         4. Cook pasta in boiling water until tender. Drain and quick-chill in ice water. Drain after chilling.

         5. Combine pasta, broccoli, onions, mushrooms, and olives.

         6. Combine the salad dressings in another bowl and mix well.

         7. Mix the salad with the dressing.

CCP-1   8. Quick-chill salad. Cool the salad to 41°F (5°C) within 4 hours. Monitor and record the temperature of the product at least once every hour. Cover and hold for service at 41°F (5°C) or below.

Service

CCP-2   9. Maintain temperature of finished product at 41°F (5°C) or below during entire serving period. Monitor and record internal temperature of the product every 30 minutes. Maximum holding time is 4 hours.

         10. Discard any portion of the product that is placed into service but is not served within the 4-hour holding time.

Storage

CCP-3 11. Store the chilled product in a covered container that is properly dated and labeled. Refrigerate at 41°F (5°C) or below.

Figure 5.8—HACCP Flow Diagram for Pasta Salad

(Adapted from: HACCP for Food Service—Recipe Manual and Guide, 1994.)

Ingredients	Amount	Servings		
		25	**50**	**100**
Clams, canned	Ounces	16	32	64
Water	Quarts	4	8	16
Potatoes, diced	Ounces	40	80	160
Salt pork	Lbs.	1	2	4
Onions, minced	Lbs.	1	2	4
Flour	Ounces	10	20	40
Milk	Ounces	80	160	320
Heavy cream	Ounces	16	32	64

Figure 5.9—Sample Recipe and HACCP Flow Chart for Clam Chowder

Receiving

1. Purchase clams from an approved source.

Pre-preparation

SOP-1 2. Wash hands before beginning food production.

SOP-2 3. Wash clams.

Preparation

4. Mince salt pork to a paste.

5. Dice potatoes to 1/4".

6. Mince onions.

Cooking

7. Heat clams in a covered pot.

8. Strain broth through a filter or cheesecloth. Hold broth at 140°F (60°C) or higher.

9. Hold clams at 140°F (60°C) or higher.

10. Cook potatoes in clam broth to 140°F (60°C) or higher. Separate potatoes and broth. Hold both broth and potatoes at 140°F (60°C) or higher.

11. Render (melt fat down into a dripping) in the soup pot; add onions and cook gently in the fat until you can see through them.

12. Add flour and cook to make blond roux.

13. Add reserve broth gradually and stir completely working out any lumps that might form.

14. Simmer for 40 minutes until the product reaches 140°F (60°C). Skim the surface as necessary.

15. Scald milk and cream and add to the soup.

16. Add seasoning.

CCP-1 17. Cook mixed product to a temperature of 145°F (63°C) or higher.

Holding/Service

CCP-2 18. Hold chowder at 140°F (60°C) or above for service. Do not mix new product with old.

Cooling

CCP-3 19. Cool in shallow pans with a product depth not to exceed 2 inches. Quick-chill the product from 140°F to 70°F (60°C to 21°C) within 2 hours and then from 70°F to 41°F (21°C to 5°C) within four hours.

Storage

20. Store the chowder in a covered container at a product temperature of 41°F (5°C) or below.

Reheating

CCP-4 21. Reheat chowder to a product temperature of 165°F (74°C) or higher within 2 hours.

5.10—HAACP Flow Diagram for Clam Chowder

(Adapted from: HACCP Reference Book, 1993.)

Ingredients	Amount	Servings		
		25	**50**	**100**
Ground beef	Lbs.	6	12	24
Onion, diced	Cups	2	4	8
Green pepper, diced	Cups	1	2	4
Celery, diced	Cups	1	2	4
Bread crumbs	Cups	3	6	12
Pasteurized eggs, frozen	Cups	1	2	4
Catsup	Cups	1	2	4
Homogenized milk	Cups	½	1	2
Pepper	Cups	½	1	2
Salt	Cups	½	1	2

Figure 5.II—Sample Recipe and HACCP Flow Chart for Meat Loaf

Pre-preparation

SOP-1   1. Wash hands before beginning food production.

SOP-1   2. Thaw ground beef and pasteurized eggs under refrigeration at 41°F (5°C).

SOP-2   3. Clean and rinse vegetables with cool running water and cut as directed. Use immediately in the recipe or cover and refrigerate at 41°F (5°C) or below.

Preparation

   4. Combine all ingredients and blend in a properly cleaned and sanitized mixer.

   5. Place the mixture in a shallow loaf pan that does not exceed 2- 1/2" in depth.

CCP-1   6. Bake the meat loaf uncovered to an internal temperature of 155°F (68°C) for a minimum of 15 seconds in a preheated conventional oven at 350°F (177°C) or a convection oven at 325°F (163°C), approximately one hour.

   7. Remove from oven and allow each cooked loaf to cool at room temperature for 15 minutes. Place loaves in a shallow service pan and slice into 3-ounce portions.**Holding/Service**

CCP-2   8. Maintain temperature of product at 140°F (60°C) or higher during service period. Record temperature of unused product every 30 minutes.

Storage

CCP-3   9. Cool in shallow pans with a product depth not to exceed 2 inches. Quick-chill the product from 140°F to 70°F (60°C to 21°C) within 2 hours and from 70°F to 41°F (21°C to 5°C) within 4 hours.

   10. Store the meat loaf in a covered container at a product temperature of 41°F (5°C) or below.

Reheating

CCP-4   11. Remove from refrigeration and heat in a preheated conventional oven at 350°F (177°C). Heat until all parts of the product reaches an internal temperature of 165°F (74°C) for 15 seconds.

   12. Discard unused, reheated product.

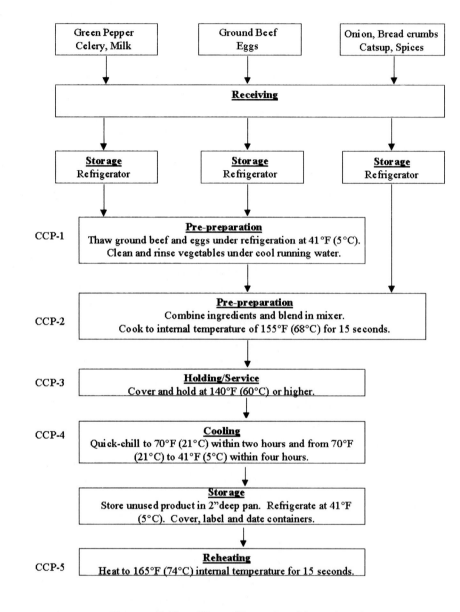

Figure 5.12—Flow Chart for Meat Loaf

(Adapted from: HACCP for Food Services—Recipe Manual and Guide, 1993)

Step 4—Establish Procedures to Monitor CCPs

In each food establishment, someone should be responsible for **monitoring critical control points**. To monitor, make observations and measurements to determine whether a critical control point is under control. This shows when a critical limit has been exceeded at a critical control point.

""You have to monitor it!"

For example, monitoring tells you whether or not the internal temperature of poultry has reached 165°F (74°C) or above for 15 seconds. **The risk of foodborne illness increases, when a critical control point is not met. Monitoring is a critical part of a HACCP system and provides written documentation that can be used to verify that the HACCP system is working properly.**

Time, *temperature*, *pH*, and *water activity* are the critical limits most commonly monitored to assure that a critical limit is under control. If a product or process does not meet critical limits, immediate corrective action is required before a problem occurs.

Monitoring can be performed either continuously or at predetermined intervals in the food production process. Continuous monitoring, such as that used to manage the temperature and time of a cook-chill operation, is performed using temperature recording charts. Continuous monitoring is preferred because it identifies defects more quickly.

If a critical limit cannot be monitored continuously, set up specific monitoring intervals that can accurately indicate hazard control. If early monitoring shows the process is very consistent, do not monitor as often.

Monitoring must be doable. More frequent monitoring catches problems earlier and provides more options for correction (ie., reheat instead of discard food).

Observations of cross-contamination control, employee hygiene compliance, and product formulation control may also be incorporated into the monitoring system. A record of actions, times, temperatures, and any departure from critical limits provides a history for that item. Once the flow is established, measurements can be recorded on a flowchart.

Food workers responsible for monitoring CCPs must know how to accurately monitor critical control points and record the information accurately in data logs. They must also be given the tools (thermometers, pH meters, etc.) needed to take measurements and record their findings. Another important part of monitoring is making employees aware of the harm that can occur if data are faked or not collected as required.

Monitoring is one of the most important activities in a HACCP system. An operation that identifies critical control points and establishes critical limits without having a monitoring system in place, has not actually implemented a HACCP system. Critical limits without monitoring are meaningless.

Step 5—Establish the Corrective Action to Be Taken When Monitoring Shows That a Critical Limit Has Been Exceeded

"What do you do when it is outside the limit?"

Serious problems can occur when critical limits are not met. If you detect that a critical limit was exceeded during the production of a HACCP monitored food, correct the problem immediately. The flow of food should not continue until all CCP's have been met.

First, determine what went wrong. Next, choose and apply the appropriate corrective action. For example, if the temperature of the BBQ pork on your steam table is not at 140°F (60°C) or higher, check the steam table to make sure it is working properly and will keep food hot. At the same time, put the pork on the stove and reheat it rapidly to 165°F (74°C). The pork should be discarded if you suspect it has been in the temperature danger zone for four hours or more.

Additional corrective actions include having employees measure the temperature of the product at more frequent intervals and stir the pork to assure the even distribution of heat throughout the product. Record the additional steps and verify that the critical limit is met using the revised system. Taking immediate corrective action is vital to the effectiveness of your food safety system.

Step 6—Establish Effective Record Keeping Systems That Document the HACCP System

An effective HACCP system requires the development and maintenance of a written HACCP plan. The plan should provide as much information as possible about the hazards associated with each individual food item or group of food items covered by the system. Clearly identify each CCP and the critical limits that have been set for each CCP. The procedures for monitoring critical control points and maintaining records procedures must also be contained in the establishment's HACCP plan.

The amount of record keeping required in a HACCP plan will vary from one food establishment to another, depending on the type of food processing used. For example, a cook-chill operation in a campus dining hall would require more record keeping than a limited menu cook-serve operation in a neighborhood cafe. The detail of your HACCP plan will be determined by the complexity of your food production operation. **Keep enough records to prove your system is working effectively, but keep it as simple as possible**.

Changing a procedure at a CCP *but not recording the change on your flowchart almost guarantees that similar problems will be repeated.* Therefore, record keeping is vital to the overall effectiveness of your HACCP system. A clipboard, work sheet, thermometer, watch or clock, and any other equipment needed to monitor and record these limits must be readily available to the food production staff. An example of the record keeping information that is suggested by the *Food Code* is presented in Figure 5.13.

---

1. List of HACCP team members and their assigned responsibilities

2. Description of the food product and its intended use

3. Flow diagram of the food preparation steps with CCPs noted

4. Hazards associated with each CCP and preventive measure

5. Critical limits

6. Monitoring system

7. Corrective action plans for deviations from critical limits

8. Record keeping procedures

9. Procedures for verification of HACCP system

Figure 5.13—Examples of Documents That Can Be Included in the Total HACCP System (Source: Food Code)

The information presented in Figure 5.14 provides an example of how the information in your HACCP plan can be organized.

Process Step	Quick-Chill	Reheating
CCP	Yes	Yes
Chemical, Physical, & Biological Hazards	Bacteria (especially spore-formers)	Bacteria
Critical Limit	140° F to 70°F in 2 hours or less. 70°F to 41°F in 4 hours or less.	Reheat to an internal temperature of 165°F or above within 2 hours
Monitoring Procedures Frequency Person(s) Responsible	Monitor product temp. every 60 minutes	Monitor product temp. every 30 minutes
Corrective Action(s) Person(s) Responsible	Discard product if CCP limit is *not* met	Continue heating until CCP limit is achieved
HACCP Records	Record data on a time/temp. chart and initial	Record data on a time/ temp. chart and initial
Verification Procedures/Person(s) Responsible	Food Manager	Food Manager

Figure 5.14—Information Commonly Included in a HACCP Plan

The method you use to record the information is not especially important, as long as it is easy for the staff to use and provides quick access to the information contained in the log.

"Have I told you lately that it's working?"

Step 7—Establish Procedures to Verify That the HACCP System Is Working

The last step in the HACCP system is verifying that your system is working properly. The **verification** process typically consists of two phases. First, you must verify that the critical limits you have established for your CCPs will prevent, eliminate, or reduce hazards to acceptable levels. Second, you must verify that your overall HACCP plan is functioning effectively. Once critical limits at each

CCP are met, minimal sampling of the final product is needed. However, frequent reviews of HACCP based food flow plans and records is necessary to insure product safety. Figure 5.15 contains guidelines that can assist you in determining how and when to implement HACCP plan verification procedures as well as the kind of information your verification reports should contain.

Verification procedures may include:

▲ Initiation of appropriate verification inspection schedules

▲ A review of the HACCP plan

▲ A review of the CCP records

▲ A review of departures from critical limits and how they were corrected

▲ Visual inspection of food production operations to determine if CCP's are under control

▲ Conducting random sample collection and analysis

▲ A review of the critical limits to verify if they are adequate to control hazards

▲ A review of written record of verification inspections which certifies compliance with the HACCP plan or deviations from the plan and the corrective action taken

▲ Validation of the HACCP plan, including on-site review and verification of flow diagrams and Critical Control Points

▲ A review of the modifications made to the HACCP plan

Verification inspections should be conducted under the following conditions:

▲ Routinely and unannounced to assure that selected CCPs are under control

▲ If it is determined that intensive coverage of a specific food is needed because of new information concerning food safety

Figure 5.15—Guidelines for Determining How and When to Implement HACCP Plan Verification Procedures
(Source: Food Code)

▲ When foods prepared at the establishment have been linked to a foodborne illness

▲ When established criteria have not been met

▲ To verify that changes have been implemented correctly after a HACCP plan has been modified

Verification reports should contain the following information:

▲ Existence of the HACCP plan and person(s) responsible for administering and updating plan

▲ The status of records associated with CCP monitoring

▲ Direct monitoring data of the CCP while in operation; certification that monitoring equipment is properly calibrated and in working order; deviations, and corrective actions noted

▲ Any samples analyzed to verify that CCPs are under control. Analyses may involve physical, chemical, microbiological, or organoleptic methods

▲ Modifications to the HACCP plan

▲ Training and knowledge of individuals responsible for monitoring CCPs

Figure 5.15—Guidelines for Determining How and When to Implement HACCP Plan Verification Procedures (Cont.)
(Source: Food Code)

The HACCP system should be reviewed and, if necessary, modified to accommodate changes in your clientele (i.e., more high risk clients), the items on your menu (addition of potentially hazardous foods or substitution of low-risk foods for high-risk foods), or the processes used to prepare HACCP products.

Your management team should review and evaluate the establishment's HACCP program at least once a year and more often if necessary.

Education and Training

"Welcome to HACCP training!"

Education and training are key to the successful implementation of a HACCP program. Your HACCP system should be integrated into each food worker's duties as well as performance plans and goals. Your training program for employees should be tailored to the operation they work in.

The content of the training program should provide employees an overview of the HACCP system and how it works to assure food safety. The training program should also include an in-depth examination of the CCP's and critical limits in your HACCP system.

The primary goal of your HACCP training program is to make employees skilled in performing the specific tasks (monitoring and recording) which the HACCP plan requires them to perform. Motivate them by stressing the importance of their roles and responsibilities to the success of the program.

HACCP training must be an ongoing activity due to high employee turnover that most establishments' experience. Keep records of employee HACCP training along with the other documents generated by your HACCP system.

Effective training and supervision will help you achieve the benefits of a HACCP based operation in a much shorter period of time. This will save you money and more importantly enhance the safety of the products you are serving to your clients.

Roles and Responsibilities Under HACCP

The role of health department personnel and other regulators is to promote the use of HACCP by the food industry. They can help you better understand the HACCP concept and how to implement a HACCP system. Regulatory personnel will also review your HACCP documents periodically to assure that critical control points are properly identified, critical limits are properly set, required monitoring is being performed, and the HACCP plan is being revised when necessary.

The role of the food establishment managers and supervisors is to develop, implement, and maintain the HACCP system. You must continuously use and improve your HACCP system if the desired outcome of safe food management is to be achieved.

Summary

Implementing a HACCP food safety system you can avoid situations like the one described in the case at the beginning of this chapter. A HACCP system would provide three levels of intervention which would prevent this type of foodborne disease outbreak. First, the HACCP recipe and flow chart would alert food handlers to potential hazards and critical control points that can be used to prevent, minimize, or eliminate them. Since the lettuce is an uncooked food, purchasing it from an approved source would be a critical control point. An even more effective critical control point would be a *no bare hands* policy whereby food handlers would be instructed not to touch lettuce and other uncooked foods with their bare hands. Instead, they would use spoons, tongs, or other utensils. A standard operating procedure that should be added to your HACCP recipe for the Caesar salad would be for food handlers to wash their hands before starting to handle uncooked ready-to-eat foods. Hands should be washed whenever they become contaminated and when employees return from a break or the toilet. The proper use of utensils and the *when* and *how* of proper handwashing must be taught to food handlers as part of your HACCP educational program.

A **hazard** means a biological, chemical, and physical property that may cause an unacceptable consumer health risk. If these hazards are not controlled, foodborne illness can occur.

The *Hazard Analysis Critical Control Point (HACCP)* system is a prevention-based safety program that identifies and monitors the hazards associated with food production. The HACCP system will help you estimate the relative risks for each hazard and determine where control procedures will be needed most. The system, when properly applied, can be used to effectively control any area or point in the food flow that could cause a hazardous situation.

A **Critical Control Point (CCP)** is a step in the food flow where loss of control could result in unacceptable risk to food safety. The most commonly used CCPs are cooking, cooling, reheating, and hot/cold holding. The *1997 Food Code* also recognizes specific food handling and sanitation practices (such as proper thawing methods), cross contamination control, and certain aspects of employee and environmental hygiene as CCPs. The food industry considers these latter types of activities to be "standard operating procedures" or SOPs rather than CCPs. This is because handwashing and cross contamination control cannot always be acurately monitored and recorded. This should in no way diminish the importance of these activities and food safety practices. It merely acknowledges that they are harder to monitor and record than are critical control points.

Monitoring is a critical activity within a HACCP system. When done properly, monitoring can help pinpoint the cause of a problem and provide an early warning that a potentially hazardous situation might exist. If monitoring indicates that a critical limit has been exceeded, immediate action must be taken. Each food establishment is different and will have different CCPs. The corrective action must also be tailored to your particular establishment and the various food operations you use. Regardless of the type of operation, corrective actions must demonstrate that the CCP has been brought under control.

Food workers and managers share the responsibility for maintaining an effective record keeping system. Food workers should measure and record all appropriate monitoring data in HACCP logs, and managers should review these logs to make certain that monitoring is being done properly. Well-organized monitoring records provide evidence that food-safety assurance is being accomplished according to HACCP principles.

The HACCP system is the most effective method yet created to ensure the safety of food processing and preparation operations. Implementation of a properly designed HACCP program will protect public health well beyond anything that could be accomplished using old style methods. Traditional inspections emphasize facility, equipment, design, and compliance with basic sanitation principles. HAACP focuses on the actual safety of the product.

Case Study 5.1

In the following exercise, a recipe for BBQ ribs is used to demonstrate application of the HACCP system. Use the recipe in Figure 5.16 and follow the decision tree in Figure 5.5 to determine why each step is needed to ensure the safety of the finished food product.

Ingredients	Amount	Servings		
		25	**50**	**100**
Hoisin sauce	Tbsp.	2.5	5.0	10
Bean sauce	Tbsp.	2.5	5.0	10
Apple sauce	Tbsp.	2.5	5.0	10
Catsup	Tbsp.	5.0	10.0	20
Soy sauce	Tbsp.	2.5	5.0	10
Rice wine	Tbsp.	5.0	10.0	20
Peanut oil	Tbsp.	2.5	5.0	10
Ginger, minced	tsp.	1.25	2.5	5
Scallion, minced	1	1.5	5.0	10
Garlic cloves, minced	2	5.0	10.0	20
Sugar	Tbsp.	2.5	5.0	10
Salt	tsp.	1.25	2.5	5
Pork spareribs, trimmed	1 rack	2.6	5.0	10
Honey	Tbsp.	7.5	5.0	30

**Figure 5.16—Sample Recipe and HACCP Flow Chart
for Barbecued Spareribs**

Pre-preparation

1. Thaw spareribs under refrigeration at 41°F(5°C) for 1 day or until completely thawed.

2. Wash hands before starting food preparation.

3. Combine all of the ingredients for the marinade in a large bowl.

Preparation

4. Score the ribs with a sharp knife. Place the ribs in the marinade. Marinate them for at least 4 hours at a product temperature of 41°F (5°C) or lower in refrigerated storage.

5. Place the spareribs in a smoker at 425°F (220°C) for 30 minutes.

6. Reduce the heat to 375°F (190°C) and continue smoking the ribs to a final internal temperature of 155°F (68°C) or higher. This phase of the cooking process should take about 50 minutes. Brush the honey on the spareribs during the last 5 minutes of the smoking process.

Holding/Service

7. Slice the ribs between the bones and maintain at 140°F (60°C) or above while serving.

Cooling

8. Transfer any unused product into clean, 2-inch deep pans. Quick-chill the product from 140°F (60°C) to 70°F (21°C) within 2 hours and from 70°F (21°C) to 41°F (5°C) within 4 hours.

Storage

9. Store the chilled product in a covered container that is properly dated and labeled. Refrigerate at 41°F (5°C) or below.

Reheating

10. Heat spareribs to an internal temperature of 165°F (74°C); or 190°F (88°C) in a microwave oven within 2 hours.

(Adapted from: HACCP Reference Book, 1993.)

The answers to the case studies are provided in Appendix A.

Discussion Questions (Short Answer)

1. What is HACCP?

2. What are HACCP's advantages over traditional food safety programs?

3. What types of foods are most commonly incorporated into the HACCP system?

4. What is a hazard? List three classes of hazards and give an example of each one.

5. What is a risk?

6. Define critical control point and give an example.

7. Why is ongoing monitoring important to a HACCP system?

Answers to the multiple choice questions are provided in Appendix A.

Quiz 5.1 (Multiple Choice)

1. The Hazard Analysis Critical Control Point (HACCP) system should be employed

   a. whenever potentially hazardous foods are prepared, regardless of the type of food establishment.

   b. only in institutional food facilities that provide food for very young or frail elderly consumers.

   c. only in convenience stores where mechanical dishwashing equipment is not available.

   d. whenever foods are sold by a food establishment for consumption off site.

2. For which of the following products would it **not** be necessary to develop a HACCP flow chart?

   a. Chicken salad

   b. Tuna salad

   c. Seafood salad

   d. Cranberry salad

3. A **hazard** as used in connection with a HACCP system is

   a. any biological, chemical, or physical property that can cause an unacceptable risk.

   b. any single step at which contamination could occur.

   c. an estimate of the likely occurrence of a hazard.

   d. a point at which loss of control may result in an unacceptable health risk.

4. A **risk** as used in connection with a HACCP system is:

   a. failure to meet a required critical limit for a critical control point.

   b. an estimate of the likely occurrence of a hazard.

   c. greatest for non-potentially hazardous foods.

   d. lowest when complex recipes are required to produce a food item

5. Which of the following statements about HACCP programs is **false**?

   a. The HACCP system attempts to anticipate problems before they happen and establish procedures to reduce the risk of foodborne illness.

   b. The HACCP system targets the production of potentially hazardous foods from start to finish.

   c. Records generated by the HACCP system can also be used to aid in foodborne disease investigations.

   d. A HACCP system should only be implemented by public health officials who have been certified by the FDA to conduct such programs.

6. Which of the following is **not** associated with the hazard analysis portion of the HACCP program?

   a. A review of the menu to identify potentially hazardous foods.

   b. A risk assessment of both the likelihood that hazards will occur and their severity if they do occur.

   c. A series of questions used to facilitate the identification of potential problems in each step in the flow of food.

   d. The identification of critical control points whereby hazards can be prevented, eliminated, or reduced to acceptable levels.

7. Which of the following statements is **false?**

   a. A critical limit is the threshold that must be met to insure that each critical control point effectively controls a microbiological, chemical or physical hazard.

   b. There must be at least two critical control points in the flow of food in order for a HACCP system to be implemented.

   c. Many steps in food production are considered control points, but only a few qualify as critical control points.

   d. A critical control point is a point, step, or procedure in food preparation where controls can be applied and a food safety hazard can be prevented, eliminated, or reduced to acceptable levels.

8. Which of the following statements about critical control point monitoring is **false**?

   a. Monitoring is a series of observations and measurements that is used to determine whether a critical control point is under control.

   b. The monitoring of critical limits can be performed either continuously or at predetermined intervals.

   c. Individuals who perform monitoring tasks must be management personnel who will do the job in an unbiased manner.

   d. An operation that identifies critical control points but does not establish a monitoring system, has not actually implemented a HACCP system.

9. The **ultimate** success of a HACCP program depends on:

   a. eliminating potentially hazardous food items from your menu.

   b. providing proper training and equipment for employees who are implementing the HACCP system.

   c. having HACCP flow charts developed for all foods sold by the establishment.

   d. food establishment managers having sole authority for implementing the HACCP system.

10. Which of the following is an example of a critical control point?

   a. Poultry and eggs are purchased from approved sources.

   b. Chicken and noodles are heated on the stove until the center of the product reaches 165°F (74°C) for 15 seconds.

   c. Only pasteurized milk is used by the establishment.

   d. The cutting board is washed and sanitized between chopping carrots and celery for the garden salad.

References/Suggested Readings

Bryan, F. L. (1992). *Hazard Analysis Critical Control Point Evaluations: A Guide To Identifying Hazards And Assessing Risks Associated With Food Preparation And Storage.* Geneva, Switzerland: World Health Organization.

Federal Register ,Volume 59, Number 149. Washington, D.C.: U.S. Government Printing Office, 1994.

Food Marketing Institute (1989). *A Program To Ensure Food Safety And Quality.* Washington, D.C.

LaVella, B. and J.L. Bostic, (1994). *HACCP For Food Service - Recipe Manual And Guide.* St. Louis, MO: LaVella Food Specialists.

J. K. Lotkin, (1995). *The HACCP Food Safety Manual.* New York, NY: Wiley Press.

Pierson, M. D. and D.A. Corlett, Jr. (1992) *HACCP Principles And Applications.* New York, NY: Van Nostrand Rheinhold.

Rue, N., and National Assessment Institute (1994). *Handbook For Safe Food Service Management.* Englewood Cliffs, NJ: Prentice Hall.

The Educational Foundation of the National Restaurant Association. (1993). *HACCP Reference Book.* Chicago, IL: National Restaurant Association.

U.S. Department of Health and Human Services. <u>1997 Food Code</u>. Washington, D.C.: U.S. Government Printing Office.

6 FACILITIES, EQUIPMENT, AND UTENSILS

Ice Machine Is Cause of Gastrointestinal Disease Outbreak

A gastrointestinal disease outbreak affected 123 of the 1,200 individuals who attended a meeting at the convention center in Columbus, Ohio. The initial assumption that the outbreak was foodborne did not pan out. Though two food items were significantly associated with the illness, their connection proved to be coincidental.

*Based on the incubation period, symptoms, and duration of the illness, investigators speculate that **Giardia lamblia** and a Norwalk-like virus caused the illness. Because both agents are commonly waterborne, investigators turned their attention to the water supply at the convention center. Of particular interest was an ice machine which supplied the portable bars. It was discovered that a flexible tube from the machine had been inserted into a floor drain. When the machine's filters were serviced, the tube formed a connection between the ice machine's water supply and raw sewage.*

Learning Objectives

After reading this chapter, you should be able to:

▲ Identify ways in which the design and layout of facilities contribute to the efficiency and effectiveness of a food establishment

▲ Describe how tasks are conducted in work centers and how the work flows through a production area

▲ Identify the criteria that should be used when determining the need for each type of equipment

▲ Understand the basic design and construction requirements that apply to floor-and table-mounted equipment

▲ Explain the role of organizations such as NSF International and Underwriter's Laboratory Inc. in the approval of food equipment

▲ Recognize the different types of cooking, refrigeration, preparation and dishwashing equipment that are available for use in a food establishment

▲ Describe how proper installation and maintenance affect the operation of equipment used during the course of food production, storage, and service

▲ Explain the role of proper lighting in food production and warewashing

▲ Explain how proper heating, air conditioning, and ventilation affect food sanitation and worker comfort and productivity

Essential Terms

Easily movable	Non-food contact surfaces
Easy-to-clean	Sealed
Equipment	Smooth
Food contact surfaces	Splash contact surfaces

Kitchenware
    Tableware
    Utensils
    Single-use articles	

Design, Layout, and Facilities

The design, layout, and facilities in a food establishment should be based on the menu to be served and menu trends. The type of equipment used will be determined by the preparation procedures required to produce menu items. A plan that is good for one operation may not be good for another site with a different menu. Food facilities are normally used for long periods of time. Try to anticipate possible technological advancements and developments in foodservice equipment in the planning stages. Seek a design that facilitates future redesign and remodeling if needed to accommodate new menu items.

The design and layout of facilities, such as the kitchen, dishroom, and dining area, should provide an environment in which work may be done efficiently and effectively. The ideally designed facility enables the use of multiple sources of energy (electric and gas) as well as energy-efficient appliances and equipment.

Facilities planning and design are often left to architects or engineers who may not be familiar with the needs of the food establishment. You and your employees can help the architects or engineers by providing practical information about your operation before and during the design phase of the project. Use a team approach to prepare and review the facility plans. Try to avoid unnecessary expense and inconvenience caused by a faulty design.

The general areas of a food establishment are:

▲ receiving

▲ storage

▲ preparation

▲ holding

▲ display

▲ service

▲ warewashing

Activities that are carried out in these different areas are called functions. Functions are further broken down into various sub-functions. When planning a food establishment, try to understand and visualize each and every function within that facility.

First, determine the tasks within the functions. Next, arrange these tasks in a way that allows a smooth and sequential flow within that area. It is important that you *develop a flow diagram* of your establishment's operation in order to plan the physical facilities for each function. A sample flow diagram is presented in Figure 6.1.

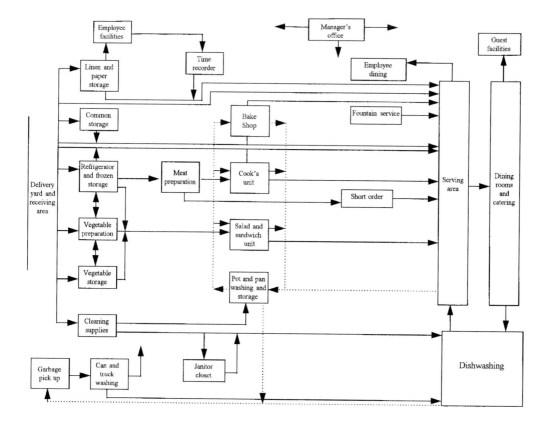

Figure 6.1—Flow Diagram Showing the Functional Relationships of Work (Source: Kotschevar and Terrell, 1985)

Attention to the design and construction of the building, the equipment, and its installation, assures high standards of sanitation and safety helps make maintenance activities easier.

Regulatory Considerations

When planning facilities for food establishments, you must know of and comply with national, state, and local standards and codes, related to:

▲ health

▲ safety

▲ building

▲ fire

▲ zoning

▲ environmental code standards

The equipment used in food establishments should meet the standards and bear the stamp of approval of recognized standard organizations (Figure 6.2). This list includes:

▲ NSF International (NSF)

▲ Underwriters Laboratories Inc. (UL)

▲ American Gas Association (AGA)

Figure 6.2—UL and NSF Seals

Buyers who purchase equipment approved by these organizations are assured that quality materials are used. Also, the items are built according to acceptable standards for the particular item.

Installation of equipment must conform to local code. Officials from local health, building, and fire protection agencies usually conduct on-site inspections of equipment installation.

Work Center Planning

The food production area is commonly organized into **work centers**. These are areas where a group of closely related tasks are performed by an individual or individuals. The number of work centers required in a food facility depends on the number of functions to be performed and the volume of material handled.

Two of the most important features to consider when planning work centers are the total space needed and the arrangement of equipment in that space. A properly designed work center provides adequate facilities and space for:

▲ efficient production

▲ fast service

▲ a pleasant environment

▲ effective cleanup

A worker should be able to complete the related tasks at the work center without moving away from it. The work center should be large enough to do the job yet compact enough to reduce travel and conserve time and energy. A simply-arranged short-order work center showing the close relationship between production, dish-up, and service to dining room is presented in Figure 6.3.

Figure 6.3—An Efficient Short-Order Cooking and Service Working Center (Source: Kotschevar and Terrell, 1985)

Equipment Selection

It is extremely important to select the right piece of equipment for the job. Compare different pieces of equipment for a particular job and look at such features as:

▲ design

▲ construction

▲ durability

▲ ability to clean easily

▲ size

▲ cost

▲ safety

▲ overall ability to do the job

Need

The basic needs of a food establishment should dictate the purchase of equipment. Need should be evaluated on the basis of whether the addition of a particular piece of equipment will:

▲ result in improved quality of food

▲ produce significant savings in labor and material costs

▲ improve sanitation

▲ contribute to the overall profitability of the food establishment

Food establishment managers should assign a priority to their equipment needs. When buying equipment, look for products that:

▲ can meet the needs and demands of the operation

▲ can be used for a long period of time

▲ do not require extraordinary repair and upkeep

▲ can meet the future needs of the operation

Cost

Some of the major costs associated with the purchase of equipment are:

▲ the purchase price

▲ installation cost

▲ repair and maintenance costs

▲ depreciation costs

▲ operating costs

▲ finance charges

Compare these costs for the different pieces of equipment that you are considering before you make a purchase. Some of these costs will be calculated by the manufacturers and provided for comparison purposes. For others, the food establishment manager or his agent will have to collect information to assist in making a purchasing decision. It is not advisable to buy equipment that is more expensive, larger, or more sophisticated than that which is required to meet the needs of the operation.

Size and Design

Equipment should easily fit into the space available in the layout of the facility. Consider future needs when selecting equipment, but it is unwise to buy oversized equipment in anticipation of future growth many years away. Oversized equipment can cause as much wasted effort as equipment that is too small.

Design is also an important feature of food equipment, since the equipment used in a food establishment is subject to constant use and abuse. Equipment and utensils must be designed to function properly when used for their intended purposes.

Equipment that sets on the floor and is not easily movable must be elevated on legs or sealed to the floor. **When legs are used, they should provide a minimum clearance of 6 inches (15 centimeters) between the floor and the bottom surfaces of the equipment.** The space makes it easier to clean the floor under and behind the equipment.

Heavy equipment such as ranges and cabinets may be mounted on a raised masonry, tile, or metal platform and sealed to the floor. This prevents trash and pests from collecting under the equipment.

In a supermarket or convenience store, display shelving units, display refrigeration units, and display freezer units located in the consumer shopping areas do not have to be elevated or sealed to the floor. However, the floor under these units must be maintained in a clean and sanitary manner.

Table mounted equipment (that is not easily movable) should be on 4 inch (10 centimeter) legs. This provides clearance between the counter top and the bottom of the equipment to make it easier to clean under and around the equipment.

Construction Materials

The *Food Code* and construction standards from NSF International require food equipment and utensils to be:

▲ smooth

▲ seamless

▲ easily cleanable

▲ easy to take apart

▲ easy to reassemble

▲ equipped with rounded corners and edges

Materials used in the construction of utensils and food-contact surfaces of equipment must be non-toxic and not impart colors, odors, or tastes to foods. Stainless steel is a preferred material for food contact surfaces.

Under normal use, the materials should be:

▲ safe

▲ durable

▲ corrosion-resistant

▲ nonabsorbent

▲ of proper weight and thickness to withstand repeated washing

▲ resistant to:

▼ chipping

▼ pitting

▼ scratching

▼ deterioration

Metals

We depend on metals for nearly everything in a food establishment. Chromium over steel gives an easily cleanable, high-luster finish. It is used for appliances, such as toasters and waffle irons, and trim where high luster is desired. Noncorrosive metals formed by the alloys of iron, nickel, and chromium may also be used in the construction of foodservice equipment.

Stainless Steel

Stainless steel is one of the most popular materials for food operations. It is commonly used for table tops, sinks, dish tables, dishwashers and ventilation hood systems.

The highly durable finish has a shiny surface which easily shows soil and makes it easier to clean and maintain. Stainless steel also resists rust and stain formation and can resist high temperatures.

Gauge refers to the thickness of sheet metal or the weight of the metal. As the number of the gauge **increases**, the thickness and weight of the metal decreases. Gauges between 8 and 22 are most commonly used in foodservice equipment.

Metal finishes are either polished or dull. However, the more polished the metal, the more easily it is scratched. Stainless steel, for example, must be polished and cleaned with great care.

Do not use abrasive cleaners and scouring pads to clean stainless because they scratch the surface of the metal which can become "germ farms." Bacteria can attach as a biofilm (see Chapter 3) which is difficult to remove from the surface.

The cost of stainless steel is based on the extent of polishing desired, because polishing requires labor, material, and energy. Finish No. 4 is most commonly preferred for food production areas while higher finishes are usually preferred in serving areas.

Plastic

Plastics and fiberglass are frequently used in foodservice equipment because they are durable, inexpensive, and can be molded into different combinations. Undoubtedly, plastics will be used more and more as components of food equipment in the future.

Some examples of plastics used in food establishments are:

▲ acrylics (used to make covers for food containers)

▲ melamines (used for a variety of dishes and glassware)

▲ fiberglass (used in boxes, bus trays, and trays)

▲ nylons (used in equipment with moving parts)

▲ polyethylene (used in storage containers and bowls)

▲ polypropylene (used for dishwashing racks)

Make sure you use only food-grade plastics. There are many different brand names for plastics. Select them on the basis of their use and durability. Harder, more durable plastics, are easier to clean and sanitize. Always follow NSF Standard No. 51 when selecting plastic materials and coverings.

Wood

Wood has both advantages and disadvantages for use in foodservice equipment. It is light in weight and economical. However, the disadvantages outweigh advantages because of problems with sanitation. Wood is porous to bacteria and moisture, and it absorbs food odors and stains. Wood also wears easily under normal use, which requires frequent maintenance and replacement.

The *Food Code* permits the use of hard maple or an equally hard, close-grained wood for cutting boards, cutting blocks, and baker's tables. Wood is also approved for paddles used in candy kitchens and pizza establishments.

Types of Equipment

In order to select the proper equipment for a food establishment, it is necessary to obtain up-to-date information about the equipment from manufacturers' brochures and catalogues, and trade journals and magazines.

NSF International has developed uniform equipment construction standards and provides independent laboratory testing of equipment and materials. The NSF seal on a piece of equipment indicates that it meets the requirements set in the standards. Sample pieces of the same design and model have been tested for performance in the laboratory and in the field.

Cooking Equipment

The types and quantities of food to be prepared in a food operation are prime considerations in selecting cooking equipment. Always consider durability and energy conservation.

The frame, door, exterior, and interior materials should not take away from the durability and ability to clean the unit as a whole. Insulation materials and their thickness contribute to the energy efficiency of this type of equipment.

For the sake of time and convenience, only buy equipment that has been tested and approved by such organizations as the American Gas Association, Underwriters Laboratory (UL), and NSF International.

Ovens

Ovens are among the most important pieces of equipment in a food establishment. They are used to cook a variety of foods to different temperatures. The heat in an oven is distributed by radiation, conduction, or convection depending on the type of oven being used.

A good oven should rise to 450°F (232°C) within 20 minutes, and proper heat circulation is important. Ovens should be able to cool quickly when a drop in temperature is required.

The *range oven* is the most commonly used oven in small food operations (Figure 6.4). It has a cooking surface above the oven which makes it suitable for doing all kinds of work. Range ovens must have good insulation and construction to prevent heat loss. They should also be equipped with heavy-duty doors and shelves. A window in the oven door makes it easier to see inside.

Figure 6.4—Range Oven

Deck ovens are the stationary type where one deck sits on top of another to conserve space (Figure 6.5). A pizza oven is a common example of a deck oven.

In these units, the heated air is circulated around the outside of the heating chamber and radiates through the lining. Deck ovens contain separate heating elements and controls for each unit, and good insulation is provided between decks. The decks are designed to provide different working heights with 7-8" clearance provided for baking and 12-16" clearance for roasting

A *convection oven* uses a high-speed fan to circulate heated air and guarantee even-heat distribution over and around foods (Figure 6.6). Cooking time in a convection oven is about 1/3 to 3/4 the

Figure 6.5—Deck Oven

amount required in deck ovens. Another advantage of the convection oven is that more cooking is accomplished in a smaller space, as food is placed on multiple racks instead of on a single deck.

Figure 6.6—Convection Oven

Microwave ovens are commonly used for thawing, heating, and reheating food (Figure 6.7). Microwaves are electromagnetic waves of radiant energy that, like light, travel in straight lines. Microwaves are reflected by metals, pass through air, and are absorbed by several food components. They pass through many, but not all, types of paper, glass, and plastic materials. When microwaves are reflected or pass through a material, they do not give off heat to the object. To the extent that microwaves are absorbed, they heat the absorbing material.

The advantage of the microwave oven is that it can cook foods rapidly. It cooks small quantities of food in seconds. A microwave oven is not useful for cooking large quantities of food due to its limited capacity. However, it is excellent as a support to quantity cooking.

Figure 6.7—Microwave Oven

Many other types of ovens are available for use in a food establishment. These include conveyor, roll-in, revolving, and infrared ovens. Each of these pieces of equipment has unique features and has been designed for special applications. You should contact your equipment supplier to determine if this type of equipment is appropriate for your operation.

Steam-jacketed Kettles

Steam-jacketed kettles are essential pieces of equipment in most food establishments. These kettles consist of two bowl-like sections of welded aluminum or stainless steel with an air space between for circulation of steam (Figure 6.8). When the steam is released inside the jacket, it condenses on the outside of the inner shell, thereby giving up its heat to the metal, from which it is then transferred to the foods. The steam does not come directly in contact with the food being heated.

Courtesy of Groen Corporation

Figure 6.8—Steam Kettle

Steam-jacket kettles may be stationary or tilting. The cooking capacity of kettles should be based on a maximum load to fill the kettle to about 2/3 to 3/4 full. More than that makes it difficult to handle and pour the food without spillage. When planning for kettles, it is important to remember that emptying the contents of the container should be as easy as possible.

Refrigeration and Low-Temperature Storage Equipment

Refrigeration and low-temperature storage equipment are widely used to protect perishable foods and preserve wholesomeness. Many foods deteriorate rapidly at room temperature. A lot of waste can be eliminated by keeping foods at lower temperatures until they are used.

Proper cooling requires removing heat from food quickly enough to prevent microbial growth. Improper cooling of potentially hazardous foods is consistently identified as one of the leading contributors to foodborne illness. Bacteria grow best at temperatures between 70°F (21°C) and 120°F (49°C). **The *Food Code* states that cooked potentially hazardous foods *must* be cooled from 140°F (60°C) to 70°F (21°C) within 2 hours and from 70°F (21°C) to 41°F (5°C) or below within 4 hours.**

Other potentially hazardous foods, such as reconstituted foods and canned tuna, must be cooled to 41°F (5°C) or below within 4 hours if prepared from ingredients that are at room temperature. A potentially hazardous food, such as shell eggs, received at a temperature *above* 41°F (5°C) during shipment from the supplier, must be cooled to 41°F (5°C) or *below* within 4 hours.

Refrigeration is important during the transportation and storage of perishable foods. Together they allow us to have an ample supply of meats, poultry, fish, dairy products, fruits, and vegetables in all parts of the country practically all seasons of the year. Refrigeration during transportation and better cold storage facilities have helped to stabilize the price of perishable foods.

The efficient operation of a refrigeration unit depends on several factors including:

▲ design

▲ construction

▲ capacity of the equipment

Proper air circulation both inside and outside the cabinet is important. The storage of **food in shallow containers, placed on slatted shelves or tray slides to permit good circulation of the chilled air**, is essential for both short- and long-term storage.

Sheet pans, foil, plastic, or cardboard should not be used to line shelves because they decrease air flow. Sturdy construction of doors, hardware, and fixtures is a necessary requirement. Doors may be full or half length, and shelving should be adjustable. Door gaskets should provide reasonable wear and be replaceable when worn.

The size of refrigerator or freezer needed depends on the size of the work area and the type and amount of food to be stored in the unit. Refrigerators and freezer units have far more capacity today than ever before. More compact compressors are usually located at the top of the unit, which means the unit can be taller, utilizing all the space and increasing capacity. The type and size of refrigeration system selected should insure reliable and efficient operation.

All types of refrigerators and freezers have a maximum capacity for cooling foods. Too often, workers put large amounts of hot food in a unit and rely on it to "cool" the food. However, the *addition of large amounts of hot food will cause the inside temperature of the unit to rise above acceptable storage temperatures.* This in turn could cause food to be stored in the temperature danger zone. Do not forget that the primary purpose of a refrigerator is to hold foods that are at or near the proper cold storage temperature.

Maintenance of the refrigerated equipment in the kitchen and other areas is an important responsibility. Clean refrigerators on a regular basis to maintain good sanitary conditions and eliminate odors. Remove shelves and other accessories and wash periodically. Wash the inside walls and the floor of a walk-in unit as needed to clean up spills and remove debris. Clean the fan grates and condenser unit periodically.

Open doors of refrigerators as briefly and infrequently as possible when taking food in and out of storage. Large amounts of warm, moist air raise the holding temperature and humidity inside a refrigerator.

Reach-in Refrigeration

There are several types of reach-in refrigerated units on the market. These include *pass-through, upright, under-the-counter, display cabinets, mobile* or *portable,* and *dispensing units* to name a few.

In a small operation, reach-in refrigerators may provide all of the cold storage that is needed. In larger operations, reach-ins may serve the storage needs of a single work center.

The capacity of reach-in refrigerators varies greatly. Small units will have only a few cubic feet of storage space while large models have a capacity of about 90 cubic feet. Upright models are generally 6 feet tall, 3 feet deep and come in various widths. These units are usually equipped with single, double, or multiple doors {Figure 6.9 (a)}.

a. Standard Upright   b. Pass-Through   c. Under-the-Counter

Figure 6.9—Reach-in Refrigerators

Pass-through refrigerator units open from both sides and are used for storage between production and service areas {Figure 6.9 (b)}. Pass-through refrigerators save labor and eliminate interference by providing access of two working areas simultaneously.

However, the ability to open these units from two sides may increase the loss of cold air if the doors are opened repeatedly or for long periods of time. Keep the doors to these refrigerators closed tight, except when food is being put into or taken out of the unit.

Another example of an in-line production refrigerator is the under-the-counter drawer unit, placed below the counter or under equipment {Figure 6.9 (c)}. It provides instant, on-the-spot storage. These units can be placed below fryers, griddles, and salad preparation areas.

Walk-in Refrigerators

Walk-in refrigerators are used to store large quantities of food in bulk at temperatures between 32° and 41°F (0° and 5°C). They are also used to safely thaw products removed from a freezer. Locate walk-ins to make the delivery of foods from receiving to production and service areas as easy as possible. The floors of walk-ins should be made of strong, durable, easily cleanable material. The walls need a washable finish that will resist the effects of moisture. A safety device for opening the door should be provided on the inside of the unit.

Some walk-in units have the door opening covered with four-inch wide plastic strips called a strip curtain. These curtains reduce air loss and conserve energy when the door is opened. An outside wall mounted thermometer or recorder will enable you to determine the air temperature inside the walk-in without opening the door.

Cook-Chill System

Cook-chill is a system in which food is:

▲ cooked using conventional cooking methods

▲ rapidly chilled using a chiller

▲ stored for a limited time

▲ reheated before service to the customer

In a standard cook-chill system, the food is cooked and then placed in sealed plastic pouches. The pouches are placed in a chill tumbler which looks a lot like a front loading clothes washing machine. The pouches are then tumbled inside the machine in ice cold water. The food is typically chilled to 37°F (24°C) in 90 minutes or less and is stored at temperatures between 33° and 38°F (1° and 4°C) for five days. Day one is counted as the day of production and day five is the day of service.

The advantages of this system include reduction of peaks and valleys in production and readily available foods. The disadvantages of this system include the high cost of the chiller and the storage-space requirements.

Other Types of Food Equipment

Slicers

The basic design of food slicers includes a circular knife blade and carriage that passes under the blade (Figure 6.10). Foods to be sliced are placed on the carriage and fed either automatically or by hand. Thickness of the slices can be controlled by changing the setting of a close adjustment to the blade.

Slicers can be dangerous if not used properly. The manufacturer's instructions should always be followed and employees should receive training on safe operation and cleaning of equipment.

Figure 6.10—Slicer

Mixers

Mixers are available as table and floor models. Their primary function is to combine or blend foods. However, mixers can perform other functions, such as shredding and grinding, by using different accessories and attachments. Mixers are designed to operate at a variety of speeds, depending on the job.

Floor model mixers have three standard attachments: (1) a paddle beater for general mixing which can be used to mash, mix, or blend foods and ingredients; (2) a whip to incorporate air into products; and (3) a dough hook used to mix and knead dough.

Some mixers are designed to accommodate accessories that attach directly to the drive shaft of the mixer. Most common among these attachments are knife sharpeners, juice extractors, and food slicers. Other popular mixer attachments are cutters, choppers, and grinders.

Figure 6.II—Floor-Mount Mixer

Ice Machines

Ice is food; and it must be handled with the same degree of care as other foods. Ice must be made from potable water, and ice machines must protect the ice during production and storage (Figure 6.12).

The parts of an ice machine that contact the ice are considered food contact surfaces. These surfaces must be smooth, durable, easily cleanable and constructed of non-toxic materials. Food contact surfaces of ice machines must be cleaned and sanitized regularly to prevent the growth of mold and other microorganisms.

The drain line from the ice machine must be equipped with an air gap to prevent the backflow of contamination into the ice. You will learn more about these concepts in Chapter 8.

Scoops used to dispense ice must be designed and constructed to meet the basic requirements of food equipment. Scoops must be stored either outside the ice machine in a protected fashion or inside the machine in a bracket that is mounted to a wall of the ice storage compartment. In either instance, the scoop must be stored in such a way that the handle can be grasped by workers without their hands coming into contact with the ice. Workers must never dispense ice by passing a glass or cup through the ice. This may cause the glass from the container to break off and become a physical hazard in the ice.

Figure 6.12—Ice Machine

Dishwashing Equipment

The effective cleaning and sanitizing of equipment and utensils is one of the most important jobs in a food establishment. Contaminated utensils, equipment (e.g., slicers), and cutting boards have been identified as sources of cross contamination of food during preparation and service. Contaminated eating utensils can aid the spread of bacteria and viruses that can cause disease.

Dishwashing is best performed in a separate room or area which is well lighted and ventilated. Noise-absorbing materials are used to aid in lowering the noise levels associated with this activity. The design of the dishwashing area is dependent upon the total volume of equipment and utensils to be washed and the time required to do the job. As business changes, periodically evaluate the dishwashing operation to make certain that it can effectively handle the current volume.

The items that are most frequently washed and sanitized in a food establishment are kitchenware and tableware. Kitchenware includes kitchen utensils such as pots, pans, and skillets soiled in the process of food preparation. Tableware includes dishes, glassware, and eating utensils that are handled by the employees or customers.

The purposes of dishwashing are to clean and to sanitize equipment, dishware, and utensils. **It requires a two-part operation:**

▲ **a cleaning procedure to remove visible soil from the surface of the item**

▲ **a sanitizing procedure to reduce the number of disease-causing microorganisms on a cleaned surface to safe levels**

Cleaning and sanitizing kitchen equipment and utensils can be done manually or mechanically. Manual cleaning and sanitizing is typically used for in-place cleaning and sanitizing of equipment and for cleaning and sanitizing portable equipment and utensils. Most food establishments will use manual dishwashing to clean and sanitize pots, pans, and utensils used to prepare and serve food.

Manual Washing

Sufficient space to store soiled equipment and utensils must be provided in the manual dishwashing area. Equipment and utensils must be pre-flushed or prescraped and, when necessary, presoaked to remove food particles and soil. Provide a hose and nozzle or similar device for pre-flushing and pre-scraping food soil into a garbage container or disposal. Locate this equipment at the soiled end of the manual dishwashing operation to prevent the contamination of cleaned and sanitized equipment and utensils.

Use a three-compartment sink for manual cleaning and sanitizing (Figure 6.13). In the first compartment, wash the scraped equipment and utensils in a detergent solution with hot water. Rinse the soap off the equipment and utensils in the second compartment. Use the third compartment to sanitize. **There are two accepted methods for sanitizing equipment and utensils:**

▲ the hot-water method

▲ the chemical method

Refer to Chapter 7 of this text for more information about proper cleaning and sanitizing techniques.

Figure 6.13—Three-Compartment Sink

The compartments of the three-compartment sink must be large enough to accommodate the largest pieces of equipment and utensils used in the food establishment. Supply each compartment with hot and cold potable running water. Provide drainboards or easily movable dish tables of adequate size, for proper handling of soiled utensils prior to washing, and for air drying cleaned and sanitized items. In a manual operation, the temperature of hot water used for sanitizing must be maintained at or above 171°F (77°C). To achieve water temperature that high, you will need a booster heater or an electrical heating element that can be immersed directly in the water in the third compartment.

Mechanical Washing

Mechanical dishwashers are among the most expensive and important pieces of equipment in a food establishment. Use them for cleaning and sanitizing any equipment or utensil that does not have electrical parts and will fit into the machine. The most common types of mechanical dishwashers are:

Immersion dishwashers, in which racks of dishes are immersed for cleaning. This arrangement is very similar to the manual dishwashing procedure already discussed.

Single-tank, stationary-rack dishwashers, in which dishes are placed on racks and washed one rack at a time with jets of water within a single tank. They are operated by opening a door, inserting a rack of dishes, closing the door, and starting the machine.

Conveyor-rack dishwashers, in which a conveyor carries the racks of dishes through the dishwasher. These machines are built with either single or multiple tanks. The racks move through the machine automatically.

Flight-type dishwashers, in which the conveyor is one continuous rack and the dishes are placed on pegs or bars. This machine operates continuously with a person stationed at each end.

Carousel-type dishwashers, in which there is a closed circuit conveyor where dishes are loaded and unloaded.

Low-temperature dishwashers, which use chemicals to sanitize equipment and utensils. This allows lower water temperatures, which conserves energy.

The design of the dishwasher should fit in the overall layout of the food operation. The capacity needed will depend on the number of dishes to be cleaned. Specifications are provided by manufacturers for different types of dishwashers. When making a selection, you should also consider the cost of installation and maintenance.

An adequate supply of very hot water (180° to 195°F, 82° to 91° C) is required for the final rinse in a high-temperature dishwashing machine. The extremely high temperatures required for effective sanitization make it expensive and unsafe to maintain general-purpose hot water at these temperatures. Therefore, a separate booster heater is needed to raise the temperature of the sanitizing rinse water to between 180° and 195°F (82° and 91° C). The booster heater must be properly sized, installed, and operated to deliver water at the volume, flow pressure, and temperature required for the operation. For more information about booster heaters, consult NSF International Standard No. 5, Commercial Hot Water Generating Equipment.

Figure 6.14—Flight-Type Mechanical Dishwasher

Installation

Proper installation is a necessity for the successful operation of all equipment. The best design and construction would be worthless if electrical, gas, water, or drain connections were inadequate or poorly done. The dealer from whom the equipment was purchased may or may not be responsible for its installation. Arrangements for installation will usually be specified in your purchase agreement.

Architects, engineers, and contractors are responsible for providing:

▲ adequate plumbing

▲ electrical wiring

▲ venting facilities for the satisfactory installation of kitchen equipment

▲ complying with the standards of local building, plumbing, electrical, health, and fire safety codes

The operation of each piece of equipment must be checked many times by both the contractors and service engineers before it is ready for actual use. Provide full instruction for the proper operation and satisfactory performance of each piece of equipment to all persons who will work with it. They must know the danger signals so that preventive measures can be taken early.

Maintenance and Replacement

The cost of care and upkeep on a piece of equipment may determine whether or not its purchase and use are justified. Successful maintenance of equipment requires definite plans to prolong its life and maintain its usefulness. Such plans place emphasis on a few simple procedures:

▲ keep the equipment clean

▲ follow the manufacturer's printed directions for care and operation

▲ post the instruction card for a piece of equipment near it

▲ stress careful handling as essential to continued use

▲ make needed repairs promptly

Some valuable suggestions for the care of equipment are:

▲ assign the care of a machine to a responsible person;

▲ check the cleanliness of machines daily; and

▲ have repairs performed promptly and by a competent person.

Lighting

Good lighting is a very important feature of a work area. Proper lighting in the kitchen increases productivity, improves workmanship, reduces eye fatigue and worker irritability, and decreases accidents and waste due to worker error.

The kitchen should be equipped with proper lighting and soft colors which reduce glare. Locate light to eliminate shadows on work surfaces, or glare and excessive brightness in the field of vision. Glaring light is unacceptable because it tends to harm vision, cause fatigue, reduce efficiency, and increase accidents.

The proper intensity of light depends on the kind of work to be done. The following intensity levels are recommended in the *Food Code*:

▲ *10 footcandles at a distance of 30" above the floor*
   ▼ Walk-in refrigeration areas
   ▼ Dry food storage areas
   ▼ Other areas and rooms during periods of cleaning
▲ 20 footcandles at a distance of 30" above the floor
   ▼ Areas where fresh produce or packaged foods are sold or offered for consumption
   ▼ Areas used for handwashing
   ▼ Areas used for warewashing
   ▼ Areas used for equipment and utensil storage
   ▼ Toilet rooms
▲ *50 footcandles at the work surface*
   ▼ Where a food employee is working with unpackaged potentially hazardous food
   ▼ Where a food employee is working with food, utensils, and equipment such as knives, slicers, grinders or saws
   ▼ Where employee safety is a factor

The recommended intensity of light for most dining areas is 15 to 20 footcandles. The food regulations in some states and local jurisdictions may require higher illumination levels in food establishments, especially during periods of cleaning. Consult the food regulation in your jurisdiction to determine what lighting levels are required for your establishment.

Heating, Ventilation, and Air Conditioning (HVAC)

An adequate supply of fresh air, suitable temperature, and humidity are necessary for worker comfort and productivity. A worker's comfort and well-being also require air that is free of obnoxious odors and other objectionable or injurious elements. Achieving this in food establishments where heat, odors, and high air moisture are commonly created presents a challenge.

Air conditioning in food establishments means more than simply "cooling the air." It includes heating, humidity control, circulation, filtering, and cooling of the air. Modern HVAC systems will filter, warm, humidify, and circulate the air in the winter and maintain a desirable and comfortable temperature in the summer.

Ventilation in kitchens is typically provided by means of mechanical exhaust hood systems. These systems keep rooms free of excessive heat, steam, condensation, vapors, obnoxious odors, smoke, and fumes. The standard ventilation system used in food establishments consists of a hood, fan, and intake and exhaust air ducts and vents (Figure 6.16). Ventilation hood systems must be designed and constructed to prevent grease or condensation from dripping onto food, equipment, utensils, linens, or single-service and single-use articles. The capacity of the ventilation system should be based on the quantity of vapor and hot air to be removed.

Figure 6.15—Ventilation Hood System

Hoods are usually constructed of stainless steel or a comparable material that provides a durable, smooth, and easily cleanable surface. The hood should be equipped with filters or other grease-extracting equipment to prevent drippage into food.

The filters or other grease-extracting equipment must be designed to be removed easily for cleaning and replacement, if not designed to be cleaned in place. Many fires in food establishments are caused by grease accumulation in filters and ducts. Filters should be cleaned or replaced regularly to assure they are working efficiently. This must be part of your regular cleaning program.

Base the frequency of filter cleaning or replacement on the amount and type of pollution products from air exhausted from kitchens. The National Fire Protection Association recommends that all hoods be equipped with a fire extinguishing system.

Clean intake and exhaust air ducts so that they are not a source of contamination by dust, dirt, and other materials. If vented to the outside, ventilation systems must not create a public health nuisance or unlawful discharge.

Pollution control devices that can be placed in hoods and ventilators are available. These devices operate with both hot water spray from nozzles, and electrostatic precipitators which use differences in electrical charge to remove particles.

Summary

Think about the situation you read about at the beginning of this chapter. Did you come up with this solution? Plumbing codes typically require a 2 inch air gap between the end of a drain tube and the floor drain. In this case, investigators speculate that someone wanted to be neat and rather than curl the tube on the floor, it was tucked into the grate of the drain. This permitted back siphonage to occur and contaminated the ice with raw sewage. This situation could have been prevented by making certain an air gap was provided on the drain line. Always make certain equipment is installed in compliance with local plumbing codes.

Good planning is essential for maximum productivity and efficiency. The total space needed and the arrangement of equipment in the space are the overall features you must consider when planning the layout of a food operation. The design of your facility should encourage a smooth flow of work, provide adequate facilities and space for efficiently completing the work, and contribute to high sanitation standards.

The basic needs of a food establishment should determine the type and size of equipment purchased. When purchasing equipment, look for items that can meet the current and future needs of the operation, can be properly cleaned and sanitized, and do not require extraordinary repair and upkeep.

The size and amount of food equipment and placement in the facility should be determined by managers of the food establishment working closely with an experienced engineer or architect. Ideally, equipment should easily fit into the available space.

Materials used in the construction of food contact surfaces should be safe, durable, corrosion-resistant, and nonabsorbent. These materials must not allow the transfer of harmful substances, or allow the transfer of colors, odors, or tastes to food.

The equipment used in food establishments should meet the standards and bear the seal of approval of the National Sanitation Foundation, Underwriters Laboratories Inc. or other recognized standards organizations.

Always install equipment in accordance with local building, plumbing, electrical, health, and fire safety codes. The best possible design and construction of equipment is worthless if electrical, gas, water, or drain connections were inadequate or poorly installed.

Case Study 6.1

The O.K. Corral Restaurant is a buffet style operation that offers customers a choice of roast beef, ham, or turkey in addition to several hot vegetables. The meat and poultry on the buffet are placed on wooden cutting boards and are carved in the dining room in front of the customers. The temperature of the meat and poultry is out of the danger zone when it leaves the kitchen. However, no effort is made to keep these products hot once they reach the dining room. The carver periodically wipes his carving utensils with a damp kitchen towel.

1. What sanitation risks exist at the O.K. Corral?

2. What steps should the manager take to correct the sanitation problems that exist in his/her facility?

Case Study 6.2

Mark Sellmore is the deli manager at Longfellow's Supermarket. Mark has been given permission to purchase a new slicer for the department. Mark's store manager has given him only one instruction... "Buy the most equipment possible for the money you spend."

1. What strategy should Mark use when purchasing the new slicer?

2. What factors should Mark use to determine the deli's *need* for the slicer?

3. What design and construction features should Mark use when he is making comparisons between slicers?

4. What standards organizations might Mark consult when evaluating different kinds of slicers?

The answers to the case studies are provided in Appendix A.

Discussion Questions (Short Answer)

1. In what ways do layout, design, and facilities planning influence a food establishment?

2. What is a work center? What layout features are important to the efficiency of a work center?

3. What design and construction factors should a manager consider before buying a particular piece of equipment?

4. What standards organizations are commonly involved in the testing of food equipment? How can these organizations be helpful to a food establishment manager?

5. What kinds of materials are commonly used in the construction of equipment and utensils? What are the advantages and disadvantages of each kind of material?

6. How does a food contact surface differ from a non-food contact surface?

7. What are some features that make a piece of equipment easily cleanable?

8. How do proper lighting and ventilation affect sanitation in a food establishment?

Answers to all multiple choice questions are provided in Appendix A.

Quiz 6.1 (Multiple Choice)

1. The design, layout and facilities in any food establishment should be based on the

   a. number of employees working in the kitchen.

   b. number of meals served each day.

   c. menu to be served.

   d. amount of space available in the kitchen.

2. Which of the following organizations does **not** routinely evaluate the design and construction of food equipment?

   a. The United States Food and Drug Administration

   b. The National Sanitation Foundation

   c. The American Gas Association

   d. The Underwriters Laboratory

3. Which of the following criteria is **not** used when determining a food operation's need for a particular piece of equipment? Will the equipment

   a. result in improved quality of food?

   b. produce a significant savings in labor and material?

   c. improve sanitation?

   d. make the facility more attractive to customers?

4. When buying equipment, food establishment managers should look for equipment that

   a. can meet the need and demands of the operation.

   b. can be used for a long time.

   c. does not require excessive repair and upkeep.

   d. all of the above.

5. Which of the following statements is **false**?

    a.   The size of equipment should be such that it can easily be fitted in the space available in the layout of the facility.

    b.   Construction requirements for equipment vary according to whether the surface or area is a "food contact surface" or a "splash zone."

    c.   Wood is a preferred material for food contact surfaces of equipment because it resists moisture and bacterial growth.

    d.   Floor-mounted equipment that is not easily movable must be elevated on 6-inch legs or sealed to the floor on a base that is sealed to the floor.

6. Which of the following statements about ovens is **false**?

    a.   A convection oven cooks food by circulating heated air around the product.

    b.   Fewer microwave ovens are sized to permit quantity cooking in a food establishment.

    c.   The range oven is the type of oven most commonly used in food establishments.

    d.   Deck ovens contain separate heating elements and controls for each unit.

7. Which of the following statements about refrigeration equipment is **false**?

    a.   The size of refrigerator or freezer needed depends on whether a walk-in unit is available, what is going to be stored, and how much.

    b.   Mechanical refrigeration during transportation and storage is important to preserve perishable foods.

    c.   Pass-through refrigeration units open from both sides and are used for storage between production and service areas.

    d.   The cleanliness and care of refrigerated equipment is not important, since it is only used to store packaged foods.

8. What type of equipment is required when a food establishment uses a manual dishwashing operation?

   a. A three-compartment sink with hot and cold potable running water and drainboards or easily movable dish tables.

   b. A two-compartment sink with hot and cold potable running water and drainboards or easily movable dish tables.

   c. A two-compartment sink with suitable facilities for pre-flushing and prescraping the dishes before they are washed.

   d. A single-tank dishwashing machine that is large enough to accommodate the largest pieces of equipment and utensils used in the operation.

9. From a sanitation perspective, what is the **most** important reason for having adequate lighting in a food production area?

   a. To provide a comfortable work environment for employees.

   b. To show when a surface is soiled and when it has been properly cleaned.

   c. To decrease accidents and waste due to worker error.

   d. To reduce glare that causes eye fatigue.

10. Which of the following statements about ventilation is **false**?

   a. Ventilation is typically provided by means of a mechanical exhaust hood system.

   b. Ventilation hood systems must be designed and constructed to prevent grease or condensation from dripping onto food and food contact surfaces.

   c. The hood should be equipped with filters or other grease catching devices to prevent drippage into food.

   d. Intake and exhaust air ducts do not need cleaning, if filters or other grease catching devices are provided to collect grease and other condensation.

References/Suggested Readings

Cichy, R. F. (1994). *Quality Sanitation Management*. East Lansing, Michigan: Educational Institute of the American Hotel and Motel Association.

Khan, M. A. (1991). *Foodservice Operations And Management*. New York, NY: Van Nostrand Reinhold.

Kotschevar, Lendal H. and Margaret E. Terrell (1985). *Foodservice Planning: Layout And Equipment*. NY: Wiley.

Longrèe, K., and G. Armbruster (1996). *Quantity Food Sanitation*. New York, NY: Wiley Interscience.

Knight, J. B., and L. H. Kotschevar (1989). <u>Quantity Food Production, Planning, and Management</u>. New York, NY: Van Nostrand Reinhold.

NSF International, Ann Arbor Michigan,.

STANDARD Number 2 - Food Equipment

STANDARD Number 3 - Commercial Spray-Type Dishwashing Machine

STANDARD Number 4 - Commercial Cooking, Rethermalization, and Powered Hot Food Holding and Transport Equipment

STANDARD Number 5 - Water Heaters, Hot Water Supply Boilers, and Heat Recovery Equipment

STANDARD Number 6 - Dispensing Freezers

STANDARD Number 7 - Food Service Refrigerators and Storage Freezers

STANDARD Number 8 - Commercial Powered Food Preparation Equipment

STANDARD Number 12 - Automatic Ice Making Equipment

STANDARD Number 13 - Refuse Compactors

STANDARD Number 18 - Manual Food and Beverage Dispensing Equipment

STANDARD Number 20 - Commercial Bulk Milk Dispensing Equipment

STANDARD Number 21 - Thermoplastic Refuse Containers

STANDARD Number 26 - Pot, Pan, and Utensil Washers

STANDARD Number 29 - Detergent and Chemical Feeders for Commercial Spray-Type Dishwashing Machines

STANDARD Number 35 - Laminated Plastics for Surfacing Food Service Equipment-

STANDARD Number 36 - Dinnerware

STANDARD Number 37 - Air Curtains for Entranceways in Food and Food Service Establishments

STANDARD Number 51 - Plastic Materials and Components Used in Food Equipment

STANDARD Number 52 - Supplemental Flooring

STANDARD Number 59 - Food Carts

CRITERIA C-2 — Special Equipment and/or Devices

Pannell, Dorothy Van Egmond (1990). *School Foodservice Management*. New York, NY: Van Nostrand Reinhold.

Scriven, C., and J. Stevens (1989). *Manual Of Equipment And Design For The Foodservice Industry*. New York, NY: Van Nostrand Reinhold.

Scriven, C., and J. Stevens (1989). *Food Equipment Facts: A Handbook For The Foodservice Industry*. New York, NY: Van Nostrand Reinhold.

West, B. B., et al. (1986) Food Service in Institutions. New York, NY: Macmillan Publishers.

7 CLEANING AND SANITIZING OPERATIONS

Dirty Meat Grinder Suspected in Salmonella Outbreak

A Salmonella outbreak involving 107 confirmed and 51 probable cases occurred in Dodge County, Wisconsin. The illness was caused by eating raw ground beef commonly known as steak tartare. Investigators suspect inadequate cleaning of the meat grinder may have been the cause of the problem. Employees of the butcher shop where the ground beef was purchased indicated the parts of the grinder were cleaned and sanitized at the end of each day. However, the auger housing, which was attached with nuts and bolts could not be easily removed for cleaning and sanitizing. Employees indicated they had been instructed not to remove the auger housing for cleaning. When inspectors from the health department removed the housing, they found meat residue. Investigators speculate improper cleaning resulted in ongoing contamination of the ground beef over several days. A stool specimen from one of the butchers, who had eaten the raw ground beef, was positive for **Salmonella typhimurium***.*

Learning Objectives

After reading this chapter you should be able to:

▲ Recognize the difference between cleaning and sanitizing

▲ Identify the different processes that can be used to clean and sanitize equipment and utensils in a food establishment

▲ Identify the primary steps involved in manually and mechanically cleaning and sanitizing equipment and utensils

▲ Describe the factors that affect cleaning efficiency

▲ Identify the procedures used to clean environmental areas in a food establishment

Essential Terms

Cleaning agent	Sanitizer
Clean-in-place (CIP)	Chlorine
Detergent	Iodophores
Soap	Quaternary Ammonium Compounds
Sanitize	Selectivity

Principles of Cleaning and Sanitizing

Cleaning and sanitizing are important activities in a food safety program. Food contact surfaces of equipment and utensils must be cleaned and sanitized at regular intervals to prevent contamination and cross contamination. Equipment and utensils used to prepare potentially hazardous foods are food contact surfaces which must be washed and sanitized:

▲ after each use

▲ after any interruption of an operation that could cause contamination

Cleaning and sanitizing are two distinct processes used for very different purposes. Cleaning is the *physical removal of soil and food residues* from surfaces of equipment and utensils.

Sanitizing (sometimes called sanitization) **is the treatment of a surface that has been previously cleaned to reduce the number of disease-causing microorganisms to safe levels.** The equipment and supplies used for cleaning are different from those used for sanitizing.

Effective cleaning consists of four separate events:

1. a detergent or other type of cleaner is brought into contact with the soil

2. the soil is loosened from the surface being cleaned

3. the loosened soil is dispersed in the wash water

4. the dispersed soil is rinsed away along with the detergent to prevent it from being redeposited onto the clean surface

Removal of Food Particles

Scrape and flush large food particles from equipment and utensils before the items are placed in a cleaning solution. Spray the equipment and utensils with warm water. Avoid using very hot water or steam because they tend to "bake" food particles on the surface of equipment and utensils and that makes cleaning more difficult.

Application of Cleaning Agents

A cleaning agent is a chemical compound formulated to remove soil and dirt. There are many methods of applying cleaning agents and solutions to the surfaces of equipment. Effectiveness and the economy of the method generally dictate its use.

Soaking

Small equipment, equipment parts, and utensils may be immersed in cleaning solutions in a sink. By soaking equipment or utensils for a few minutes before scrubbing, you will increase the effectiveness of manual and mechanical dishwashing.

Spray Methods

Spray cleaning solutions on equipment surfaces with either fixed or portable spray units that use hot water or steam. These methods are extensively used in meat departments of grocery stores and in food processing plants.

Clean-in-Place Systems

The **clean-in-place** method is an automated cleaning system generally used in conjunction with permanent-welded pipeline systems. The strength and velocity of the cleaning solution moving through the pipes are chiefly responsible for soil removal in clean-in-place (CIP) operations.

Abrasive Cleaning

Abrasive type powders and pastes are used to remove soil that is firmly attached to a surface. Always rinse these cleaners away completely and avoid scratching the surface of equipment and utensils. Abrasive type cleaners are not recommended for use on stainless steel surfaces. Never use metal or abrasive scouring pads on food-contact surfaces because small metal pieces from the pads may promote corrosion or may be picked up in food to become a physical hazard.

Rinsing

Thoroughly rinse all equipment surfaces with hot, potable water immediately after cleaning to remove the cleaning solution. This very important rinse step is necessary because the product or detergent used for washing can interfere with the germ-killing power of the sanitizer.

Factors Effecting Cleaning Efficiency

Many factors effect the efficiency of a cleaning process in terms of how well and how easily soil is removed. Among the most important factors are:

▲   type of soil to be removed

▲   water quality

▲   the detergent or cleaner to be used

▲   water temperature

▲   water velocity or force

▲   time detergent remains in contact with the surface

▲   the concentration of cleaner

Each of these factors is important for effective cleaning and can be modified to meet the needs of a particular type of problem or set of conditions.

Type of Soil to Be Removed

Soil may consist of:

▲   food deposits (protein and carbohydrates)

▲   mineral deposits (salts)

▲   microorganisms (bacteria, viruses, yeasts, and molds)

▲   fats and oils

▲   dirt and debris

When you know the type and condition of the soil you are working with, it is easier to determine the physical and chemical methods best suited to remove soil effectively and economically.

Water Quality

Water is the primary component of cleaning materials used in food establishments. The water supply serving food establishments must be safe to drink. Water must be free from harmful microorganisms, chemicals, and other substances that can cause disease. While the water supply must be safe to drink, it may contain substances that affect hardness, taste, and odors. Therefore, adjust cleaning agents to fit the characteristics of your water supply and type of operation.

"Hard" water is caused by dissolved salts of calcium, magnesium, and iron. Water hardness reduces the effectiveness of detergents and leaves "lime" scale deposits on the surface of equipment. The degree of water hardness varies considerably from place to place. For effective cleaning, hard water requires softening. If the water is not softened, the cleaner must contain a sequestering (softening) agent that inactivates the iron and manganese without settling them out.

Detergents and Cleaners to Be Used

A **detergent** is defined as a cleaning or purifying agent - a solvent. The origin of the word is from the Latin, "detergeo," meaning "to wipe away." Water acts as a detergent when soils are readily soluble. However, we can improve the detergent action of water by adding soap, alkaline detergents, acid detergents, degreasers, abrasive cleaners, detergent sanitizers, or other cleaning agents to it.

Soaps

Bar **soaps** are cleaning agents made by chemical reaction of alkali on fats or fatty acids. Soaps are only used as cleaners in food establishments in a limited way. In soft water, they are effective for washing hands. However, most soaps do not dissolve in cold water, and are not compatible with quaternary ammonium compounds (QUATS). In hard water, soaps form troublesome precipitates and films that lose their cleaning power and break down to fatty acids. Bar soaps have largely been replaced by synthetic detergents in today's food establishments.

Alkaline Detergents

An alkali is the principal detergent ingredient of most cleaners. Alkalis combine with fats to form soaps, and with proteins to form soluble compounds easily removed by water. Some alkalis are good buffers which enhance detergency. However, in varying degrees, alkalis corrode aluminum, galvanized metal, and tin.

Sodium hydroxide (caustic soda or lye) is the strongest and cheapest of strong alkalis. It has high detergency but is also highly corrosive for nearly all surfaces, including skin. It rinses with difficulty. Wetting agents improve rinsing and wetting while inhibiting corrosion.

Mild alkalis have moderate dissolving power and are much less corrosive than strong alkalis. Some skin contact with mild alkalis is possible. Sodium carbonate competes with sodium hydroxide as the cheapest of the alkalis. Sodium carbonate is safer and less corrosive and therefore is a common ingredient in cleaners.

Alkaline detergents are good general-purpose cleaners that are commonly used to clean equipment, utensils, floors, walls, and ceilings in food establishments.

Acid Detergents

Acid cleaners dissolve mineral deposits, such as calcium and magnesium precipitates, from equipment surfaces. Acid detergents are frequently used to remove food and hard water deposits from the surfaces of equipment and utensils.

The acids may be categorized into two groups: inorganic and organic. The inorganic acids, also called mineral or strong acids, include hydrochloric (HCl), sulfuric (H_2SO_4), nitric (HNO_3) and phosphoric (H_3PO_4). The strong acids are extremely corrosive to metals and are used only in special cases. Cleaners to remove milk films often contain nitric acid, and those to remove hard water films often contain phosphoric acid. The organic acids are the active ingredients of a wide variety of acid cleaners. The organic acids are not as corrosive to metals and are less irritating to the skin.

Degreasers

Degreasers are specialty products that remove grease and greasy/oily soil. Surfactants, their basic ingredients, penetrate and break up grease and oil. Degreasers are designed more for hard surfaces than for fabrics. They may be used for pre-treatment or as the sole cleaning agent, but their use should always be followed by rinsing.

Abrasives

Abrasives, when mixed with a detergent, are useful for jobs that require scrubbing, scouring, or polishing. Such naturally occurring mineral abrasives as pumice, quartz, and sand are ground into small particle size and supply scouring and polishing action to cleansers, hand soaps, and soap pads.

Abrasives should be used with care since they can cause scratches on metal surfaces, including stainless steel. In addition, the particles of the cleaner, along with metal particles scraped from equipment, may also contaminate food.

Detergent Sanitizers

As the name would suggest, detergent sanitizers are compounds that contain both a detergent and a sanitizer. These products effectively clean and sanitize a food contact surface provided a two-step process is used. That is, the detergent sanitizer must be applied to a food contact surface two times. The first time to clean the surface and a second time to sanitize it. Food contact surfaces should be thoroughly rinsed to remove chemical residues that may remain on the surface after the cleaning and sanitizing process.

Water Temperature

Heat-stable detergents work best when the water temperature of the solution is between 130°F (54°C) and 160°F (71°C). The temperature of the wash water needs to be hot enough to effectively remove soil, but it should not be so hot that the soil will be "baked" onto the food contact surface. Increased wash water temperatures help decrease the strength of the bonds that hold soil to the surface being cleaned.

Some detergents are designed specifically for cold water. Check the manufacturer's directions to determine the appropriate temperatures. A good rule of thumb is to apply cold-water detergents at tap-water temperature.

Velocity or Force

In manual cleaning procedures, force is applied by "elbow grease." For mechanical and clean-in-place systems the velocity and force of the cleaning solution helps remove soil and film from food contact surfaces. The importance of velocity and force on cleaning decreases as the effectiveness of the detergent increases. In other words, less "elbow grease" will be required when the detergent is formulated to effectively remove soil from the surfaces of equipment and utensils.

Amount of Time the Detergent or Cleaner Remains in Contact with the Surface

Cleaning efficiency is increased by use of longer contact times. The amount of scrubbing necessary to remove soil can be decreased by "soaking" items in detergents or cleaners before cleaning.

Concentration of the Detergent or Cleaner

Increasing the strength of a detergent increases the reaction rate and magnifies its cleaning power. However, there is an upper limit beyond which higher concentrations neither increase nor decrease efficiency. Always follow the manufacturer's recommendations for detergent concentration. Using too much detergent is a waste of money.

Sanitizing Principles

Heat and chemicals are the two types of sanitizers most commonly used in food establishments. **Sanitizers destroy disease-causing organisms which may be present on equipment and utensils even after cleaning.** Sanitization is not sterilization, because some bacterial spores and a few highly resistant vegetative cells generally survive.

In all instances, a food contact surface must be cleaned and then thoroughly rinsed to remove loosened soil and detergent residues that tend to inhibit the sanitizer's action.

Heat Sanitizing

Heat has several advantages over chemical sanitizing agents because it:

▲ can penetrate small cracks and crevices

▲ is non-corrosive to metal surfaces

▲ is non-selective to microbial groups

▲ leaves no residue

▲ is easily measurable

▲ is usually economical

Heat destroys vegetative bacteria cells by disrupting some of the protein molecules in the cells. Moist heat is much more efficient in killing microorganisms than dry heat. Heat sanitization is used in both manual and mechanical warewashing operations.

Heat sanitizing in manual warewashing operations involves immersing cleaned equipment and utensils for at least 30 seconds in hot water that is maintained at 171°F (77°C) or above. A properly calibrated thermometer must be kept on hand to routinely check the temperature of the sanitizing water. Use dish baskets or racks to lower equipment and utensils into the sanitizing water. This allows employees to cover the items completely with the hot water without being scalded. Use extreme care with this process. Enforce procedures that protect the safety of the employees involved in manual dishwashing operations.

Sanitizing with hot water can also be performed in mechanical warewashing equipment. The *Food Code* requires a temperature of not less that 180°F (82°C) for the hot water sanitizing rinse in mechanical warewashers. However, in single tank, stationary rack, and single-temperature machines, the final rinse temperature must be at least 165°F (74°C). For safety reasons, the temperature of the hot water sanitizing rinse in a mechanical warewashing machine must not be more than 194°F (90°C).

Steam is an excellent agent for treating pieces of food equipment. Steam flow in cabinets should be sufficient to achieve 171°F (77°C) for at least 15 minutes or 200°F (94°C) for at least 5 minutes.

When using heat for sanitization, it is the temperature at the utensil surface that is most important to insure proper destruction of microorganisms. The temperature at the utensil surface can be measured by using irreversible heat-sensitive labels or tapes that are attached directly to equipment and utensils by a self-adhesive. The silver labels will turn black when the required sanitization temperature is reached.

Another popular device for measuring the temperature of hot water sanitizers is the "maximum registering" or "holding" thermometer. This type of thermometer will continue to hold the highest temperature measured until shaken down like a medical thermometer. An example of a maximum registering thermometer is presented in Figure 7.1.

Courtesy Cooper Instrument Corporation

Figure 7.1—Maximum Registering Thermometer

Chemical Sanitizing

Chemically sanitize by either immersing an object in a sanitizing solution or by swabbing, brushing, or pressure spraying a sanitizing solution directly on the surface to be sanitized.

The *effectiveness of a chemical sanitizer weakens* as bacteria and other microorganisms are destroyed. Also, water from the wash and rinse stages of the warewashing process will dilute the sanitizer. Keep a chemical test kit or test strips on hand to permit personnel to routinely check the strength of the sanitizing solution. Replace the sanitizing solution in the sink whenever it is contaminated or if the concentration falls below the minimum recommended by the chemical manufacturer.

There are a wide variety of chemicals whose properties destroy or inhibit the growth of microorganisms. However, many of these chemicals are not suitable for use on food-contact surfaces because they may corrode, stain, or leave a film on the surface. Others may be toxic or too expensive for practical use. Therefore, the chemical sanitizing agents discussed in this section will be limited to those agents commonly used in food establishments.

Chlorine

Chlorine is a chemical component of hypochlorites which are commonly used as chemical disinfectants in food establishments.

Hypochlorites offer many advantages as sanitizers for food establishments. The chief advantages are that they:

▲ control a wide range of microorganisms through germicidal action

▲ deodorize *and* sanitize

▲ are non-toxic to humans when used at recommended concentrations

▲ are colorless and non-staining

▲ are easy to handle

▲ are economical to use

Hypochlorites are available as powders or liquids. Calcium hypochlorite is generally available in powder form and contains 70% available chlorine. Sodium hypochlorite, more commonly called household bleach, comes in a liquid form and contains between 1 and 15% available chlorine. Hypochlorites release hypochlorous acid in solution. It is the hypochlorous acid that provides chlorine's germ-killing power.

The germicidal effectiveness of chlorine-based sanitizers depends, in part, on water temperature and pH of the solution. According to the *Food Code*, a chlorine solution must satisfy the minimum concentration requirements presented in Figure 7.2.

Maximum Concentration	Minimum Temperature	
ppm	pH 10 or less	pH 8 or less
25	120°F (49°C)	120°F (49°C)
50	100°F (38°C)	75°F (24°C)
100	55°F (13°C)	55°F (13°C)

Figure 7.2—Minimum Concentration of Chlorine-Based Sanitizers

The *Food Code* recommends that food contact surfaces be exposed to chlorine-based sanitizers for at least 10 seconds to insure proper destruction of microorganisms. Most state and local food codes require that equipment and utensils be immersed in chlorine sanitizers for at least 60 seconds (Figure 7.3). Consult with the food regulatory personnel in your area to determine the sanitizing requirements for your establishment.

Wash-Rinse-Sanitize

Figure 7.3—Chemical Sanitizing in a Three Compartment Sink

The *effectiveness of hypochlorites is reduced by organic matter (i.e., food soil) even in small amounts.* Therefore, rinse the detergent off of equipment and utensils before immersing them in the sanitizing solution. A chlorine test kit or strips must be available to measure the concentration of the chlorine at least once per hour. Replace the sanitizer whenever the concentration falls below the required strength.

Iodine

Iodine is chemically related to chlorine and has long been used to kill germs. The iodine-containing sanitizers commonly used in food establishments are called **iodophors**. Iodophors are effective against a wide range of bacteria, small viruses, fungi, and the spores of several disease-causing bacteria. Iodophors kill more quickly than either chlorine or the quaternary ammonium compounds.

Iodophors function best in acidic solutions at temperatures between 75° and 120°F (24° and 49°C). It is recommended that iodophors be applied at 12.5 parts per million in immersion sanitizing and 25 parts per million in swab and spray applications. Expose a surface to an iodophor for at least 60 seconds to assure proper sanitizing.

Iodophors are less influenced by organic matter than are hypochlorites and quaternary ammonium compounds. However, they are more expensive to use, and they will discolor and stain some surfaces such as silver, silverplate, and copper. Iodophors are also slippery and harder to handle than hypochlorites.

Quaternary Ammonium Compounds (quats)

Quaternary ammonium compounds (quats) are ammonia salts that are used as chemical sanitizers in food establishments.

Quats are effective sanitizers, but are frequently selective for certain types of bacteria. The *Food Code* recommends using quats at 200 parts per million (ppm) for immersion sanitizing of food contact surfaces. Quats are non-corrosive and non-irritating to skin and have no taste or odor when used in the proper dilution. Other advantages include stability to heat and effectiveness in a wide pH range (although they are most effective in solutions that are slightly alkaline). Quats are less affected by organic matter than is chlorine.

Quats are ineffective in hard water (above 500 ppm hardness). At high concentrations, quats will leave a residue on the surface of an item. This is undesirable for food contact surfaces. It is generally recommended that quats not be used at concentrations above 200 ppm. Follow the manufacturer's directions for proper uses and concentration of quats. Also consult with the regulatory agency in your jurisdiction about the uses of these and other chemical sanitizers.

Factors that Affect the Action of Chemical Sanitizers

The effectiveness of chemical sanitizers is affected by many different factors. Some of the most important are:

▲ **Contact of sanitizer**—in order for a chemical to react with microorganisms, it must achieve intimate contact.

▲ **Selectivity of sanitizer**—certain sanitizers are non-selective in their ability to destroy microorganisms while others exhibit a degree of selectivity. Chlorine is relatively non-selective. However, both iodophors and quaternary compounds have a selectivity which may limit their application.

▲ **Concentration of sanitizer**—in general, increasing the concentration of a chemical sanitizer proportionately increases the rate of microbial destruction. But there are certain limitations. The increased activity only extends to a certain maximum, then levels off so that a further increase in concentration has no advantage. In rare instances, the activity actually decreases with increased concentration. Always follow the EPA-approved manufacturer's label use instructions to assure peak effectiveness of chemical sanitizers.

▲ **Temperature of solution**—all of the common sanitizers increase in activity as the solution temperature increases. This is partly based on the principle that chemical reactions in general are speeded up by raising the temperature. The recommended range of water temperatures for chemical sanitizing solutions is between 75°F (24°C) and 120°F (49°C). Water temperatures above 120°F (49°C) should be avoided because at high temperatures the potency of the sanitizer is lost by its evaporation into the atmosphere.

▲ **pH of solution**—water hardness can effect the pH of water which exerts a significant influence on most sanitizers. Quaternary compounds react differently to changing pH depending on the type of organism being destroyed. Chlorine and iodophors generally decrease in effectiveness with an increase in pH. Most soaps and detergents are alkaline with a pH between 10 and 12. That's why the soap or detergent must be rinsed off before a surface is sanitized.

(Continued)

▲ **Time of exposure**—allow sufficient time for chemical reactions to destroy the microorganism. The amount of exposure time depends on the preceding factors as well as the size of the microbial populations and their susceptibility to the sanitizer.

Mechanical Dishwashing

The mechanical dishwashing machine has been used in food establishments for many years to clean and sanitize multiple-use equipment and utensils. A dishwashing machine is designed to clean and sanitize large quantities of equipment and utensils that will fit into the machine and that have no electrical parts. When properly operated and maintained, machine dishwashing is more reliable than manual dishwashing for removing soil and bacteria from equipment and utensils.

Mechanical Dishwashing Process

The mechanical dishwashing process employs eight separate steps to remove soil and produce bacteriologically safe equipment and utensils. See Figure 7.5. A summary of the mechanical process follows. You must:

1. Pre-scrape and pre-flush soiled equipment and presoak utensils to remove visible soil.

2. Rack equipment and utensils so that wash and rinse waters will spray evenly on all surfaces and the equipment will freely drain.

3. Wash equipment and utensils in a detergent solution that satisfies the temperature requirements prescribed in Figure 7.4.

4. Rinse equipment and utensils in clean water at a temperature consistent with the type of dishwashing machine being used. See Figure 7.4.

5. Rinse equipment and utensils in a fresh hot water sanitizing rinse between 180° and 194°F (82° and 90°C) except for a single tank, stationary rack; single temperature machine where the final rinse may not be less than 165°F (74°C). The recommended final rinse temperature for a low-temperature chemical sanitizing dishwashing machines is 120°F (49°C) or less.

6. Air dry equipment and utensils.

7. Store clean and sanitary items in a clean, dry area where they are protected from contamination.

8. Clean and maintain the machine to keep it in proper working condition.

Type of Machine	Wash Temperature	Rinse Temperature
Single tank, stationary rack, single temperature machine	165°F (74°C)	165°F (74°C)
Single tank, conveyor, dual temperature machine	160°F (71°C)	180°F (82°C)
Single tank, stationary rack, dual temperature machine	150°F (66°C)	180°F (82°C)
Multitank, conveyor, multi-temperature machine	150°F (66°C)	160°-180°F (71°-82°C)
Chemical sanitizing machine	120°F (49°C)	120°F (49°C)

**Figure 7.4—Minimum Wash and Rinse Temperatures
of Mechanical Dishwashing Machines**
(Source: Food Code)

The majority of commercial spray-type dishwashing machines on the market today will work efficiently. The major problems with this type of equipment are operational and require ongoing supervision and surveillance. Selection of a particular machine for a given food establishment requires knowledge of the demands to be placed on the machine. This includes the type of utensils to be washed and the quantity of equipment and utensils to be processed during peak periods.

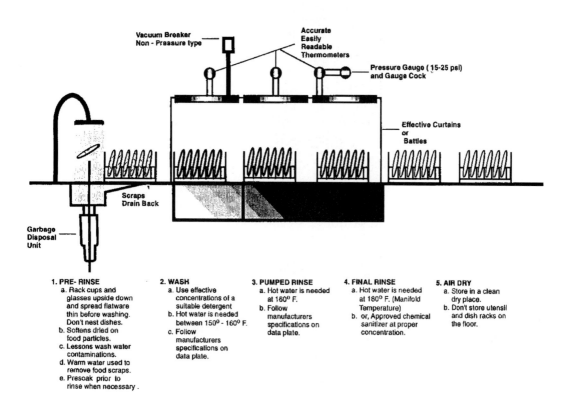

Figure 7.5—Diagram of Machine Dishwashing System

Provide sufficient counter or table space for the accumulation of soiled equipment and utensils and keep them separate from items that are clean and sanitary. Scrape food debris into a garbage disposal or garbage can. Freshly deposited soil is the material that remains on equipment and utensils after a meal or preparation of a meal. This is the easiest type of soil to remove because washing usually occurs while the soil is still moist.

Dried deposits of soil result when used dishes and utensils stand for a long period of time or are exposed to high temperatures. This allows fresh soft soil to dry, harden, and form a crusty deposit that is hard to remove. Dried soil frequently requires pre-soaking to soften and loosen it from the surface.

Once items are pre-flushed and pre-scraped, position them in a rack or on a conveyor so that wash and rinse water and the sanitizer will spray evenly on all surfaces. Glasses and small equipment are racked with their bottom side up. Dishes are racked on their edge and eating utensils are placed in baskets with the mouth piece up. After the utensils are washed, rinsed, and sanitized, invert them into another basket with the handles up and repeat the warewashing process.

The temperature of the wash water (and power rinse if applicable) is extremely important in providing effective sanitizing of equipment and utensils. Minimum wash and rinse water temperatures are provided in Figure 7.4. Equipment and utensils should be exposed to the wash water for at least 40 seconds.

Some machines provide a power rinse which removes soil and detergent residues. The final rinse is designed to sanitize at a temperature of not less than 165°F (74°C) for at least 30 seconds in single tank, stationary rack, single temperature machines. Sanitizing in all other machines requires a final rinse temperature between 180° and 194°F (82° and 90°C) for at least 30 seconds. The flow pressure of the hot water sanitizing rinse must be between 15 and 25 pounds per square inch (psi) to insure the water makes good contact with the surface of the items being sanitized.

Wash and power rinse water temperatures less than those prescribed in the Food Code will not effectively sanitize equipment and utensils even when the final rinse (sanitizing) temperature is properly maintained. This is because effective sanitizing of dishes is the result of the cumulative temperature effects of wash, power rinse, and final rinse waters.

Cleaned and sanitized equipment and utensils *must be air dried* before storage (Figure 7.6). Soiled, multi-use cloth towels can recontaminate cleaned and sanitized equipment and utensils. The *Food Code* prohibits cloth-drying of equipment and utensils, except that air-dried utensils can be "polished" with cloths that are clean and dry.

Manual Dishwashing

Manual warewashing is typically performed in a sink that has at least three compartments (Figure 7.7). **The first compartment is used for washing, the second for rinsing and the third compartment is used for sanitizing.** Each compartment must be large enough to accommodate immersion of the largest equipment

Figure 7.6—Clean Dish Storage

and utensils used in your food establishment. If equipment or utensils are too large for the warewashing sink, they must be cleaned and sanitized using a mechanical dishwashing machine or alternative manual warewashing equipment, such as high pressure.

Figure 7.7—Three Compartment Sink

detergent sprayers, low or line-pressure spray detergent foamers, or other task-specific cleaning equipment

The manual warewashing sink must be equipped with sloped drain boards or dish tables of adequate size to store soiled items prior to washing, and clean items after they have been sanitized. Hot and cold potable water must be supplied to each compartment of the sink, and the sink should be cleaned and sanitized prior to use.

Equipment and utensils should be scraped, flushed, and when necessary, presoaked to remove food residues and other soil. Proper pre-flushing and pre-scraping helps preserve the cleanliness of the wash water in the first compartment of the sink.

Equipment and utensils are washed in the first compartment with warm water and an effective cleaning agent. Washing removes visible food particles and grease. The correct amount of detergent, based on the quantity of water used in the compartment, should always be used. The temperature of the wash solution must be maintained at not less than 110°F (43°C) unless a different temperature is specified by the manufacturer of the cleaning agent.

A nylon brush, cloth, or other approved cleaning device should be used to loosen and remove soil.

Equipment and utensils are rinsed in clean, warm water in the second compartment. Rinsing removes cleaning agents, soap film, remaining food particles, and abrasives that may interfere with the sanitizer agent. For best results, the rinse water must be kept clean and the temperature should be at least 120°F (49°C).

Items are sanitized in the third compartment by submerging them in hot water or a chemical sanitizer solution. **When hot water is used as a sanitizer, the temperature of the water must be maintained at 171°F (77°C) or above at all times.** Items must be immersed in the hot water for at least 30 seconds. Chemical sanitizers are frequently preferred in food establishments because they do not require large amounts of hot water, which saves energy. The *Food Code* recommends that items being chemically sanitized be submerged in the sanitizer solution for at least 10 seconds for a chlorine compound and 30 seconds for other chemical sanitizers. Most state and local food codes require immersion in all chemical sanitizers for at least 60 seconds. You should consult the regulatory authority in your jurisdiction to find out what rules apply in your area. **The recommended range of water temperatures for chemical sanitizing solutions is between**

75°F (24°C) and 120°F (49°C). Water temperatures above 120°F (49°C) must be avoided because at high temperatures the potency of the sanitizer is lost by evaporation into the air. Soil and other deposits can shield bacteria from chemical sanitizing solutions. Therefore, always make certain that all surfaces are properly cleaned before they are sanitized.

As with mechanical warewashing, items that have been manually cleaned and sanitized must be air dried before they are put into storage. Avoid wiping cleaned and sanitized equipment and utensils with cloths or towels because this can recontaminate the sanitized surfaces.

The effectiveness of the manual warewashing process depends to a great degree on the condition of the wash, rinse, and sanitize water. When the cleaning agent disappears in the first compartment, the wash solution should be completely drained and replaced with fresh detergent. When detergent builds up in the second compartment, the fresh water rinse should be drained and replaced with clean, fresh water. When the sanitizer in the third compartment is depleted, it should be drained completely and a new solution made. The concentration of a chemical sanitizer solution must be tested periodically with a chemical test kit or strips to make sure that it remains at the strength required by the regulatory agency in your jurisdiction. Obtain test strips from the manufacturer of your sanitizer. These strips provide a color comparison to indicate the strength of the sanitizer.

Cleaning Fixed Equipment

Some equipment such as soft-serve yogurt machines, mixers, slicers, and grinders cannot be cleaned and sanitized using either mechanical or conventional manual warewashing processes. This equipment should be disassembled to expose food contact surfaces to cleaning and sanitizing agents.

Basic Steps for Cleaning Fixed Equipment

▲ To avoid electrocution and other injury, always disconnect power to the equipment before disassembling it for cleaning

▲ Equipment must be disassembled as necessary to allow access of the detergent solution to all parts

Basic Steps for Cleaning Fixed Equipment (Cont.)

▲ Use a plastic scraper to clean equipment parts and remove food debris that has accumulated under and around the equipment. Scrape all debris into the trash

▲ Carry the parts that have been removed from the equipment to the manual warewashing sink where they will be washed, rinsed, and sanitized

▲ Wash the remaining parts of the equipment using a clean cloth, brush, or scouring pad and warm, soapy water. Clean from top to bottom

▲ Rinse thoroughly with fresh water and a clean cloth

▲ Swab or spray a chemical sanitizing solution, mixed to the manufacturer's recommendations, onto all food-contact surfaces

▲ Allow all parts to drain and air dry

▲ Reassemble the equipment

▲ Resanitize any food-contact surface that might have been contaminated due to handling when the equipment was being reassembled

Large equipment such as preparation tables and band saws can be cleaned by using a foam or spray method. In this process, detergents and degreasers, fresh water rinse, and chemical sanitizer are applied using foam or spray guns. The hoses, feed lines, and nozzles that make up the foam or spray unit should be in good condition and attached properly.

The bucket method is often used to clean equipment that could be damaged by pressure spraying or immersion in the manual warewashing sink. This system employs separate buckets for washing, rinsing, and sanitizing. Three buckets are required when sanitizing with a clean cloth and sanitizer solution. Only two buckets (one for wash and another for rinse) are required if the sanitizer is sprayed on the equipment from a spray bottle.

Figure 7.8—Soft Serve Ice Cream Machine

The clean in place (CIP) method is used for equipment that is designed to be cleaned and/or sanitized by circulating chemical solutions through the equipment. An example of this type of equipment is a soft serve ice cream or yogurt machine (Figure 7.8). When the CIP method is used, the following steps should be followed:

1. Empty food product and waste from the equipment.

2. Disconnect the power to the equipment.

3. Disassemble if parts are removable and cleanable in the manual warewashing sink.

4. Clean and sanitize the removable parts using the three compartment warewashing sink and process.

5. Clean and sanitize the main unit by circulating wash, rinse, and sanitizing solutions through it. Combination detergent sanitizers can also be used on equipment that is designed for CIP cleaning.

6. Reassemble parts that were removed from the main unit.

7. Re-sanitize by circulating a manufacturer approved sanitizing solution through the equipment.

The cleaning frequency for kitchen equipment depends on the location and product processed. In most operations, the equipment should be cleaned at least once every four hours or between different types of products. Always check the manufacturer's instructions for recommended cleaning frequency and procedures.

Cleaning Environmental Areas

Walls, ceilings, floors, and drains are non-food contact surfaces that must be cleaned regularly to minimize contamination, odors, and insect and rodent infestations. Use only chemicals accepted for food contact equipment when cleaning and sanitizing walls, ceilings, and floors of rooms used for food processing. For these surfaces, it is all right to use sanitizers at concentrations higher than those permitted for food-contact surfaces. It is important to prevent dirt and chemicals from falling or splashing onto food-contact equipment or into open containers.

Ceilings

Ceilings should be checked regularly to make certain they are not contaminating food production areas. Ceilings, lights, fans, and covers can be cleaned using either a wet or dry cleaning technique. When wet-cleaning ceilings and fixtures, it is best to use a bucket method to keep water away from lights, fans, and other electrical devices. Whenever possible, disconnect power before cleaning fixtures.

Walls

Some parts of the walls in a food production area, such as those around a sink or food production equipment, should be considered food contact surfaces. These areas should be washed, rinsed, and sanitized whenever the other food contact surfaces in the area are cleaned. Other wall areas are considered non-food contact surfaces and do not need to be cleaned as often.

Walls may be cleaned using either the bucket or spray methods. However, walls should not be spray cleaned if spraying will damage the walls or contaminate exposed equipment and supplies in the area.

Floors

The floor is an important part of production, warewashing, and food storage areas. Floor construction and condition are important factors in maintaining a sanitary operation. Floors in all areas of a food establishment are subject to harsh treatment. Cleaning solutions, hot water, steam, scrubbers, food wastes, and heavy traffic all contribute to floor deterioration.

The cleanliness of floors depends on the ability of an employee to remove soil from the surface of the floor. Floors are usually cleaned using a spray system for washing, rinsing, and sanitizing. If floors will be damaged by spray cleaning, they can be cleaned using the bucket method. All floors should be sloped to drains to help remove soil and the water used to clean floors.

If floor drains are not properly maintained, they can be a source of disease, vermin, and odors. Floor drains under refrigeration cases should be flushed, washed, rinsed, and sanitized.

The steps commonly used to clean these types of floor drains are listed below:

1. Remove the grate or cover over the drain.
2. Clean out waste and other debris from the drain.
3. Use a sprayer or hose to flush the drain and grate or cover.
4. Pour in drain cleaner to break up grease and other waste in the drain.
5. Wash the drain using a brush or water pressure from the sprayer.
6. Rinse the drain with hot water.
7. Pour or spray sanitizer into the drain.

Odor problems from floor drains can be solved by regularly flushing drains with hot water. This should be the last step in the daily cleaning program.

Equipment and Supplies Used for Cleaning

Managers must make certain that employees have the proper equipment and supplies needed to clean food contact and non-food contact surfaces in the food establishment. Some examples of equipment commonly used during cleaning are nylon brushes, cleaning cloths, scouring pads, squeegees, mops, buckets, spray bottles, hoses, and spray or foam guns. Commonly used cleaning supplies include hot water, cleaners, degreasers, and sanitizers. Cleaning equipment and supplies should be stored in areas away from where food and utensils are stored. If possible, cleaning supplies should be stored in a separate room. If space does not permit storage in a separate area, chemicals used for cleaning and pest control must be stored in a locked and labeled cabinet to avoid accidental contamination of food and food contact surfaces.

The Occupational Safety and Health Administration (OSHA) requires that employees have the "Right-to-Know" about the hazardous chemicals to which they may be exposed on the job. Information about hazardous substances in the workplace is provided to employees by way of material safety data sheets (MSDS). Material safety data sheets are developed by chemical manufacturers, and they must be maintained on file in the food establishment (Figure 7.9). Examples of information contained in an MSDS include:

▲ Ingredients

▲ Physical and chemical characteristics

▲ Fire, explosion, reactivity, and health hazard data

▲ How to handle hazardous chemicals safely

▲ How to use personal protective equipment and other devices to reduce risk

▲ Emergency procedures to use if required.

Failure to produce the required MSDS upon demand can result in a substantial fine from OSHA.

Material Safety Data Sheet

HEALTH	2*
FLAMMABILITY	0
REACTIVITY	1
Personal Protection	B

I Chemical Identification

NAME: REGULAR BLEACH   **CAS no.** N/A

DESCRIPTION: CLEAR, LIGHT YELLOW LIQUID WITH CHLORINE ODOR   **RTECS no.** N/A

Other Designations	Manufacturer	Emergency Procedure
EPA Reg. No. 5813-1 Sodium hypochlorite solution Liquid chlorine bleach Liquid Bleach	12 Broadway Broad Oak, CA. 94612	Notify your Supervisor Call your local poison control center or Rocky Mountain Poison Center (303) 573-1014

II Health Hazard Data

*Causes severe but temporary eye injury. May irritate skin. May cause nausea and vomiting if ingested. Exposure to vapor or mist may irritate nose, throat and lungs. The following medical conditions may be aggravated by exposure to high concentrations of vapor or mist: heart conditions or chronic respiratory problems such as asthma, chronic bronchitis or obstructive lung disease. Under normal consumer use conditions the likelihood of any adverse health effects are low. FIRST AID: EYE CONTACT: Immediately flush eyes with plenty of water. If irritation persists, see a doctor. SKIN CONTACT: Remove contaminated clothing. Wash area with water. INGESTION: Drink a glassful of water and call a physician. INHALATION: If breathing problems develop remove to fresh air.

III Hazardous Ingredients

Ingredients	Concentration	Worker Exposure Limit
Sodium hypochlorite CAS# 7681-52-9	5.25%	not established

None of the ingredients in this product are on the IARC, NTP or OSHA carcinogen list. Occasional clinical reports suggest a low potential for sensitization upon exaggerated exposure to sodium hypochlorite if skin damage (eg. irritation) occurs during exposure. Routine clinical tests conducted on intact skin with Liquid Bleach found no sensitization in the test subjects.

IV Special Protection Information

Hygienic Practices: Wear safety glasses. With repeated or prolonged use, wear gloves.

Engineering Controls: Use general ventilation to minimize exposure to vapor or mist.

Work Practices: Avoid eye and skin contact and inhalation of vapor or mist.

V Special Precautions

Keep out of reach of children. Do not get in eyes or on skin. Wash thoroughly with soap and water after handling. Do not mix with other household chemicals such as toilet bowl cleaners, rust removers, vinegar, acid or ammonia containing products. Store in a cool, dry place. Do not reuse empty container; rinse container and put in trash container.

VI Spill or Leak Procedures

Small quantities of less than 5 gallons may be flushed down drain. For larger quantities wipe up with an absorbent material or mop and dispose of in accordance with local, state and federal regulations. Dilute with water to minimize oxidizing effect on spilled surface.

VII Reactivity Data

Stable under normal use and storage conditions. Strong oxidizing agent. Reacts with other household chemicals such as toilet bowl cleaners, rust removers, vinegar, acids or ammonia containing products to produce hazardous gases, such as chlorine and other chlorinated species. Prolonged contact with metal may cause pitting or discoloration.

VIII Fire and Explosion Data

Not flammable or explosive. In a fire, cool containers to prevent rupture and release of sodium chlorate.

IX Physical Data

Boiling point------------------------212°F/100°C (decomposes)
Specific Gravity (H$_2$O=1)------------1.085
Solubility in Water------------------complete
pH------------------------------------11.4

Figure 7.9—Material Safety Data Sheet

Summary

Think about the situation you read about at the beginning of this chapter. Did you come up with a solution? Equipment, such as the meat grinder in the example, must be cleaned and sanitized whenever it becomes contaminated. This should occur at least once a day and more often if necessary to control contamination. Some types of food processing equipment, such as a meat grinder, cannot be cleaned and sanitized in a three compartment sink or a dishwashing machine. Instead, they are designed to be cleaned in place. This type of equipment must be disassembled to provide access to all food contact surfaces. The parts that are removed are cleaned and sanitized in a three compartment sink or a dishwasher. The remaining food contact surfaces are commonly cleaned and sanitized using a three bucket technique for washing, rinsing, and sanitizing. Do not forget to resanitize all food contact surfaces that have been touched when reassembling the equipment.

A good sanitation program starts with a neat, clean, and properly maintained building. A well-maintained facility will help protect food products from contamination, make proper stock rotation easier, prevent entrance of pests, reduce fire hazards, and contribute to the overall safety of the work environment.

The most important step in the development of a food facility's sanitation program is the establishment of sanitation standards and procedures which are designed to correct deficiencies and to assist in emergency situations. Sanitation standards are the facility's policies, and they should reflect the requirements of government regulations.

The effectiveness of a food establishment's sanitation program is directly related to the degree of commitment and concern demonstrated by top management. In both large and small operations top management must instill the proper attitude among employees and convey incentive and motivation by personal participation and interest in the program.

Proper education and training of food establishment employees are vital to assure that sanitation requirements are met. Employees responsible for handling food, equipment, and cleanup of the building and grounds must be trained to accept good sanitation as one of their responsibilities. A clean, well-maintained facility can become a source of pride for employees.

For a sanitation program to be effective, cleaning tasks must be scheduled and individual employees assigned to complete the tasks. Employees must be given instructions that include what they are to clean, how to clean it, and what tools and supplies are required to effectively clean it. Cleaning activities must be carried out by properly trained employees, and they must be closely monitored by supervisors to identify and correct problems when they occur.

A good sanitation program is a preventive program which anticipates and eliminates potential hazards before they become serious problems. The value of an effective program is difficult to measure in terms of dollars. Nonetheless, the value of effective sanitation can be evident in the form of diminished problems and increased goodwill with customers and the local regulatory community.

Case Study 7.1

Ted is night manager of the deli at the Regal Supermarket. One evening Ted noticed that there was a large amount of detergent suds in the third compartment of the manual equipment and utensil washing sink. The deli uses chlorine as a sanitizer. When asked about the soap suds in the sanitizing water, the dishwasher indicated this was a common occurrence when there were many things to wash, especially toward the end of the cleaning and sanitizing process.

1. Should Ted be concerned about what he observed? Why?

2. What should Ted tell the dishwasher to do when there is a large amount of detergent in the sanitizer?

3. What could the dishwasher do to prevent detergent from getting into the sanitizer?

Case Study 7.2

On a Sunday morning the food manager of the Shady Rest long-term care facility noticed that the mechanical dishwasher was not producing water hot enough to properly sanitize equipment and utensils that were being run through the machine. It was not possible to get someone to repair the machine until first thing Monday morning.

1. How should the facility wash and sanitize dishes until the dishwasher is fixed?

2. Are there other alternatives that might be used in the interim?

3. Do you think the food service should be suspended at the facility until the machine is repaired? Why or why not?

Answers to case studies are provided in Appendix A.

Discussion Questions (Short Answer)

1. What is the difference between cleaning and sanitizing?

2. Briefly discuss some of the factors that affect cleaning efficiency.

3. What are the main functions of detergents in the cleaning process?

4. What are the basic steps in the manual dishwashing process?

5. Why must cleaned and sanitized equipment and utensils be air dried?

6. How does water temperature affect chemical sanitizers?

7. What are some of the factors that affect the action of chemical sanitizers?

8. What is the best way to measure the strength of a chemical sanitizer?

9. What steps are commonly used to clean fixed equipment that is too large to be placed in a dishwashing machine or three compartment sink?

10. What purposes do material safety data sheets serve in a food establishment?

Answers to the multiple choice questions are provided in
Appendix A.

Quiz 7.1 (Multiple Choice)

1. What are the proper steps in a manual dishwashing
   operation after pre-flushing?

   a. Wash, rinse, sanitize, and towel dry.

   b. Rinse, wash, sanitize, and air dry.

   c. Wash, rinse, sanitize, and air dry.

   d. Rinse, wash, sanitize, and towel dry.

2. When sanitizing with hot water in a manual dishwashing
   operation, the temperature of the water in the final rinse
   must be maintained at:

   a. 161°F (72°C)

   b. 171°F (77°C)

   c. 181°F (83°C)

   d. 191°F (88°C)

3. Which of the following statements is false?

   a. Dishes should be washed in very hot water (above
       171°F, 77°C) to effectively remove soil from the surface.

   b. Prescraping helps to remove larger food particles from
       dishes, which helps keep the wash water clean.

   c. The cleaning compounds used in a food establishment
       must be tailored to the individual water supply.

   d. Cleaning is a process which removes soil and prevents
       accumulation of food residues on equipment, utensils,
       and surfaces.

4. The recommended range of water temperatures for
   chemical sanitizing solutions is between _____
   and _____.

   a. 75° and 95°F (24° and 35°C)

   b. 75° and 120°F (24° and 49°C)

   c. 95° and 140°F (35° and 60°C)

   d. 120° and 171°F (48° and 77°C)

5. The strength of the chemical sanitizer in the third compartment of the three compartment sink must be checked frequently because

    a. If the chemical is too strong, it may ruin fragile dishware.

    b. The chemical strength increases over time which may leave a toxic residue on the surface of equipment and utensils.

    c. The strength of chemical sanitizers may drop off as germs are killed off.

    d. The strength of the chemical increases as germs are killed off.

6. The first step in developing a cleaning program for environmental areas is to

    a. determine the cleaning needs.

    b. assign cleaning jobs to employees.

    c. obtain the equipment and supplies needed to implement the cleaning.

    d. conduct a training program to teach employees how to clean properly.

7. Which of the following information is not provided by a material safety data sheet?

    a. Information about the physical and chemical characteristics of hazardous substances used in the facility.

    b. Information about how to use personal protective equipment and other devices to reduce a worker's risk of injury.

    c. Information about emergency procedures to use when exposed to a hazardous chemical.

    d. Information about approved hazardous waste sites that will accept unused portions of the hazardous materials.

8. Which of the following statements is false?

    a. Keeping things clean is the responsibility of every person working in the food industry.

    b. Cleanliness goes beyond the removal of visible soil.

    c. A good sanitation program, if properly organized, will function successfully without the support of top management.

    d. A good sanitation program starts with a neat, clean, and properly maintained building.

References/Suggested Readings

Cichy, R.F. (1994). *Quality Sanitation Management*. East Lansing, MI: Educational Institute of the American Hotel and Motel Association.

Educational Foundation of the National Restaurant Association (1992). *Applied Foodservice Sanitation*. NY: Wiley.

Gravini, R. B. and D.C. Rishoi (1993). *Food Store Sanitation*. NY: Chain Store Publishing Company.

8 ENVIRONMENTAL SANITATION AND MAINTENANCE

Cockroaches Deserve Bad Rap

Scientists from North Carolina State University have demonstrated how easily cockroaches can spread Salmonella among themselves and to foods. The research, reported in the February, 1994 issue of Journal of Food Protection, confirms that cockroaches are capable of acquiring and infecting other cockroaches and objects.

Cockroaches are attracted by the warmth, darkness, food, and moisture. Given the number of ways cockroaches can become contaminated -- by feeding on infected food or feces, contacting an infected cockroach directly or indirectly, or by drinking an infected water source -- the risk they pose should be taken seriously. The fact that cockroaches can acquire and infect each other and other objects with Salmonella bacteria is an important point for the food industry to remember.

Learning Objectives

After reading this chapter, you should be able to:

▲ Describe how the premises of a food establishment can affect customers' opinions about the cleanliness and sanitation of the operation

▲ Identify the criteria that should be used when selecting materials for floors, walls, and ceilings in kitchen, warewashing, and serving areas of a food establishment

▲ Identify the equipment and supplies that must be provided in a properly equipped restroom facility

▲ Identify the main components of a properly equipped handwashing station and explain how conveniently located handwashing facilities contribute to good personal hygiene

▲ Identify the types of plumbing hazards that can have a negative effect on public health and the devices that are commonly employed to prevent these hazards

▲ Explain how proper disposal and storage of garbage and refuse help prevent contamination and pest problems in a food establishment

Essential Terms

Air gap	Garbage
Backflow	Integrated Pest Management (IPM)
Coving	Refuse
Cross connection	Vacuum breaker

Condition of Premises

The premises of a food establishment are made up of the physical facility, its contents, and the surrounding land or property. The exterior of a food establishment includes building structure, parking, landscaping, doors and windows. The objective of the exterior design is to attract customers. To accomplish this function, the exterior must make a good impression on the customer.

The exterior of the facility must be free of litter and debris that could attract pests and detract from the aesthetics of the facility. Grass and weeds should be regularly mowed to eliminate harborage areas for insects, rodents, and other pests. Walking and driving surfaces should be constructed of concrete, asphalt, gravel, or similar materials to facilitate maintenance and control dust. These surfaces should also be properly graded to prevent rainwater from pooling and standing on parking lots and sidewalks.

Condition of Building

The entrance area to a facility creates a lasting impression. The adequacy, cleanliness, and attractiveness of a building influences the quality of a consumer's overall dining or shopping experience. The entrance should be easy to find and have an inviting appearance. Locate entrance doors for easy access from streets or parking areas.

Use self-closing to discourage the entrance of flying insects. Clearly mark the doors for *entrance* and *exit* to prevent accidents between those entering and leaving the facility.

Floors, Walls, and Ceilings

Proper construction, repair, and cleaning of floors, walls, and ceilings are important elements of an effective sanitation program. Consider the specific needs of food areas when making a selection of floors and walls, including:

▲ sanitation

▲ safety

▲ durability

▲ comfort

▲ cost

Smooth and easy-to-clean surfaces are needed in food preparation areas, store rooms (including dry storage areas and walk-in refrigerators) and warewashing areas.

For floor coverings, walls, wall coverings, and ceilings, use non-absorbent materials that are free from cracks or crevices where soil may lodge, and from imperfections that might cause accidents. Choose surfaces that are resistant to damage and deterioration from water, cleaning agents, and repeated scrubbing used to keep them in good condition.

Floors

The preferred floor materials in food preparation and warewashing areas include:

▲ terrazzo

▲ quarry tile

▲ asphalt tile

▲ ceramic tile

Concrete may also be used if it has been properly sealed with an epoxy or similar material to make it durable and non-absorbent.

The *Food Code* prohibits the use of carpeting in:

▲ food preparation areas

▲ walk-in refrigerators

▲ warewashing areas

▲ toilet room areas where handwashing lavatories, toilets, and urinals are located

▲ refuse storage rooms or other areas subject to moisture

In food production and warewashing areas avoid the use of:

▲ wood

▲ vinyl

▲ carpeting

These materials are not easy to clean and they tend to absorb water, soil, and other forms of contamination.

Floors graded to drains are needed in food establishments where water-flush methods are use for cleaning. In addition, the floor and wall must be coved and sealed. **Coving** is a curved sealed edge between the floor and wall that eliminates sharp corners or gaps that would make cleaning difficult and ineffective (Figure 8.1). In food establishments where cleaning methods other than water flushing are used for cleaning floors, the floor and wall juncture must be coved with a gap of no more than 1/32 inch (1mm) between the floor and wall.

Figure 8.1—Coving

Slips and falls are the most common types of accidents in food establishments. In many instances, slippery floors cause accidents which result in personal injury and broken equipment. Use mats and other forms of anti-slip floor coverings where necessary to protect the safety of workers (Figure 8.2). These devices should also be impervious, non-absorbent, and easy-to-clean. The *Food Code* prohibits the use of sawdust, diatomaceous earth, or similar materials on floors except where they are applied in small amounts to collect liquid spills or drippage immediately before spot cleaning.

Figure 8.2—Anti-Slip Mat

Walls and Ceilings

Smooth, nonabsorbent, and easy-to-clean walls and ceiling must be provided in food preparation and warewashing areas, walk-in refrigerators, and toilet facilities. Light colors enhance the artificial lighting in these areas and make soil easy to see for better cleaning. In areas that are cleaned frequently, use walls and wall coverings that are constructed of materials such as ceramic tile, stainless steel, or fiberglass. Concrete, porous blocks, or bricks should only be used in dry storage areas unless they are finished and sealed to provide a smooth, nonabsorbent, and easily cleanable surface.

Ceilings should be constructed of nonporous, easily cleanable materials. Studs, rafters, joists, or pipes must not be exposed in walk-in refrigeration units, food preparation and warewashing areas, and toilet rooms. Light fixtures, ventilation system components, wall mounted fans, decorative items, and other attachments to walls and ceilings must be easy-to-clean and maintained in good repair.

Restroom Sanitation

Toilet facilities are required for all employees. Employee restrooms must be conveniently located and accessible to employees during all hours of operation. Toilet facilities near work areas promote good personal hygiene, reduce lost productivity, and permit closer supervision of employees. A toilet room on the premises must be completely enclosed and provided with a tight-fitting and self-closing door.

Materials used in the construction of toilet rooms and toilet fixtures must be durable and easily cleanable. The floors, walls and fixtures in toilet areas must be clean and well maintained. Supply toilet tissue at each toilet. Provide easy-to-clean containers for waste materials, and have at least one covered container in toilet rooms used by women.

Poor sanitation in toilet areas can spread disease. Dirty toilet facilities can also have a negative effect on the attitudes and work habits of the establishment's employees. Include these areas in the routine cleaning program to assure they are kept clean and in good repair. Never store food in restroom areas.

Handwashing Facilities

In earlier chapters of this book, you learned about the importance of food handlers' hands as sources of contamination and cross contamination. Food handlers must know when and how to wash their hands in order to do their jobs safely. Conveniently located and properly equipped handwashing facilities are key factors in getting employees to wash their hands. Locate handwashing stations (Figure 8.3) in food preparation, food dispensing and warewashing areas. Handwashing stations must also be located in or adjacent to restrooms. The number of handwashing stations required and their installation are usually set by local health or plumbing codes.

Figure 8.3—Handwashing Station

A handwashing station must be equipped with hot and cold running water under pressure, a supply of soap, and a means to dry hands. Water at a temperature of at least 110°F (43°C) through a mixing valve or combination faucet is required. If a self-closing, slow-closing or metering faucet is used, it must provide a flow of water for at least 15 seconds without the need to be reactivated.

Equip each handwashing station with a dispenser containing liquid or powdered soap. **The use of bar soap is not permitted**. Individual disposable towels and mechanical hot-air dryers are the preferred hand-drying devices.

Most local health departments do not recommend retractable cloth towel dispenser systems because there are too many possibilities for contamination. Common cloth towels, used multiple times by employees to dry their hands, are also prohibited.

Keep handwashing stations clean and well maintained and **never use them for purposes other than handwashing**. It is equally important to remember that sinks used for **preparing produce and warewashing must not be used for handwashing**.

Plumbing Hazards in Food Establishments

The *Food Code* includes many different components within the definition of a plumbing system. In particular, it identifies the

▲ water supply and distribution pipes

▲ plumbing fixtures and traps

▲ soil, waste and vent pipes

▲ sanitary and storm sewers

▲ building drains, including their respective connections and devices within the building and at the site

A properly designed and installed plumbing system is extremely important to food sanitation. Contamination of the public water supply in a food establishment is a real public health problem. Numerous outbreaks of gastroenteritis, dysentery, typhoid fever and chemical poisonings have been traced to cross connections and other types of plumbing hazards in food establishments.

Cross Connections

A **cross connection** is any physical link through which contaminants from drains, sewers, or waste pipes can enter a potable (safe to drink) water supply. A cross connection may be either direct or indirect.

A *direct cross connection* occurs when a potable water system is directly connected to a drain, sewer, non-potable water supply, and other sources of contamination. An *indirect cross connection* is where the source of contamination (sewage, chemicals, etc.) may be blown across, sucked into, or diverted into a safe water supply.

One of the most common cross connections in the food industry is a garden hose attached to a service sink with the end of the hose submerged in soapy water that is used to clean floors.

Backflow

Backflow is the backward flow of contaminated water into a potable water supply. It is caused by back pressure. It occurs under two conditions:

▲ backpressure where contamination is forced into a potable water system through a connection that has a higher pressure than the water system

▲ backsiphonage when there is reduced pressure or a vacuum formed in the water system (Figure 8.4). This might be caused by a water main break, the shut-down of a portion of the system for repairs, or heavy water use during a fire

©Wise 1997

In the event of water pressure drop... backsiphonage occurs.

Figure 8.4—Backsiphonage

Methods and Devices to Prevent Backflow

The plumbing system in your food establishment must be designed, constructed, and installed according to the plumbing code in your jurisdiction. A properly designed and installed plumbing system will keep food, equipment, and utensils from becoming contaminated with disease-causing agents found in sewage and other pollutants. Cross connections and backflow can be prevented by using the following devices:

▲ air gap

▲ atmospheric vacuum breakers

▲ pressure type vacuum breakers

▲ double check valves

▲ reduced pressure principle backflow preventers

Air Gap

An **air gap** is the physical separation of the potable and non-potable system by a vertical air space (Figure 8.5). The vertical distance between the supply pipe and the flood rim must be at least two times the diameter of the supply pipe (2D), but never less than 1-inch (25mm). An air gap is the most dependable backflow prevention device.

Figure 8.5—Air Gap

Atmospheric Type Vacuum Breaker

The most commonly used *atmospheric type anti-siphon* **vacuum breakers** incorporate an atmospheric vent in combination with a check valve. Their operation depends on a supply of potable water to seal off the atmospheric vent, admitting the water to downstream equipment.

If a negative pressure develops in the supply line, the loss of pressure permits the check valve to drop, sealing the opening. At the same time, the vent opens admitting air to the system to break the vacuum. Atmospheric vacuum breakers can be used on most inlet type water connections which are not subject to back-pressure. This includes low inlet feeds to receptacles containing toxic and non-toxic substances.

Pressure Type Vacuum Breakers

Pressure type vacuum breakers are designed for use under continuous supply pressure, but are not good under backpressure. The device is usually spring loaded and designed to operate after extended periods of hydrostatic pressure. These devices should only be used where non-pressure vacuum breakers cannot be used.

Double Check Valve

A *double check valve* assembly may be used as protection of all direct connections through which foreign materials might enter the potable water system.

Reduced Pressure Principle Backflow Preventers

Reduced pressure zone devices may be used on all direct connections which may be subject to back-pressure or back-siphonage. Use this device when there is the possibility of contamination by material that is a potential health hazard.

These devices are commonly installed as main line protection to protect the municipal water supply. They should also be used on branch line applications where non-potable fluid would constitute a health hazard if introduced into the potable water supply system.

Garbage And Refuse Sanitation

Proper disposal and storage of garbage and refuse protect food and equipment from contamination. Good management of waste decreases attraction of insects, rodents and other pests to the food establishment. Typically, this involves proper handling and short-term storage of the materials inside the operation. Outdoor storage bins hold refuse and garbage for slightly longer periods until pickup. **Refuse** is solid waste which is not disposed of through the sewage disposal system. **Garbage** is the term applied to food waste that cannot be recycled.

An inside storage room, and all containers must be large enough to hold any refuse, recyclables, and returnables that accumulate in the food establishment.

Provide a trash container in each area of the food establishment or premises where refuse is generated or commonly discarded, or where recyclables or returnables are placed. Do not put containers in locations where they might create a public health nuisance or interfere with the cleaning of nearby areas. Use durable, cleanable, insect and rodent-resistant, leak-proof, and non-absorbent equipment and receptacles to store refuse, garbage, recyclables, and returnables. Use plastic bags and wet strength paper bags to line receptacles for storage inside the food establishment or within closed outside receptacles. You must keep equipment and receptacles covered if they contain garbage and are not in continuous use or after they are filled.

Equipment and containers used for holding refuse, recyclables, and returnables must be cleaned regularly. Remember, dirty equipment and containers attract insects and rodents. When cleaning this equipment, be careful not to contaminate food, equipment, utensils, linens, or single-service and single-use articles.

Provide suitable cleaning equipment and supplies such as high pressure pumps, hot water, steam and detergent to thoroughly clean equipment and receptacles. Waste water produced while cleaning the equipment and receptacles is considered to be sewage. It must be disposed of through an approved sanitary sewage system or other system that is constructed, maintained and operated according to law.

Each food establishment should also have an outside storage area and enclosure (Figure 8.6) to hold refuse, recyclables, and returnables that accumulate. An outdoor storage surface should be durable, cleanable, and maintained in good repair. Keep equipment and receptacles covered with tight-fitting lids, doors or covers to discourage insects and rodents.

Refuse and garbage should be removed from the premises at least twice per week during warm months to prevent objectionable odors and other conditions that attract or harbor insects and rodents. Refuse removal may be required less frequently during winter months when the air temperature is colder.

Outdoor storage areas must be kept clean and free of litter. Suitable cleaning equipment and supplies must be available to clean the equipment and receptacles. Refuse storage equipment and receptacles must have drains, and drain plugs must be in place.

Figure 8.6—Outside Garbage and Refuse Station

Compactors and other equipment for refuse and recyclables, must be installed to minimize the accumulation of debris. Make sure that you clean under and around the unit to prevent insect and rodent harborage.

Cardboard or other packaging material (that does not contain food residues) may be stored outside for regularly scheduled pickup for recycling or disposal. If materials are stored so they do not create a rodent-harborage problem, a covered receptacle is not required.

Some food establishments may provide redeeming machines for recyclables or returnables. According to the *Food Code*, a redeeming machine may be located in the packaged food storage area or consumer area of a food establishment if food, equipment, utensils and linens, and single-service and single-use articles are not subject to contamination from the machines and a public health nuisance is not created.

Pest Control

All food establishments must have a pest control program. Insects and rodents which spread disease and damage food are the target. These include rats, house mice, house flies, cockroaches, small moths, and beetles. Insects and rodents carry disease-causing bacteria in and on their bodies.

The benefits of proper cleaning and sanitizing of equipment and utensils, time and temperature controls, and food handling, can all be wasted if insects and rodents are allowed to contaminate foods and food contact surfaces. Any food establishment may have an occasional insect or rodent problem. However, their continual presence causes major problems and indicates a lack of good sanitation and control measures.

The key element of a successful pest control program is prevention. However, no single measure will effectively prevent or control insects and rodents in food establishments. It takes a combination of three separate activities to keep pests in check. You must:

▲ prevent entry of insects and rodents into the establishment

▲ eliminate food, water, and places where insects and rodents can hide

▲ implement an integrated pest management program to control insect and rodent pests that enter the establishment

Insects

What insects lack in size, they more than make up for in numbers. Insects may spread diseases, contaminate food, destroy property, or be nuisances in food establishments. Insects need water, food, and a breeding place in order to survive. The best method of insect control is good sanitation supported by integrated pest management when needed.

Flies

House flies, blow-flies, and fruit flies are the types of flies most commonly found in food establishments.

The house fly is the one most likely to spread disease. When a fly walks over filth, such as human and animal feces or garbage, some of the material, including bacteria, sticks to its body and leg hairs. When a fly feeds on waste material, it takes some bacteria into its body. When the fly goes into an area where food is prepared or eaten, it walks on food and food contact surfaces thereby contaminating them (Figure 8.7). The house fly cannot chew solid food. Instead, the fly vomits on solid food to soften it before eating it. In vomiting, some of the bacteria are spread on food and cause the food to become contaminated.

Figure 8.7—Flies spread bacteria

Blow-flies are usually larger than house flies and are a shiny blue, green, or bronze color. Blow-flies have a keen sense of smell and are attracted by the odors produced by food establishments and food-processing plants.

Fruit flies are the smallest of the three flies and are attracted by decaying fruit.

Fly Control

Eliminate the insect's food supply as a first step to fly control. Store food properly to protect it from flies. In many cases the main source of flies is improperly stored garbage. Store garbage and other wastes in fly tight containers that are cleaned regularly.

Good sanitation includes proper cleaning of kitchen, dining, and toilet facilities and should be a routine practice.

Equip windows, entrances and loading and unloading areas with tight fitting screens or air curtains (Figure 8.8) to prevent the entry of flying insects. Air curtains and electrocution devices may be used at receiving doors to prevent flying insects from entering the establishment.

Figure 8.8—Air Curtain

Chemical insecticides should be applied by a professional pest control operator. Remember, insecticides are a supplement to, never a substitute for, a clean food establishment.

Cockroaches

The four most common cockroaches in the United States are the American, Oriental, German, and Brown Banded. The German cockroach is the one most frequently found in food establishments (Figure 8.9).

Similar to flies, cockroaches are capable of carrying disease organisms on their body. They crawl from toilets and sewers into kitchens, running over utensils, food preparation areas, and unprotected food. They carry bacteria on their hairy legs and body as well as in their intestinal tract.

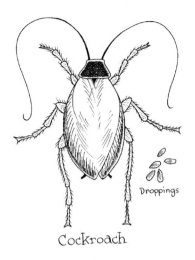

Droppings

Cockroach

Figure 8.9—Cockroach

Roaches avoid light and commonly hide in cracks and crevices under and behind equipment and facilities. It is possible to have a cockroach infestation and not realize it until they are caught by surprise some night when a light is turned on suddenly in a room.

Cockroach Control

To control cockroaches, maintain good housekeeping indoors and outside. Eliminate hiding places by picking up unwanted materials, such as boxes and rags. Also fill cracks and crevices in floors and walls and around equipment. Doors and windows should be tight fitting. Doors and windows, if kept open for ventilation or other purposes, must be protected by screening, air curtains, or other effective means.

Check incoming food and supplies for signs of infestation. Store food in containers that are insect proof and have tight-fitting lids. Keep floors, tables, walls and equipment clean and free of food wastes. Frequent cleaning will help remove egg cases and reduce the roach population.

Chemical control is only recommended in combination with the other control procedures and not as the primary method. Insecticides are made to kill. It is recommended that insecticides be applied by a reputable, professional pest control operator. These individuals know how to handle insecticides safely to avoid contamination of food and food contact surfaces.

Cockroaches are best controlled by insecticides that remain active for several days and are sprayed into cracks and crevices. Make certain the pest control operator remembers to treat baseboards, windows, door trim, and under and around appliances. Commercially available baits can be used in "blind" areas, such as false ceilings. Re-treatment in a few days may be necessary to kill any young roaches that may have recently hatched.

Moths and Beetles

Moths and beetles cause concern since they invade certain foods and can do extensive damage. The saw-toothed grain beetle, confused flour weevil, and rice weevil are examples of stored product beetles that can be found in food establishments. These insects feed on a variety of products including corn, rice, wheat, flour, beans, sugar, meal, and cereals. Small moths and beetles create problems of wasted food and nuisance rather than disease.

Control of Moths and Beetles in Stored Foods

Control of moths and beetles begins with proper stock rotation. Use the FIFO (first in first out) system of stock rotation. All opened packages or sacks should be either used immediately or stored in covered containers. Clean shelves and floors frequently. These pests thrive on flour, meal, and cereal products that are spilled on the floor or shelving.

Examine incoming shipments for signs of infestation, and keep infested products away from other stock until they are ready for disposal. Keep dry food storage areas cool. Cool temperatures limit growth of these insects and reduce egg laying. Insecticides may have to be use to prevent re-infestation of stored food. Pest control operators must treat only along baseboards, cracks, crevices, and under pallets to avoid contaminating food.

Rodents

Rodents adapt easily to human environments and tolerate a wide range of conditions. They may carry a number of diseases including salmonellosis, plague, and murine typhus. Rodents also consume and damage large quantities of foods each year (Figure 8.10).

The term "domestic" rodents includes *Norway rats, roof rats,* and *house mice.* The Norway rat is the most commonly found rat in the United States. Common names for the Norway rat are the brown rat, sewer rat, and wharf rat.

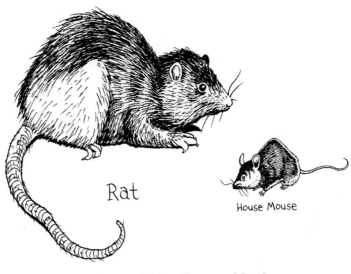

Rat

House Mouse

Figure 8.10—Types of Rodents

The *Norway rat* is primarily a burrowing rat. It hides in burrows in the ground and around buildings and in sewers. Norway rats will eat almost any food but prefer garbage, meat, fish, and cereal. They stay close to food and water, and their range of travel is usually no more than 100 to 150 feet.

The *roof rat* is smaller than the Norway rat but is a very agile climber. It generally harbors in the upper floors of buildings but is sometimes found in sewers. Roof rats prefer vegetables, fruits, cereal and grain for food. The range of travel for the roof rat is also about 100 to 150 feet.

The *house mouse* is the smallest of the domestic rodents. It is found primarily in and around buildings, nesting in walls, cabinets, and stored goods. The house mouse is a nibbler, and it prefers cereal and grain. Its range of travel is 10 to 30 feet.

Signs of Rodent Infestation

It is unusual to see rats or mice during the daytime, since they are nocturnal. It is necessary to look for signs of their activities. From rodent signs you can determine the type of rodent, whether it is a new or old problem and whether there is a light or heavy infestation.

Droppings

The presence of rat or mouse feces (Figure 8.11) is one of the best indications of an infestation. Fresh droppings are usually moist, soft and shiny, while old droppings become dry and hard. Norway-rat droppings are the largest and have rounded ends. They look a lot like black jelly beans. Roof-rat droppings are smaller and more regular in form. The house mouse's droppings are very small and pointed at each end.

Norway Rat Droppings   Roof Rat Droppings   House Mouse Droppings

Figure 8.11—Rodent Droppings

Runways and Burrows

Rats stay in a limited area. They are very cautious and repeatedly use the same paths and trails. Outdoors in grass and weeds, you can see paths worn down that are 2 to 3 inches wide.

The Norway rat prefers to burrow for nesting and harborage. Burrows are found in earth banks, along walls, and under rubbish. Rat holes are about three inches in diameter while mouse holes are only about one inch in diameter. If a burrow is active, it will be free of cobwebs and dust. The presence of fresh food or freshly dug earth at the entrance of the burrow also indicates an active burrow.

Rubmarks

Rats prefer to stay close to walls where their highly sensitive whiskers can keep in contact with the wall. By using the same runs, their bodies rub against the wall or baseboard. The oil and filth from the rat's body are deposited and create a black mark called a rubmark. Mice do not leave rubmarks that are detectable, except when the infestation is heavy.

Gnawings

The incisor teeth of rats grow 4 to 6 inches a year. As a result, rats have to do some gnawing each day to keep their teeth short enough to use. Gnawings in wood are fresh if they are light colored and show well-defined teeth marks.

Tracks

Tracks may be observed anywhere along rat or mouse runs both indoors and outdoors. Dust in little-used rooms and in mud around puddles are good places to look for tracks. Rat tracks may be 1-1/2" long.

Miscellaneous Signs

Rodent urine stains can be seen with an ultraviolet light. Rats leave a different pattern than mice. Rat and mouse hairs may be found along walls, etc. When examined under a microscope they can be distinguished from other animal hairs.

Rodent Control

Effective rodent control begins with a building and grounds that will not provide a source of food, shelter, and breeding areas. The grounds around the food establishment should be free of litter, waste, refuse, uncut weeds, and grass. Unused equipment, boxes, crates, pallets and other materials should be neatly stored to eliminate places where pests might hide.

Get rid of all unwanted materials that may provide food and shelter for rodents. This means storing trash and garbage in approved-type containers with tight-fitting lids. Plastic liners help to keep cans clean, but they will not exclude rats and mice. Garbage must be removed frequently from the food establishment to cut off the food supply.

Rats can enter a building through holes as small as 1/2 inch. Mice can enter through even smaller holes. Buildings and foundations should be constructed to prevent rodent entry, and all entrances and loading and unloading areas should be equipped with self-closing doors and door flashings that will serve as suitable rodent barriers. Metal screens with holes no larger than 1/4 inch should be installed over all floor drains.

Traps are useful around food establishments where rodenticides are not permitted or are hazardous. Live traps can be used for collecting live rats. Check traps at least once every 24 hours. Killer or snap traps can also be used as part of a rodent-control program.

When using these types of traps, place them at right angles to the wall along rodent runways. Glueboards can be used to catch mice. These boards have a very sticky surface, and the mouse's feet stick to the board when they walk on it.

Rodenticides are dangerous chemicals that can contaminate food and food contact surfaces if not handled properly. These substances should be applied by a professional pest control operator. Always make certain that pesticides are stored in properly labeled containers away from food, in a secure place. Dispose of containers safely and know emergency measures for treating accidental poisoning.

Integrated Pest Management (IPM)

Modern pest control operators use integrated pest management to control pests in food establishments. **Integrated pest management** is a system that uses a combination of sanitation, mechanical, and chemical procedures to control pests. Chemical pesticides are used only as a last resort and only in the amount needed to support the other control measures in the IPM program.

The National Pest Control Association recommends a five-step program for IPM:

▲ inspection

▲ identification

▲ sanitation

▲ application of two or more pest management procedures

▲ evaluation of effectiveness through follow-up inspections

There are many benefits of an integrated pest management program. It is cost effective and more efficient than programs using only chemicals. IPM is also longer lasting and safer to you, your employees, and your customers.

Summary

Think about the situation you read about at the beginning of this chapter. Did you come up with this solution? Pest control is an essential part of a food safety program. The first step to controlling cockroaches and other pests is good sanitation. Cockroach control involves keeping the insects out of the establishment and depriving them of food and shelter. Cockroaches are hardy insects that resist pest control measures. This makes an adequate pest control program all the more critical.

Proper construction, repair and cleaning of floors, walls, and ceilings are important parts of an effective sanitation program. Sanitation, safety, durability, comfort, and cost are the main criteria you will use when selecting materials for floors and walls. Surfaces of floors and walls should be resistant to damage and deterioration from the water, detergents, and repeated scrubbing used to keep them clean. Walls and ceilings should be light colored to show soil, and enhance the artificial lighting used in kitchen areas.

Good personal hygiene, which includes proper handwashing, is an important factor in preventing the spread of foodborne disease organisms. Handwashing stations must be conveniently located to allow food handlers to do the frequent hand cleaning required to do their job safely.

Clean and suitably equipped toilet facilities must be provided for employees. These facilities must be kept clean and in good repair to prevent the spread of disease and promote good personal hygiene.

A properly designed, constructed and installed plumbing system is very important to food sanitation. Numerous outbreaks of gastroenteritis, dysentery, typhoid fever, and chemical poisonings have been traced to cross connections and other types of plumbing hazards in food establishments. Air gaps and mechanical vacuum breakers are used to protect the municipal water supply. Consult a professional plumber or your local plumbing code for details about the plumbing requirements in your jurisdiction.

Proper storage and disposal of garbage and refuse are necessary to prevent contamination of food and equipment and avoid attracting insects, rodents, and other pests to the food establishment. Proper facilities and receptacles must be provided inside and outside the establishment to hold refuse, recyclables, and returnables that may accumulate. Refuse and garbage should be removed from the premises frequently enough to minimize the development of objectionable odors and other conditions that attract or harbor insects, rodents, and other pests.

Case Study 8.1

John Smothers is in charge of remodeling the meat department at Kelly's Supermarket. The meat department provides a variety of meat, poultry, and fish items; and specializes in customized orders. The equipment in the facility is not new but still meets current design and construction standards. However, the floors and walls in the department are old and need to be upgraded.

1. What criteria should John use when considering alternative floor and wall materials for the facility?

2. Why is wood flooring not recommended for this area?

3. What color wall materials are recommended? Why?

4. What features about a meat department should influence the selection of floor and wall materials?

Case Study 8.2

Ryan's Hamburgers is a small restaurant that specializes in hamburgers and tacos. A prep cook at Ryan's was recently diagnosed with Hepatitis A. As a result, several employees and customers were required to be immunized against the disease. An inspection by the local health department revealed that the handwashing lavatory in the food prep area at Ryans was out of service. The only lavatories available to employees on duty were the ones in the restrooms.

1. Does the handwashing situation at Ryan's pose a health risk for customers? How?

2. What action should the local health department take against Ryan's?

3. What action should the owner/operator of Ryan's take to prevent a similar incident in the future?

4. What are some of the likely effects this episode will have on Ryan's restaurant?

Answers to all case studies are provided in Appendix A.

Discussion Questions (Short Answer)

1. What do customer opinion surveys show is one of the top reasons people choose a place to dine or shop for food?

2. How can the premises of a food establishment be used to make a positive impression on customers?

3. Identify four characteristic that floors, walls, and ceilings should have when they are used in kitchens and warewashing areas?

4. List the primary components of a handwashing station?

5. How does the location of handwashing facilities influence sanitation and personal hygiene?

6. How does proper refuse and garbage disposal contribute to the pest control activities of a food establishment?

Answers to all multiple choice questions are provided in Appendix A.

Quiz 8.1 (Multiple Choice)

1. Which of the following statements about toilet facilities is **false**?

   a. Toilet facilities must be available for all employees.

   b. Employee toilet facilities must be conveniently located and accessible to employees during all hours of operation.

   c. Separate toilet facilities should be provided for men and women.

   d. Poor sanitation in toilet facilities will influence customers' opinions about cleanliness but will not promote the spread of disease.

2. The most effective device for protecting the potable water system from contamination by backflow is a (an)

   a. air gap.

   b. double check valve.

   c. hose bib.

   d. vacuum breaker.

3. When an air gap is used, the vertical distance between the supply pipe (faucet) and the flood rim must be

   a. At least two times the diameter of the supply pipe, but never less than 1/2 inch.

   b. At least two times the diameter of the supply pipe, but never less than 1 inch.

   c. At least three times the diameter of the supply pipe, but never less than 2 inches.

   d. At least four times the diameter of the supply pipe, but never less than 3 inches.

4. Which of the following statements about garbage and refuse sanitation is false?

   a. Proper disposal and storage of garbage and refuse are necessary to prevent contamination of food and equipment and avoid attracting insects and rodents.

   b. A trash receptacle must be provided in each area of the establishment where refuse is generated.

   c. The equipment and receptacles used to store refuse, garbage, etc. must be durable, clean, non-absorbent, leakproof, and pest-proof.

   d. Trash may be stored outdoors in plastic bags provided the bags are stored at least 15 inches off the ground.

5. You are surveying your food establishment for unsafe conditions. Which one of the following situations requires corrective action?

   a. A trash receptacle with the lid off while in use.

   b. A handwashing station with a multi-use cloth towel for hand drying.

   c. Light colored ceramic tile being used for the walls of the food-preparation area.

   d. Anti-slip flooring is provided in the warewashing area.

6. Backsiphonage is likely to occur if

   a. the pressure in the potable water system drops below that of a non-potable or contaminated water source.

   b. contamination is forced into a potable water system through a connection that has a higher pressure than the water system.

   c. pressure builds up in a sewer line due to blockage.

   d. the water seal in a kitchen trap is siphoned out.

7. The primary responsibility of food establishment managers in pest control is

    a. assure good sanitation that will eliminate food, water, and harborage areas.

    b. assure that pesticides are applied safely.

    c. assure that the pest control operator they use employs integrated pest management.

    d. assure that the parking area is kept free of litter.

8. The best way to encourage employees to wash their hands when needed is to

    a. provide a separate restroom for employees and customers.

    b. provide properly equipped handwashing stations convenient to work areas.

    c. provide hand sanitizers instead of handwashing lavatories in food-preparation areas.

    d. put up a sign in the employee locker room reminding them of the importance of proper handwashing.

9. Coving is a (an)

    a. curved sealed edge between the floor and wall that eliminates sharp corners to make cleaning easier.

    b. anti-slip floor covering used to protect workers from slips and falls.

    c. plastic material used to seal cracks and crevices under and around equipment in a food establishment.

    d. a device used to prevent backsiphonage.

10. What factor has the greatest influence on where people choose to eat or shop for food?

    a. Cost of the food

    b. Nutrition of food

    c. Quality of service

    d. Cleanliness of food and facilities

Suggested Reading/References

Cichy, R. F. (1994). *Quality Sanitation Management.* East Lansing, MI: Educational Institute of the American Hotel and Motel Association.

Khan, M. A. (1991). *Foodservice Operations And Management.* New York: Van Nostrand Reinhold.

Longrèe, K. and G. Armbruster (1996). *Quantity Food Sanitation.* New York: Wiley.

Knight, J. B. and L.H. Kotschevar (1989). *Quantity Food Production.* New York: Van Nostrand Reinhold.

Kopanic, R. J., B.W. Sheldon, and C.G. Wright (1994). "Cockroaches as Vectors of Salmonella: Laboratory and Field Trials" *Journal of Food Protection*, Vo. 57., No. 2, pp. 125-32, February, 1994.

Pannell, D. V. (1990). *School Foodservice Management.* New York: Van Nostrand Reinhold.

West, B. B., et al. (1986) *Food Service in Institutions.* New York: Macmillan Publishers.

9 ACCIDENT PREVENTION AND CRISIS MANAGEMENT

Accident Prevention

As a new employee was refilling the deep fat fryer, some excess cooking oil spilled onto the floor. Later that morning, the fry cook fell due to the slippery floor. After the fall, the cook was still in severe pain and was unable to return to work. As you read this chapter, consider why this accident happened, how you can help the cook, and how you can prevent future falls.

Learning Objectives

After reading this chapter, you should be able to:

▲ Recognize how human error leads to accidents

▲ Discuss the importance of a safety audit

▲ Recognize the value of safety inservice training

▲ Identify public health rules and regulations that pertain to accidents and crisis management

▲ Develop a first aid plan

▲ Discuss the need for a fire exit plan, fire drill practice, and fire extinguisher use

▲ Identify the types and required locations of fire extinguishers

▲ Post a list of emergency phone numbers by the telephone

▲ Identify the responsibility to comply with Occupational Safety and Health Administration (OSHA) rules

Essential Terms

Cardiopulmonary resuscitation (CPR)

Dead man's switch

Safety in Food Establishments

Food establishments contain many hazards that can cause accidents and injuries. Falls, cuts, scrapes, puncture wounds, and burns occur when food handlers become careless or equipment is not in good repair. The main point to remember is that accidents, like foodborne illness, can be prevented.

Accident prevention programs typically involve three types of activities:

▲ Eliminating hazards in the environment

▲ Providing personal protective equipment for workers

▲ Training workers about hazards and how to prevent or avoid them

Hazards can be eliminated by putting safety devices on equipment, keeping equipment in proper working condition and keeping the environment free of obstacles and potential hazards.

Built-in safety guides keep hands away from moving blades during grinding and slicing operations.

Cuts can be prevented by wearing steel and nylon woven fiber gloves when using slicers and deboning equipment. Hot pads protect hands against burns. Work shoes with closed toes and rubber soles protect the worker's feet from injury.

Workers must be taught how to prevent and avoid hazards that cause injury. They must know such things as:

▲ when and how to use ladders for climbing

▲ how to lift things properly

▲ why safety devices must be left in place on equipment

▲ how to dress for safety

Give employees instructions on specific procedures and safety measures related to the assigned tasks before they start to work. An ounce of prevention is worth far more than a pound of cure.

Each establishment needs a basic first aid kit placed in a readily accessible area but away from all food, equipment, utensils, linens, and single-use articles. Depending on the size of the operation, more than one kit may be needed. The kit should include an instruction manual describing basic first aid treatment and a checklist of contents. Check expiration dates on supplies monthly and replace them as needed. Post a list of important telephone numbers such as fire department, police, emergency medical system, and nearest hospital emergency room beside the telephone in a readily accessible area.

When an accident occurs:

1. Stay calm. Information is needed to determine the seriousness of the injury.

2. Examine the injury and decide whether outside help is needed. If in doubt, call for help.

3. Administer first aid according to the type of injury.

4. Keep unnecessary personnel away from the victim.

5. Record the victim's name, the date and time of accident, type of injury or illness, any treatment given, and amount of time it takes for emergency assistance to arrive.

Common Types of Injuries

Falls

Falls are preventable. Keep floors clean and free from debris and spills. Wet floors, grease, or spilled food are hazards. Use signs to alert others of newly mopped wet floors. Use non-skid mats to cover areas that have high traffic and are frequently wet. If someone falls, ask them to stay still, then determine the extent of injury. Seek medical assistance if there is a question about their ability to move. Improper use of ladders or climbing on chairs, boxes, etc., instead of using a ladder can cause employee falls. Always use the proper equipment according to directions and intended use.

Cuts

Cuts are common injuries in food establishments. Carelessness with knives, slicers, choppers, grinders, mixers, and broken glass cause most problems. Keep knives sharp and store separately from other utensils. Accidents occur frequently when dull tools slip and cause an injury. Never leave knives on counters or submerged in a sink full of soapy water. Always use the proper tool for the task. Do not try to catch a falling knife. Let it fall to the floor. Do not try to clean the circular blade of a slicer while the equipment is still assembled. *Always make sure the equipment is unplugged before taking it apart for cleaning.*

When treating a cut, first find out the extent of the wound. Then apply pressure to the site with a clean cloth or towel and elevate the part. If the cut is minor, wash thoroughly in running water and apply a water-resistant bandage. More severe cuts should be checked by a medical professional.

Always use power equipment according to the manufacturer's directions. Leave guard devices in place—they protect from injury. A dead man's switch is commonly provided on large pieces of equipment, such as mixers, grinders, and cutters. A **dead man's switch** allows equipment to operate only when it is engaged. If the switch is released, the equipment will shut off immediately thereby reducing the risk of injury. Usually the switches are located so that you have to stretch your arms to each side to maintain the pressure. Thus, you cannot accidentally grab for something in or on the machine without releasing contact with the switches and the machine stops. Overriding the switch with duct tape or other such material is illegal. Caution employees against such actions. The switch is there to protect them from serious harm.

Burns

Burns are classified as first degree (redness and pain), second degree (blisters, redness, and pain), or third degree (charring of skin layers, little or no pain). The extent of a burn is important. If a small area is burned, either first or second degree, first aid is usually all that is needed. Third degree burns must be checked by a medical professional. Burn treatment includes the following:

▲ Remove the source of the burn. If the burn is caused by an electrical source, rescuers must first determine if the electricity is off before touching the victim.

▲ Use cool running water or ice to soothe minor burns.

▲ Do not apply ointments, sprays, antiseptics, or home remedies such as butter.

▲ Apply a clean dry dressing. Do not puncture blisters.

▲ Keep the victim calm and quiet.

▲ Seek medical assistance if needed. Burns on the face, hands, or groin area are considered serious and should be checked by a medical professional.

Chemical burns require immediate treatment. Call for medical help and check the material safety data sheet (MSDS) for emergency interventions. Chemical burns are often caused by mishandling dishwashing compounds and cleaning solvents.

Poisoning

Poisoning can occur when food contaminated by chemical substances is eaten. If there is any question that a food is contaminated by chemicals, do not wait, call for medical assistance immediately. Poison Control Centers should be contacted, and you should follow instructions until help arrives.

Body Mechanics Classes

A body mechanics class can be used to teach workers how to lift, reach, and pull correctly in order to prevent back injuries. Back injuries are very expensive when you factor in lost productivity, workmen's compensation, and medical care. Insurance companies and many local health departments may provide pamphlets, videos, and class materials to promote back safety.

Employee Medications

According to the *Food Code,* only those medications necessary for the employee's health are allowed in a food establishment. This does not apply to medicines that are stored or displayed for retail sale. Employee medication shall be clearly labeled and stored in an area away from food, equipment, utensils, linens, and single use items like straws, eating utensils, and napkins. Medications stored in a food refrigerator must be kept in a clearly labeled and covered container located on the lowest shelf of the refrigerator.

Cardiopulmonary Resuscitation (CPR) and First Aid for Choking

Unless it is a requirement in your jurisdiction, you do not have to know how to administer first aid for choking or **Cardiopulmonary Resuscitation (CPR)**. However, posting charts with instructions for these procedures can be helpful in emergencies (Figures 9.1 and 9.2). These charts are available from the American Red Cross and American Heart Association. It is desirable to have at least one person on each shift trained in emergency response procedures and first aid. Remember, knowing how to do the right thing at the right moment can save a life.

Local public health departments, American Red Cross, American Heart Association, National Safety Council, insurance companies, emergency medical systems, fire departments, and hospitals can provide classes, demonstrations, posters, videos, and other materials for use in food establishments. Personnel who volunteer to take safety related courses for use in the establishment are tremendous assets to the establishment.

Incident Reports

When an accident does occur, it is always advisable to fill out an incident report. Insurance companies require this documentation when processing claims. The time of the incident, conditions that contributed to the problem, extent of observed injury, any treatment provided at the establishment or a medical facility, and prescribed aftercare should be recorded. Notify insurance companies as soon as possible after an accident has occurred.

Safety Training Programs

Provide instructions on how to operate machinery and equipment in an easy-to-use format. Place a procedure book with detailed information on care and use of equipment in a central place. Post individual instruction sheets in the work area. Determine if employees can read signs and instructions. If you don't think they can, use picture diagrams to show steps for safe operation. In the case of foreign speaking persons, they may not be able to read English. Some may not be able to read their own language, either. Merely posting instructions in their language does not mean the information has been received.

American Red Cross First Aid:
When an Adult Stops Breathing

1 *Does the Person Respond?*
- Tap or gently shake victim.
- Shout, "Are you OK?"

2 *Shout, "Help!"*
- Call people who can phone for help.

3 *Roll Person Onto Back*
- Roll victim toward you by pulling slowly.

4 *Open Airway*
- Tilt head back and lift chin.

5 *Check for Breathing*
- Look, listen, and feel for breathing for 3 to 5 seconds.

6 *Give 2 Full Breaths*
- Keep head tilted back.
- Pinch nose shut.
- Seal your lips tight around victim's mouth.
- Give 2 full breaths for 1 to 1½ seconds each.

7 *Check for Pulse at Side of Neck*
- Feel for pulse for 5 to 10 seconds.

8 *Phone EMS for Help*
- Send someone to call an ambulance.

9 *Begin Rescue Breathing*
- Keep head tilted back.
- Lift chin.
- Pinch nose shut.
- Give 1 full breath every 5 seconds.
- Look, listen, and feel for breathing between breaths.

10 *Recheck Pulse Every Minute*
- Keep head tilted back.
- Feel for pulse for 5 to 10 seconds.
- If victim has pulse but is not breathing, continue rescue breathing. If no pulse, begin CPR.

Figure 9.1—First Aid for When Victim Stops Breathing
(Source: American Red Cross - used with permission)

American Red Cross First Aid:

When an Adult Is Choking

1 Ask, "Are You Choking?"

2 Shout, "Help!"

Call for help if victim—
- Cannot cough, speak, or breathe.
- Is coughing weakly.
- Is making high-pitched noises.

4 Do Abdominal Thrusts
- Wrap your arms around victim's waist.
- Make a fist.
- Place thumbside of fist on middle of victim's abdomen just above navel and well below lower tip of breastbone.
- Grasp fist with your other hand.
- Press fist into abdomen with a quick upward thrust

3 Phone EMS for Help
- Send someone to call an ambulance.

Repeat abdominal thrusts until object is coughed up, or victim starts to breathe or cough.

If victim becomes unconscious, lower victim to floor.

5 Do a Finger Sweep
- Grasp tongue and lower jaw and lift jaw.
- Slide finger down inside of cheek to base of tongue.
- Sweep object out.

6 Open Airway
- Tilt head back and lift chin.

7 Give 2 Full Breaths
- Keep head tilted back.
- Pinch nose shut.
- Seal your lips tight around victim's mouth.
- Give 2 full breaths for 1 to 1½ seconds each.

8 Give 6 to 10 Abdominal Thrusts

If air won't go in—
- Place heel of one hand against middle of victim's abdomen.
- Place other hand on top of first hand.
- Press into abdomen with quick upward thrusts.

Repeat steps 5, 6, 7, and 8, until airway is cleared, or ambulance arrives.

Figure 9.2—First Aid for Choking
(Source: American Red Cross - used with permission)

Hold demonstrations and discussions of procedures or proper use of equipment at the beginning of the shift or other appointed time when the majority of staff can attend. These mini-inservice sessions are extremely helpful and ensure that all personnel hear the same information. During the meeting, encourage employees to contribute to the discussion or share their views on how to improve operational flow. Managers and supervisors are responsible for teaching employees basic safety practices, and they must monitor work habits to assure compliance. Employees who are careless in their work or use equipment improperly can cause harm to themselves and others.

Self-Inspection Safety Checks

Just as self-inspection programs help identify food safety problems in food establishments, safety audits can help prevent accidents. Conducting a safety audit can be one of the most cost-effective tasks you can perform. Fire and accident prevention can result in considerable cost savings.

Fire Safety

Fires are common problems in food establishments. Grease fires (in the plenum of the hood canopy) are the number one cause of fires in food establishments. Electrical fires are number two. Regular inspections of electrical equipment and prompt repair of faulty wiring or equipment can decrease this problem. Avoid overloading circuits and improper venting or grounding. Teach and monitor employees on the hazards of pulling electrical plugs out of sockets by the wire. They must grasp the plug head and then pull.

Keep hoods, ventilating fans, filters, and adjoining walls clean and clear of greasy buildup. Perform regular maintenance according to the manufacturer's directions.

Fire Extinguishers

Fire extinguishers must be operable, easy to find, and employed according to type of fire (Figure 9.3).

Pressurized water is not recommended for food production areas because it might be used on a grease fire by mistake. Grease floats on water and would be easily spread. Water on electrical fires could cause extensive damage, too. Carbon dioxide (CO_2) is recommended

Type of Fire Extinguisher	Material Burning	Most Common Type of Extinguisher Used
Type A	wood, paper, cloth	Pressurized water or ABC
Type B	grease, gasoline, solvents	CO2 or B or BC
Type C	motors, switches, electrical	CO2 or C

Figure 9.3—Types of Fire Extinguishers

because it leaves no damaging residue on machinery or food contact surfaces. Any exposed food must always be discarded. ABC multipurpose extinguishers do leave a residue. Local fire departments can provide information and demonstrations on the proper type of fire safety equipment and how to use it.

Because personnel can ignite their clothing when working around stoves, a safety blanket should be stored in an area where it can easily be reached, if needed. Use the blanket to smother the flames and then call for help.

If a fire that you cannot extinguish quickly is detected, call for help. Then shut off exhaust fans, turn off equipment, close all doors and windows, and evacuate the area. Every food establishment needs a fire safety plan. Clearly mark routes of evacuation. Hold fire drills at periodic intervals to assure that all employees know how and where to exit if the building is on fire. Battery powered emergency lights are required in most jurisdictions. They automatically provide light when power is interrupted.

Fire safety inspectors check fire extinguishers to certify them as operable. Most types of extinguishers should be checked or serviced every six months and marked with tags that specify the next due date for service. Fines can be levied for out-of-date equipment. If an extinguisher weighs less than forty pounds, it can be mounted five feet from the ground. If it weighs more than forty pounds, it may be stored no more than three and one-half feet off the ground (*Food Code*).

Hood Systems

Hood systems are usually installed over cooking equipment and dishwashers to remove vapors, heat, and smoke. Some hood canopies may have a built-in extinguishing agent. These devices, called ansul systems, can effectively extinguish a fire. Employees need to know how they work. Hood systems should be installed and periodically serviced by fire prevention professionals.

Sprinkler Systems

Sprinkler systems are often required by law in new or remodeled buildings. Supplies must be stored the regulated distance from sprinkler heads. If a sprinkler head is accidentally broken off, contact your sprinkler service immediately.

Crisis Management

A crisis can occur at any time. Besides natural disasters such as fire, flood, storms, or earthquakes, food establishments must deal with interference in normal operations that can literally cripple production. An outbreak of foodborne illness, media or regulatory investigation, unexpected loss of personnel, delivery problems or any other event that impacts the ability to operate, can cause a crisis. How do you handle difficult situations? Develop a plan to handle the crisis with a problem-solving approach.

First, evaluate the extent of the problem. Check the facts and decide what possible outcomes can be expected. Are you going to need outside help? If you are working with a group of employees and supervisors, analyze their talents and use a team approach. One spokesperson is better than having too many individuals giving out information. Maintain control within your organization.

Set priorities according to the resources that exist. Remain calm. Look for positives. Follow established rules and regulations as set up in codes. Identify any outside resources that can help solve the problem. Keep a log of actions and communications in case it should be needed. In all situations, be honest.

Foodborne Illness Incident or Outbreak

If dealing with a suspected foodborne illness problem, cooperate with the customer and seek help from your local food regulatory agency. Work with the local regulatory agency to determine what may have caused the customer's illness. Establish the time the suspected food was eaten and, if a sample of the product is still available, preserve it for laboratory analysis. You may ask the customer to save samples of products eaten recently at home, too. Has medical attention been sought? Listen to everything the consumer says and look for clues that might explain the problem. Do not try to diagnose the problem or belittle the consumer's complaint. Keep a record of the interview. Assure the consumer that you will get back to them after investigating the problem. Make sure that you do contact them again after facts are gathered. Do not admit that your establishment is at fault—you have no proof of that until facts are checked.

Check the Flow of Food

If, after checking the flow of food, you find no evidence to support the consumer's claim you may decide to keep the problem in-house. As long as only one person is affected, an outbreak is not suspected. However, if two or more persons report the same problem, consult outside resources on how to proceed. When preparing food samples for testing, it is wise to keep a sample in your freezer for cross validation of laboratory results. Public health officials, insurance agents, and, if needed, an attorney can help you manage the problem.

Formal Investigations

Remove suspect items from use. Health inspectors may need to conduct an investigation of the premises. Employees may be required to have medical examinations. Closing a facility for a period of time to facilitate cleaning may be needed. Keep in mind that whatever must be done should be accomplished as quickly as possible. Cooperation to protect public health is the end goal. In the final analysis, it does not matter where the error occurred. It must be corrected and prevented from happening again.

Whatever the crisis may be, use a calm, systematic approach and evaluate actions as much as possible. Crisis management is not an easy task. It is always useful to have some kind of protocol to guide you through the event. Put together a team or committee consisting of management and employees to regularly brainstorm worst case scenarios. Plan disaster drills to keep employees informed and trained in crisis management skills. Designate a spokes person who is responsible for talking to the media, should they become involved. Keep a notebook with instructions on how to proceed in emergency situations.

Summary

If the new employee had been taught the importance of cleaning up spills, immediately, the cook might not have fallen. Call for help if needed. The risk of falls could be reduced by putting anti-skid mats around the fryer. The design and material of these mats should be approved by the local health department. Anyone who falls should remain on the floor until someone checks for injury.

Accident prevention programs are good investments. Use community resources to help build an effective plan. Insurance companies and vendors can supply training aids on accident prevention. Fire departments and emergency healthcare providers can provide demonstrations and advice that prepares you for accidents or other problems linked to safety. If you never need the plan, consider yourself lucky. However, be prepared.

Case Study 9.1

It was 1989, a beautiful fall day in San Francisco. The World Series was just getting underway in Candlestick Park; and then, the ground began to shake!

Across the city, a banquet was just getting started at the culinary arts school. As the ground shook and buildings swayed, guests, students, and staff evacuated the building as quickly as possible.

Meanwhile, in the dining room, a large ornate crystal chandelier was loosened from the ceiling and came crashing down, spraying fragments of glass across the area, including the buffet tables that were loaded with food. When the tremors stopped, the managers in charge of the food service were faced with immediate decisions concerning how to proceed after this catastrophic event. Because it was evening, the keys for supplies kept for emergencies were not available.

1. Make a list of the problems faced in this emergency and decide what should be done first, second, and so forth.

2. What community resources are needed to cope with this disaster?

3. How would you manage the food without electricity and a potable water supply?

Answers to all fill in the blank questions are provided in Appendix A.

Quiz 9.1 (Fill in the blanks)

1. Employees should wear _____ _____ when slicing or removing bones meat.

2. Apply _____ to stop the flow of blood from a cut.

3. Employee medications that require refrigeration must be stored in a _____ and _____ container on the lowest shelf of the refrigerator.

4. If a consumer reports a foodborne illness from something eaten at your establishment, you should listen attentively; and if the item is still present, _____ it from use.

5. If an employee has a burned hand and arm that appear charred and they are not complaining of pain, it is a _____ _____ burn and should be seen by a medical professional.

6. The fire inspector checks all _____ _____ for expiration dates and location in the establishment.

7. List at least four sources that supply instructional assistance for health and safety training.

8. When someone falls in the establishment, your first action is to tell them to _____ _____.

9. If someone is choking, use the _____ _____ to help them breathe.

10. Post _____ of _____ _____ in prominent locations to assist in evacuation during a fire.

References/Suggested Readings

Educational Foundation, (1993). *Applied Food Service Sanitation.* Chicago: Wiley. National Restaurant Association.

Food and Drug Administration (1997). 1997 Food Code. Washington: United States Public Health Service.

Rue, N., National Assessment Institute (1994). *Handbook For Safe Foodservice Management.* Englewood Cliffs: Prentice Hall.

10 EDUCATION AND TRAINING

Why Training?

The U-Go market decided to expand their business by opening a delicatessen section to serve fried chicken, potato salad, macaroni salad, and cold cuts of meat. After the equipment arrived, the vendor offered to give employees training on how to safely operate the equipment. At first, the owner refused saying, "Training takes time and time is money." The certified food manager in charge of this area objected, "The products to be sold are all potentially hazardous foods." Why did he say that? What would you do in this situation? In the summary, you can check your decisions against this manager.

In this chapter, you will explore the needs of the adult learner. If training is offered in a way that the learner is devalued, little behavioral change occurs. Putting together an effective training curriculum takes time and effort. The rewards, however, are well worth it.

Objectives

After reading this chapter, you should be able to:

▲ Identify how problems related to poor employee training affect food safety

▲ List tasks that require training

▲ Identify training resources

▲ Discuss principles of adult learning

▲ Analyze a task

▲ Develop a plan of action to train employees

▲ Discuss evaluation of training outcomes

Essential Terms

Adult learning

Competency Based Training (CBT)

Evaluation procedures

Task analysis

Training

Managers and supervisors are responsible for the way their employees perform their jobs. And keep in mind, high employee turnover is an ongoing problem. These facts verify the need for an *active* and *effective* training program with measurable goals and outcomes.

The final report from the FDA Ad Hoc Committee on Training states that "80% of all foodborne illness can be traced to a procedural problem due to actions by employees who either did not know or understand the value of using designated procedures to keep food from becoming contaminated."

Employees need:

▲ **Knowledge** of what is expected and how to perform correctly

▲ **Motivation** to do the right thing at the right time

▲ **A Work Environment** that encourages and rewards correct behaviors

Establishments that use the HACCP process to ensure food safety can use their evaluation lists to pinpoint what food handlers must know about food safety. Remember, most of the problems related to foodborne illness are due to errors related to time and temperature management, personal health and hygiene, and cross contamination.

The HACCP system monitors food during production so that any contaminated food can be made safe or discarded before it is eaten. Food handlers must know how to monitor critical control points (CCPs) and take corrective action when a critical limit is not being met.

A well-trained staff serving safe food can make any manager look good.

Adult Learners

Adults learn differently than young children. Their need to achieve is strong and egos are very fragile. Adults are usually motivated by the need to earn a living. Next is the need for recognition of achievement or making a difference. Their anxiety is high and lack of recognition or failure is hard for them to accept. Attempt to relate, whenever feasible, to the employee's own work environment. This helps to connect a topic to their own work site. **Adult learning** principles, as listed in Figure 10.1, can help you design training that uses the adult's "need to achieve" to the best advantage.

▲ Motivation to learn is critical. Adult learners need to feel that they will benefit from the training.

▲ Adults retain that which is *relevant* to them. If they see where they will apply the information, they have a better chance of retaining information.

▲ People learn in different ways at varying speeds.

▲ People learn best by doing and actively participating in the learning process.

▲ Adults will learn best if a variety of training materials are used. Everyone does not learn the same way. Use video, audiotapes, posters, pictures, pamphlets, demonstrations, or any other method of presenting material that provides different ways to learn.

▲ Reinforce learning that is achieved by praising and use other rewards as indicated. The employee who is praised or rewarded for applying learning to the job creates an incentive to other employees to increase their performance, too.

▲ Treat adult learners with respect. There is no such thing as a "dumb" question. The meaning was not clear and if one person did not understand, there may be others who are too shy to ask. Adults embarrass easily and need positive feedback to overcome feelings of inadequacy.

▲ Short sessions (30-60 minutes) are most effective. Whenever possible, keep sessions from becoming boring or tiresome.

Figure 10.1—Principles of Adult Learning (Source: Rue, N., 1994)

▲ All learners like feedback on ability to perform. Evaluate and inform learners about their progress.

▲ Know the level of understanding of your adult learners and present material in a way that they can easily understand. When employees know what is expected and how to do it, the usual result is satisfactory performance.

Figure 10.1—Principles of Adult Learning (Cont.) **(Rue, N., 1994)**

Competency Based Training (CBT)

The use of competency based training methods helps prepare staff to perform their jobs with maximum efficiency. **Competency Based Training (CBT)** is possible when the task to learn is defined as a *skill* or *direction* necessary to do the job at hand. Each job is made up of several tasks. To determine what the worker needs to learn, decide what skills and behaviors are required to complete the job. This process is called **task analysis**. For example, all employees need to know how to use principles of sanitation in their work. By the time sanitation training is completed, the employee must be able to:

▲ distinguish the difference between cleaning and sanitizing

▲ use cleaning and sanitizing products according to the manufacturer's directions

▲ demonstrate how to disassemble a piece of equipment to expose surfaces for cleaning and sanitizing

▲ demonstrate how to clean and sanitize a surface

▲ demonstrate how to reassemble equipment and re-sanitize a surface that may have been touched during re-assembly

▲ understand the public health significance of the food safety concerns associated with the tasks they perform

After you analyze the job, the list of expected behaviors is your road map for training. Break each job into small teachable tasks. Base the training on exactly what the employee needs to know. Never assume that the employee already knows any single fact. Communicate clearly to the employee the steps to be learned. Present training in a simple-to-complex sequence of activities that lead to mastery of the task. Focus on achieving identified skills. Employee evaluation based on performance of learned skills gives you an excellent way to validate awards, promotions; or if necessary, discipline or terminations.

Managers in establishments that must have defined job descriptions for all positions to qualify for accreditation (such as in all health care institutions) may find this a useful tool.

Who Trains Employees?

Managers, supervisors, and trained employees usually provide the instruction in food service establishments. If the organization is large enough, corporate resources may be available in the form of trainers and learning materials. However, even if the materials and training outlines are already in place, you must know how to put them to use. When you assign someone else to conduct the training session, the final responsibility for the information is still yours.

Frequently, an existing employee is asked to show the new person how to do a task. The new employee then performs the task as the other employee taught them to do it. A concern with this method of on-the-job training is that it can perpetuate and prolong any errors that the existing employee currently practices.

If you, as the manager, work one-to-one with new employees, valuable training time is spent with very few people. There are times when one-to-one training is justified—but use it wisely.

Staff persons who are high performers are given the task of training new employees. When this occurs, there is usually no reduction in the workload of the trainer. Soon, the employees who were doing a good job are slowly pushed until their own successes are impossible. You should support the employee-trainer who provides valuable services in the training of new personnel. Give them tangible rewards for a job well done and until that is possible, try reducing their workload.

Passive learning is one of the *least* effective methods in employee training. Examples of this are lectures, slides, and videos. Merely telling someone how to do a job rarely produces a good result. They forget what they heard. In stressful situations, only 10% of what is said can be remembered. **Show the learner what has to be done and then have them demonstrate what they have seen.** Return demonstration of skills is a tried and true method to prove that the learner really can perform the task.

How Long Should Training Sessions Last?

Training sessions for lower level workers should be less than an hour. Consider the attention span of the learner. Recognize that if skills are put to work soon after a learning period, there is a better chance that the employee will perform successfully.

Regular training sessions, which include all staff, help keep everyone informed and up-to-date. Choose the method of instruction (one-to-one, groups by level of job, or entire staff) according to the nature of the lesson to be learned. Whenever possible, use different media such as videotapes, slides, posters, games, quizzes or demonstrations to help the learners visualize and remember what they have been taught. When VCR's and television sets are available, you can get videos from the FDA, health departments, industry, and professional associations.

Have fun. Never be afraid to put a little humor into the session. When learning is fun, it enhances retention. Offer positive verbal encouragement. Use contests, games, rewards, and recognition to acknowledge a job well done. These tactics can help to increase quality and productivity, and do wonders for employee moral and loyalty.

When there is a problem with contaminated food, wasted products, employee health or accidents, an inspection, or a customer satisfaction issue, the immediate response is usually to conduct an educational session. A "quick fix" inservice class is usually your first thought. After the crisis has passed, evaluate your own actions. Always ask yourself what could have been done to prevent this incident. If training could make a difference, add it to your program. However, very often the problem is motivation. Recognize this and do not expect repeat training sessions to create the needed change in behavior.

Employees who handle food must know how to:

▲ recognize common causes of food contamination

▲ use sanitary practices to keep food safe

▲ apply the HACCP system, if possible

▲ safely operate the equipment they are assigned to use

▲ keep an establishment clean and control pests

▲ contribute to his or her own safety and that of other workers

▲ respond in emergency situations such as fire

▲ recognize that individual responsibility contributes to the safe
workplace

When considering what to teach new employees, **keep it brief and
to the point**. There is a story about the little boy who asked his
father where he came from. After the father had gone into detail
describing how an egg is fertilized, then proceeded to the moment
of birth, the boy looked up and said, "Gee, I thought I was born in
Minneapolis."

When to Schedule Training Sessions

In a busy food establishment, choosing the time and place for
training is often difficult. Determine priorities by checking reports
from inspections or audits, and observe employee practices to
determine if there are problems that need immediate attention. Set
up the master schedule based on those identified needs. A lot of
on-the-spot training is done in food establishments. When you have
taught the same thing to six different people, it is not hard to see
that one group session could have saved time and energy. You can
use the master training schedule to:

▲ reinforce principles of sanitary food practices

▲ review fire safety plans

▲ update pest control information and any current topics
employees need to know or review

There will always be a need for special sessions on specific
problems or events; so, build in some flexibility. Classes can be held
in the dining room, kitchen, or storage areas depending upon the
material being taught. Try to choose an environment that is
conducive to learning. It should be quiet, well lighted, and have
comfortable room temperatures. Always try to plan training for the
least stressful part of the day when employees are not too tired to
learn.

Reinforce managerial commitment to learning by giving training
priority treatment. Schedule classes ahead, post dates in advance,
avoid cancellations, and make sure that employees are able to
attend. This sends the message that training is valued.

Evaluation

All employees deserve to know how they are performing by undergoing **evaluation**. Once needs are identified, objectives written, and training is completed, a change in behavior should be noticeable. The whole training process is focused on the improvement of performance by employees.

Short-term evaluation usually accompanies the training session when a return demonstration or quick paper and pencil exercise is done. Long-term evaluation is completed when observation of work behavior demonstrates whether or not a favorable change occurred. Written tests can check for long-term retention of learning; but in food establishments, performance is what counts.

Records of how learning needs were identified, when training was done, and how the employee performed on the job are valuable tools when promotions, choice assignments, bonuses, salary increases, or hiring and firing issues arise. The record can be a simple file box with a 3x5 or 5x7 card for each employee with notes on training, performance, and evaluation. Printed forms are sometimes used by larger organizations. In a HACCP based operation, whole procedures and standards are built-in, job performance is routine, and irregularities such as dumping product due to employee error become quite obvious.

Planning a Sanitation Training Program

Now that you have the information on how to train employees, here is a sample plan of action:

▲ **Determine what information needs to be taught**

▲ **Consider what the learners already know about the subject**

▲ **Establish the learning objective(s) that can be achieved**

▲ **Choose the training method and materials that are most appropriate for the topic**—Make sure the choice is within the scope of your available time and resources.

▲ **Select the instructor**—this is important. That person must know the subject they are to teach and demonstrate a positive attitude toward the learners. Enthusiasm is contagious and can turn ho-hum topics into interesting presentations. Humor is always welcome as long as it does not include sarcasm and ridicule.

▲ **Schedule training at appropriate times**—Schedule training sessions with emphasis on the physical and mental state of the learner. If they are too stressed or tired, results immediately diminish.

▲ **Use guest speakers**—Invite someone from the local health department, environmental control agency, county extension, vocational school, or college to assist. They can help link technical information to local rules and regulations.

▲ **Select a training area**—Demonstrations of equipment and procedures can be held right in the food preparation site. Seldom will you have the luxury of a formal classroom. Make sure lighting, ventilation, and temperatures are comfortable enough to keep distractions to a minimum.

▲ **Prepare the trainer**—If that person is you, do not trust your ability to "think on your feet." Anyone who trains others will need a solid knowledge of the subject and have a plan to follow. It is amazing how your mind can go blank when you face the audience. It never hurts to have a trial run.

▲ **Check your materials**—Do you have everything you will need? Does the equipment work? Are there any handouts to be given to students?

▲ **Present the training and get ready to evaluate the results.**

Training Resources

When you are in charge of a food establishment, training materials are often hard to find. The last thing you want to do is dig for information on how to train your employees. However, you know that problems related to untrained personnel can ruin any of your other efforts. With this in mind, the authors of your text have compiled a list of resources. The following agencies have materials that are available to help train employees in food safety and sanitation. Many of them have catalogues that you can request.

American Red Cross - Local Chapter

FDA State Training Branch, HFC-153
Room 1536
5600 Fishers Lane
Rockville MD 20857-1706
301-443-5871

**Catalogue of State Training Branch Courses
and Training Materials 1997**
Division of Human Resource Development
State Training Branch
5600 Fishers Lane, HFC-61
Rockville, Maryland 20857
301-4431-5871
Fax 301-594-1966
http\\www.fda.gov

FDA Center for Food Safety and Applied Nutrition
200 C Street SW
Washington, D.C. 20204-0001

USDA Food Safety and Inspection Service
Publications Office
Room1165-South
14th Street and Constitution Avenue
Washington D.C. 20250
202-447-9351

Home Study Program
247 Warren Hall
Cornell University, Ithica, NY 14853-0399
607-255-3028

Food Protection Report
Charles Felix and Associates
P. O. Box 1581
Leesburg, VA 22075
703-777-7448

**The Educational Institute
of the American Hotel Association**
1407 South Harrison Road
East Lansing, MI 48823

Food Marketing Institute
1750 K Street NW
Washington, D.C. 20006
202-452-8444

**NSF International
(formerly National Sanitation Foundation)**
3475 Plymouth Road
Ann Arbor, MI 48105
313-769-8010

National Automatic Merchandising Association
20 North Wacker Drive, Suite 3500
Chicago, IL 60606
312-346-0370

National Educational Media, Inc.
21601 Devonshire
Suite 3000
Chatsworth, CA 91311
818-709-6009

Customer Service Section PY
8700 Edgeworth Drive
Capitol Heights, MD 20743-3701
301-763-1896

**Educational Foundation
of the National Restaurant Association**
250 S. Wacker Drive, Suite 1400
Chicago, IL 60606
312-782-1703

National Pest Control Association
8100 Oak Street
Dun Loring, VA 22027

National Restaurant Association
1200 17th Street, NW
Washington, D.C. 200036-3097
202-331-5900

**Occupational Safety and Health Administration
(OSHA)**
200 Constitution Ave., NW Room N-3101
Washington, D.C. 20210
88-424-5156

U. S. Government Printing Office
Superintendent of Documents
Washington D.C. 20402-9325
202-783-3238

Food Service Sanitation Manual
DHEW Publication No. (FDA) 78-2081

This manual is also available in Spanish.

Also contact the state and local regulatory agencies and restaurant associations in your jurisdiction for assistance in setting up and delivering a food safety education program for your employees. Good training is a critical factor to the smooth operation of any food production operation (Figure 10.2).

Figure 10.2—Good Training

Industry Training Competencies

The Conference for Food Protection, meets every two years, to discuss current issues related to retail food safety. Councils within the group study different issues. Council II (Administration, Education, and Certification) has developed a list of competencies that a certified food manager is expected to know.

Specific Elements of Knowledge

I. Identify terms related to foodborne illness.

A. Define terms associated with foodborne illness.

1. foodborne illness

2. foodborne outbreak

3. foodborne infection

4. foodborne intoxication

5. disease communicated by food

6. foodborne pathogens

B. Recognize the major microorganisms and toxins that can contaminate food and the problems that can be associated with the contamination.

1. bacteria

2. viruses

3. parasites

4. fungi

C. Define and recognize potentially hazardous foods.

D. Define and recognize chemical and physical contamination and associated illness.

E. Define and recognize the major contributing factors for foodborne illness.

F. Recognize how microorganisms cause foodborne illness.

II. Identify time/temperature relationships with food.

A. Recognize the relationship between time/temperature and microorganisms (survival, growth, and toxin production) during the following stages:

1. receiving

2. storing

3. thawing

4. cooking

    5. holding/displaying

    6. serving

    7. cooling

    8. storing (post-production)

    9. reheating

  10. transporting

B. Describe the use of thermometers in monitoring food temperatures.

    1. types of thermometers

    2. techniques and frequency

    3. calibration and frequency

III. Describe the relationship between personal hygiene and food safety.

A. Recognize the association of hand contact and foodborne illness.

    1. hand washing, technique and frequency

    2. proper use of gloves, including how often to replace

    3. minimal hand contact with food

B. Recognize the association of personal habits and behaviors and foodborne illness.

    1. smoking

    2. eating and drinking

    3. wearing clothing that may contaminate food

    4. personal behaviors, including coughing, sneezing, etc.

C. Recognize the association of the health of the food handler to foodborne illness.

    1. free from communicable disease symptoms

    2. free of infections that can be spread through contact with food

    3. protect food from contact with open wounds

D. Recognize how policies, procedures, and management can improve food safety and hygiene practices.

IV. Describe methods for preventing food contamination from purchasing to serving.

  A. Define terms associated with contamination:

    1. contamination

    2. adulteration

    3. damage

    4. approved source

    5. sound and safe condition

  B. Identify potential hazards and methods prior to and during delivery.

    1. approved source

    2. sound and safe condition

  C. Identify potential hazards and methods to minimize or eliminate hazards after delivery.

    1. personal hygiene

    2. cross contamination

      a. food to food

      b. equipment and utensils

    3. contamination

      a. chemical

      b. additives

      c. physical

    4. service/display—customer contamination

    5. storage

    6. re-service

V. Identify and apply correct procedures for cleaning and sanitizing.

  A. Define terms associated with cleaning and sanitizing.

    1. cleaning

    2. sanitizing

B. Apply principles of cleaning and sanitizing.

C. Identify material: equipment, detergent, sanitizer.

D. Apply appropriate methods of cleaning and sanitizing.

    1. manual warewashing

    2. mechanical warewashing

    3. clean-in-place

E. Identify frequency of cleaning and sanitizing.

VI. Recognize problems and potential solutions associated with facility, equipment, and layout.

A. Identify facility, design, and construction suitable for food establishments:

    1. refrigeration

    2. heating and cooling

    3. floors, walls, and ceilings

    4. pest control

    5. lighting

    6. plumbing

    7. ventilation

    8. water supply

    9. wastewater disposal

    10. waste disposal

B. Recognize problems and potential solutions associated with temperature control, preventing cross contamination, housekeeping, and maintenance. **Implement:**

    1. self-inspection program

    2. pest control program

    3. cleaning schedules and procedures

    4. equipment and facility maintenance program

These are the elements that every certified food manager should know. This text provides the information needed to satisfy these requirements. These examinations are designed to link food safety theory to practice. By passing a certification examination, the food manager is able to demonstrate proficiency in food protection management. The following organizations/agencies offer food sanitation exams for certification:

David Cox, President
Professional Testing Inc.
1200 Hillcrest Street, Suite 300
Orlando, FL 32803-4717
407-894-6405
407-894-8164 Fax.
davcox@juno.com

Anthony W. Mitchell, Ph.D.
National Assessment Institute
5500 Rio Vista Dr.
Clearwater, FL 34620-3144
813-535-3775
813-532 -9989 Fax.

Louise Miller
Manager of Certificationand Instructional Services
Educational Foundation of the National Restaurant Assn.
250 S. Wacker Drive, Suite 1400
Chicago, IL 60606-5834
1-800-765-2122-ext. 703
312-715-1217 Fax.

Mr. Kevin Hawley
Program Management and Development, Senior Associate
Chauncey Group International
Room 349
506 Carnegie Center
Princeton, NJ 08540
Tel: 609-951-6168 Fax: 609-951-6767

Summary

In reference to the situation at the beginning of this chapter, did you agree with what the manager told the owner? He said, "We cannot afford the loss of business and reputation, let alone individual problems from contaminated food." Employees who are not trained to handle fryers, slicers, hot and cold holding areas, and food safety and sanitation problems can harm themselves, the equipment, and consumers.

A training program is a good investment for a food service establishment. Savings gained from the correct behavior of trained employees justify the expense of preparing staff to function safely and efficiently in their jobs. Training is important. Give it the attention it deserves and you will benefit from the result.

Discussion Questions (Short Answer)

1. Discuss how the problems related to temperature abuse, cross contamination, and poor personal health and hygiene can be prevented through training.

2. Discuss what educational resources are available from health departments, vendors, professional associations, fire departments, hospitals, FDA State Training Branch, and other regulatory agencies.

3. How can principles of adult education help you design effective training?

4. Select a task (such as making sandwiches or cleaning a refrigerator) to analyze and then choose a method to teach this activity.

5. Develop a plan to orient a new employee to the job of preparing sliced tomatoes and lettuce leaves for sandwiches.

6. Identify the benefits of a training and performance record when considering an employee for a promotion.

Answers to the multiple choice questions are provided in Appendix A.

Quiz 10.1 (Multiple Choice)

1. A new employee's first training for food safety should start with

   a. warewashing duties

   b. cleaning and sanitizing

   c. basic health and personal hygiene

   d. waste disposal procedures

2. You should never take for granted that an employee

   a. knows how to read and write.

   b. understands what cleanliness and sanitation means.

   c. has worked in food service before and will not require training.

   d. all of the above.

3. Mary is a new employee assigned to work with Jack to learn how to prepare vegetables for salads. You will

   a. leave them alone so Mary can focus on what Jack is doing.

   b. consider your responsibility over and return to work.

   c. monitor what Jack is teaching Mary.

   d. add more tasks to Jack's duties so that Mary can observe.

4. You have just shown Allen how to operate the warewashing machine. To determine if he can operate the equipment correctly you should ask him to

   a. show you how to operate the machine.

   b. answer questions about the machine on a paper and pencil test.

   c. teach another person how to work the machine.

   d. go to the next task for further instruction.

5. Adult learners often have

   a. high levels of confidence.

   b. little capacity to learn.

   c. need for written instructions.

   d. high anxiety and fragile egos.

6. A supervisory position is open in your establishment. Two employees, who have been with the organization for the same length of time, want the job. You are well prepared to back your decision because you

   a. took a vote among employees to choose the staff favorite.

   b. have kept a record of training, performance, and evaluation for each employee.

   c. picked the employee who meets government guidelines for affirmative action.

   d. went outside the organization to hire someone who is already trained.

7. Training sessions should not be longer than

   a. three hours.

   b. two hours.

   c. one hour.

   d. 30 minutes.

8. When an establishment uses the Hazard Analysis and Critical Control Point System, training can be based on

   a. code requirements.

   b. FDA State Training Branch guidelines.

   c. Critical Control Points.

   d. menu selection.

9. How many "wrongs" can you find in this picture?"

References/Suggested Reading

Esque, T. J., and T. F. Gilbert (1995). "Making Competencies Pay Off." *Training*. January. Vol. 32, No.1, pp. 44-50.

Felix, C. (1996). *Food Protection Report*. Leesburg, VA: Charles Felix Publications.

Longrèe, K., and G. Armbuster (1996). *Quantity Food Sanitation* New York: Wiley and Sons.

Odiorne, G. S., and G. A. Rummler (1988). *Training And Development: A Guide For Professionals*. Chicago: Commerce Clearing House, Inc.

Rue, N, (1994). *National Assessment Institute Handbook For Safe Foodservice Management*. Englewood Cliffs: Prentice Hall.

11 FOOD SAFETY REGULATIONS

Are You Ready for Inspection?

Inspector Jones arrives at Jon's food establishment for the quarterly inspection. Jon is really busy and tells Mr. Jones to go ahead. When Mr. Jones returns with the result of the inspection, Jon is surprised. Mr. Jones has noted that the sanitizer dispenser in the chemical dishwasher is broken. What should Jon do? Individual jurisdictions may have different rules. As you read, see if the information in this chapter can help you avoid an incident like this.

Learning Objectives

After reading this chapter, you should be able to:

▲ Recognize the role of federal, state, and local jurisdictions in regulating and monitoring food safety

▲ Identify aspects of food operations that are included in inspections and audits

▲ Utilize this chapter as a reference for federal, state, and local authorities

▲ Identify organizations related to the food industry

Essential Terms

Adulterated
Generally Recognized as Safe Substances (GRAS)
Misbranded
  Recall of a food product
Department of Health
Environmental Protection Agency (EPA)
Food and Drug Administration (FDA)
United States Department of Agriculture (USDA)

State and Local Regulations

State and local agencies that are responsible for enforcing food and safety requirements may be under environmental health, public health, or department of agriculture. It varies from state to state. Contact your local authorities to find out who is in charge of food safety in your jurisdiction.

Most food establishments will work most closely with their local health department. This agency can provide you with a copy of their current food safety code. **Your state and local code contains the food safety standards and regulations that would apply to your type of operation**. Familiarize yourself with the key food safety provisions of the code.

Permit to Operate

Operating a food establishment usually begins when you obtain a permit from the local authority to operate. You cannot operate a food establishment unless you have a valid permit issued by the regulatory authority in your jurisdiction. Apply for the permit well in advance of the anticipated date for opening the food establishment. Many health agencies require submission and approval of blueprints and specifications for an establishment before new construction or extensive remodeling can begin. Contact your local health agency to find out what level of plan review is required.

When a permit is obtained, post it in a prominent location where it can be seen. Permits are generally not transferable from one person to another, from one food establishment to another, or from one food operation to another. If you add a partner or incorporate, these actions are considered ownership change and may necessitate application for a new permit to operate.

The minimum number of inspections or audits that must be performed each year is usually prescribed in the retail food code. However, many health departments are currently using a risk-based approach for setting inspection frequencies. Under this system, the risk a food establishment poses is calculated using such factors as the overall sanitation history of the establishment and number of:

▲ meals served

▲ potentially hazardous foods on the menu

▲ critical violations observed

Low-risk facilities are usually inspected one time per year or less. High-risk facilities, on the other hand, may be inspected four or more times per year. A risk-based inspection system enables local health departments to target their scarce resources at those establishments that need them most.

Always cooperate with health department personnel. Greet the inspector when he or she arrives and ask to see official identification. Whenever possible, accompany the inspector during an inspection or audit. A routine inspection or audit normally consists of **three phases:**

Phase I is a pre-inspection conference where the environmental health specialist or sanitarian and the person in charge review previous inspection results and discuss information that is relevant to the current inspection.

Phase II is the inspection itself.

Phase III is the post-inspection conference where the results of the current inspection are reviewed and discussed.

Most inspections will focus on:

▲ foods and supplies

▲ personal hygiene and employee health

▲ temperatures of food and food-holding equipment

▲ cleaning and sanitizing procedures

▲ equipment and utensils

▲ water supply and waste disposal

▲ pest control and other aspects of the operation that might compromise food safety

If a critical violation such as temperature abuse or cross contamination is discovered during an inspection, corrective action must be taken immediately. Failure to do so could result in fines and possible closure of the establishment. Lesser violations should be corrected by the next inspection or audit.

Food managers should periodically conduct self-inspections of their establishment to assure proper sanitation and food safety between health department inspections. During a self-inspection, the manager will look for signs of contamination or conditions that might be a hazard to food safety.

Federal Agencies

The primary federal agencies that protect our food supply include the:

▲ Food and Drug Administration (FDA)

▲ United States Department of Agriculture (USDA)

▲ Environmental Protection Agency (EPA)

Other important government agencies include the:

▲ National Marine Fisheries Service (NMFS)

▲ Centers for Disease Control and Prevention (CDC)

▲ Occupational Safety and Health Administration (OSHA)

▲ Consumer Product Safety Commission (CPSC)

▲ Federal Trade Commission (FTC)

Please note that states have counterparts of agriculture, health, OSHA, and EPA.

Food and Drug Administration (FDA)

The Food and Drug Administration (FDA) is an agency of the United States Department of Health and Human Services. **FDA is recognized as the leading food and drug regulatory agency in the world.** This agency regulates the processing, manufacturing, and interstate sale of all food products except meat, poultry, and eggs. All foods, except meat, poultry, and eggs, transported and sold over state lines, must comply with FDA regulations.

FDA protects the public's health by preventing food adulteration and misbranding. **Adulterated** food is food that contains filth, is decomposed or otherwise unfit, is produced in unsanitary conditions, or contains poisons or harmful substances damaging to health. **Misbranded** food is falsely or misleadingly packaged or labeled. It may be represented as a specific food product or contain ingredients not included on the label but does not meet national standards for that food. Misbranded food may also be packaged in such as way as to be misleading. For instance, it may be an imitation of another food, but the label does not notify the consumer that it is an imitation.

FDA's goal is to assure that food shipped in interstate commerce is safe, pure, wholesome, sanitary, and honestly packaged and labeled. The agency also helps to prevent milk-borne and shellfish diseases and assists in the control of sanitation related to shellfish production.

The FDA also sets standards with respect to composition, quality, labeling, and safety of foods and food additives. FDA's duties include performing routine audits of food processing plants, food storage, and imported foods to ensure that safety standards are maintained. The agency is also responsible for the toxicological safety of food packaging materials.

If a food does not meet with the approval of the FDA, a **recall of a food product** may be issued. Three types of food recalls, Class I, Class II, or Class III, can be issued depending on the severity of the health risk (Figure 11.1). It is important that all food retail establishments have a policy regarding the handling of food recalls. Recalled foods should be promptly removed from retail shelves and cannot be sold.

Class I	Foods that may cause serious adverse health consequences
Class II	Foods that would result in a temporary or reversible health problem
Class III	Foods that are not likely to cause danger to health

Figure II.I—Food Recalls

The FDA has published the *Food Code* which serves as a model for state and local retail food programs throughout the United States. The *Food Code* is not a law. Rather, it is a set of recommendations put forth to protect food sanitation and safety nationwide. Each state has its own law governing food establishments. These state laws typically contain all or a portion of the guidelines contained in the FDA's *Food Code*.

The FDA works closely with state and local health departments in matters of food protection. There is also close cooperation between the FDA and the food processing industry in their concern for the cleanliness and wholesomeness of the nation's food supply.

U.S. Department of Agriculture (USDA)

The **United States Department of Agriculture (USDA)** has many agencies engaged in food protection. The Agricultural Marketing Service (AMS) conducts programs that aid the marketing of agricultural products. The AMS develops quality standards and offers voluntary grading services for red meats, poultry and eggs, dairy products, and fruits and vegetables.

Many types of quality standards have been developed to help insure food quality and define differences in quality that affect the usefulness and value of a food. Grade or quality standards cover the whole range of a product's natural quality. The number of grades for a particular food depend on its variability. For instance, eight grades are necessary to cover the range of beef quality, while only three are needed for poultry. Beef grades usually encountered are USDA Prime, Choice, and Good. Choice is the grade most widely available; it denotes a high degree of tenderness, juiciness, and flavor. USDA Grade A poultry has more meat and a better appearance. Lower grades, such as B and C are seldom offered for retail sale, but are used in processed foods such as soup, and pot pies.

The Food Safety and Inspection Service (FSIS) of the USDA inspects domestic and imported meat, poultry, and processed meat and poultry products. Employees of the FSIS inspect meat in accordance with the federal *Meat Inspection Act of 1906*, to assure a clean wholesome, disease-free meat supply. Inspections are made by veterinarians or persons under their supervision at places of animal slaughter and at meat processing facilities. Poultry is inspected under the provisions of the *Poultry Products Inspection Act*. This law requires poultry to be processed in plants having full-time government inspection service. Poultry is inspected live prior to slaughter, during evisceration (removal of the internal organs) and during or after packaging.

Purchasers should be aware of the difference between inspection and grading. Inspection refers to an official examination of food to determine whether it is wholesome and free from adulteration. Grading refers to the process of evaluating foods relative to specific, defined standards in order to assess its quality. Inspection is often required by law, but grading is optional. Most purchasers prefer to buy graded products because they know those products have met specific quality standards. Of the two services, inspection for wholesomeness is the most important for food safety.

U.S. Department of Commerce (USDC)

Grade standards for processed fishery products have been established by the Voluntary Inspection Service of the U.S. Department of Commerce. The Department's National Marine Fisheries Service (NMFS) administers these programs on a voluntary, fee-for-service basis. A fish processor may decide to have an inspector stationed in his plant on a permanent basis to assess the premises for sanitary conditions, determine that wholesome ingredients are used, and grade the product. This type of inspection is strictly voluntary. The product gets evaluated and graded as A, B, or C in quality, the last grade being the lowest acceptable quality. Examples of NMFS regulated products include frozen raw and fried breaded fish portions, shrimp, frozen fried scallops, and frozen sole and haddock fillets.

Environmental Protection Agency

The **Environmental Protection Agency (EPA)** was established in 1970. It was created to prevent, control, and reduce air, land, and water pollution. Related to food safety, the EPA regulates the use of toxic substances (pesticides, sanitizers, and other chemicals), monitors compliance, and provides technical assistance to states. One very important responsibility of the EPA is enforcement of the *Federal Insecticide, Fungicide, and Rodenticide Act (FIFRA)*. This Act authorizes EPA to regulate pesticide products sold or distributed in the United States. The *Food, Drug, and Cosmetic Act* authorizes EPA to establish tolerance levels for pesticide residues in or on food and food products.

The EPA is also mainly responsible for the implementation of ten major environmental laws. These laws cover an enormous range of environmental problems including air pollution, water pollution, hazardous wastes, noise pollution, and contaminated drinking water. Some of these laws, especially those controlling the handling and disposal of solid and hazardous wastes, may affect food establishment operations. The store manager should contact their state and local environmental agencies to be sure their store is in compliance with current regulations.

Centers for Disease Control and Prevention (CDC)

The **Centers for Disease Control and Prevention** (CDC) is the federal agency that is responsible for protecting public health through the prevention and control of diseases. CDC supports foodborne disease investigation and prepares annual summaries and statistics on outbreaks of foodborne diseases including all those transmitted through food and water.

Occupational Safety and Health Administration (OSHA)

The **Occupational Safety and Health Administration (OSHA)** was created in the Department of Labor to enforce the Occupational Safety and Health Act. It enforces health standards and regulations on safety, noise, and other workplace related hazards. The agency conducts investigations and inspections to assess health and safety conditions in places of employment.

Federal Trade Commission (FTC)

The **Federal Trade Commission (FTC)** is involved in enforcing various laws regarding marketing practices and national advertising of foods and other products.

Other Federal Food Safety Related Organizations

Other organizations also help to protect our food supply. Many of the following organizations have good information and training materials:

▲ The American Public Health Association (APHA)

▲ The Association of Food and Drug Officials (AFDO)

▲ The Food Marketing Institute (FMI)

▲ The Frozen Food Industry Coordinating Committee (FFICC)

▲ The Food Research Institute (FRI)

▲ Institute of Food Technologists (IFT)

▲ The International Association of Milk, Food, and Environmental Sanitarians (IAMFES)

▲ The National Environmental Health Association (NEHA)

▲ The National Pest Control Association (NPCA)

▲ The National Restaurant Association (NRA)

▲ NSF International (NSF)

▲ The National Shellfish Safety Program (NSSP)

▲ Underwriters Laboratories Inc. (UL)

Food Law

Federal Food, Drug, and Cosmetic (FD&C) Act

The FDA administers the federal *Food, Drug, and Cosmetic Act* which was originally passed by Congress in 1938 to assure that foods are safe, pure, wholesome, and produced under sanitary conditions. Several amendments have been added to the law since then. Among the most notable amendments are the *Miller Pesticide Amendment of 1954*, the *Food Additives Amendment of 1958*, and the *Color Additives Amendment of 1960*.

The *Miller Pesticide Amendment* establishes a procedure for the setting of safe amounts (tolerances) for residues of pesticides which may remain on fresh fruits, vegetables, and other raw agricultural commodities when shipped in interstate commerce.

The *1958 Food Additives Amendment* has a two-fold purpose: (1) to protect the public health by requiring proof of safety before a substance may be added to food, and (2) to advance food technology and improve the food supply by permitting the use of substances which are safe at the levels of intended use. Before something is approved for use by the FDA, data must be supplied proving the substance is free from harm. If approved, the FDA will then define limits that can be used in foods. Currently, there is a list of over 3000 approved food additives. Excluded are those food additives which have been designated as **GRAS** or *generally recognized as safe* substances. These are additives that have been used in foods for years and with no apparent ill effects. Substances that typically fall into the GRAS category are spices, natural seasonings, flavoring materials, fruit and beverage acids, and baking powder chemicals. The purpose of establishing a GRAS list is to recognize the safety of basic substances without the requirement for rigorous safety testing.

The *Color Additive Amendments of 1960* were enacted to control the use of natural and synthetic color additives. Color additives are substances added only for the color they give. Color additives must be safe under normal conditions of use and must not cause cancer when ingested by humans.

1906—Federal Meat Inspection Act

This law provides for the mandatory inspection of animals, slaughtering conditions, and meat processing facilities. It helps to assure that meat and products containing meat are clean, wholesome, free from disease, and properly represented. Such products are stamped "U.S. Inspected and Passed by Department of Agriculture." This stamp is necessary for interstate commerce and imported goods. This law is enforced by the Food Safety Inspection Service of the Department of Agriculture.

For products not crossing state lines, the Wholesome Meat Act is enforced (usually governed by state health departments).

1957—Federal Poultry Products Inspection Act

This law provides for the mandatory inspection of poultry, slaughtering conditions, and poultry processing facilities. It helps to ensure that poultry and products containing poultry are clean, wholesome, free from disease, and properly represented.

1993—Nutrition Labeling and Education Act

This law provides information on specific nutritional guidelines and defines what needs to be on a Nutrition Label (Fig. 11.2). This label, which provides information on protein, fat, carbohydrate, and mineral content, helps consumers make informed choices when selecting foods.

Meltaway/French Mint Combo 5¹/₂ oz.

Nutrition Facts

Serving Size: 42.0g, 5 pieces
Serving Per Container: 4

Amount Per Serving

Calories 248   Calories from Fat 150

	% Daily Value*
Total Fat 17g	26%
Saturated Fat 10g	50%
Cholesterol Less then 5mg	0%
Sodium 50mg	2%
Total Carbohydrate 22g	7%
Dietary Fibers 1g	4%
Sugars 20g	
Protein 2g	

Vitamin A 0%	Vitamin C 0%
Calcium 6%	Iron 2%

* Percent Daily Values are based on a 2,000 calorie diet. Your daily values may be higher or lower depending on your calorie needs:

	Calories	2,000	2,500
Total Fat	Less than	65g	60g
Sat Fat	Less than	20g	25g
Cholesterol	Less than	300mg	300mg
Sodium	Less than	2,400mg	2,400mg
Total Carbohydrate		300g	375g
Dietary Fiber		25g	30g

19361

Figure II.2—The Nutrition Label

Summary

The inability to sanitize equipment and utensils is a very serious situation for a food establishment. During the post-inspection conference, Jon should discuss his options with Inspector Jones. The only solution to the problem is to have a service person come to the establishment and fix the dispenser as soon as possible. In the meantime, Jon should have his staff wash and sanitize the equipment and utensils using the 3-compartment sink. Jon might reduce the volume of items to be washed manually by using disposable items such as plastic utensils and paper cups. Jon should notify Inspector Jones when the sanitizer dispenser has been repaired so that a follow-up inspection of the dishwashing machine can be performed.

Federal, state, and local food safety regulations are important for maintaining a safe food supply. State and local health departments are critical when it comes to monitoring and enforcing each state or local food code. They evaluate food establishments to help assure delivery of safe food to consumers.

Food establishments and regulatory agencies should work together to protect the health of customers and meet their expectations for food quality and safety.

Case Study 11.1

A few hours after lunch, a customer returns to a restaurant and complains to a waiter that he got sick after eating the chicken salad. The customer claims that the chicken salad he had eaten for lunch was responsible for his illness. How should the waiter handle this customer complaint?

Answers to the case study and all multiple choice questions areprovided in Appendix A.

Quiz 11.1 (Multiple Choice)

1. Before opening a food establishment and serving food to the public, which of the following must be done?

   a. pass a food certification exam
   b. acquire a Permit to Operate
   c. attend 16 hours of training in food safety
   d. all of the above

2. Which federal agency prepared the model *Food Code*?

   a. Centers for Disease Control and Prevention
   b. Environmental Protection Agency
   c. Food and Drug Administration
   d. Occupational Safety and Health Administration

3. Which federal agency is responsible for ensuring the safety of meat, poultry, and egg products?

   a. Centers for Disease Control and Prevention

    b. Environmental Protection Agency

    c. Food and Drug Administration

    d. United States Department of Agriculture

4. Which federal agency is responsible for ensuring the safety of all foods except meat, poultry, and egg products?

    a. Centers for Disease Control and Prevention

    b. Environmental Protection Agency

    c. Food and Drug Administration

    d. United States Department of Agriculture

5. Which federal agency is responsible for regulations on safety, noise, and other working conditions?

    a. Centers for Disease Control and Prevention

    b. Environmental Protection Agency

    c. Food and Drug Administration

    d. Occupational Safety and Health Administration

6. If the FDA determines that the ingestion of a food may "cause serious adverse health consequences" a food recall may be issued. This would be an example of what kind of recall?

    a. Class I

    b. Class II

    c. Class III

    d. Class IV

7. Which legal document does the FDA abide by to protect the food supply?

    a. Federal Food, Drug, and Cosmetic Act

    b. 1906 - Federal Meat Inspection Act

    c. 1957 - Federal Poultry Products Inspection Act

    d. None of the above

8. During an inspection of food establishment, a manager should:

    a. ask to see credentials

    b. assist the inspector whenever possible

    c. discuss any violations

    d. all of the above

9. When a suspected foodborne illness claim is reported to a wait person, what should be the first cause of action?

    a.   remove all customers from the restaurant immediately

    b.   call the health inspector

    c.   locate the food manager and assure that the suspect food is not served

    d.   contact CDC

10. Responsibilities of a food manager include:

    a.   obtaining copies, understanding, and complying with rules and regulations regarding their facility

    b.   handling food establishment inspections

    c.   handling claims of foodborne illness

    d.   all of the above

References/Suggested Reading

IFT Publication (1992). Government Regulation of Food Safety: Interaction of Scientific and Societal Forces. *Food Technology*. 46(1).

Potter, N.N., J. H. Hotchkiss, (1995); *Food Science.* New York: Chapman and Hall.

Labuza, T. P., and Baisier (1992); 6. Critical Reviews Science and Nutrition. 31(3): 167-176.

APPENDIX A

Answers to Case Studies and Quizzes

Chapter 1

Quiz 1.1	Quiz 1.2
1. c	1. False
2. a	2. False
3. b	3. True
4. a	4. True
5. c	5. True

Chapter 2

Case Study 2.1

Hazard: The foodborne hazard associated with this illness was likely a toxin produced by the bacterium *Staphylococcus aureus*. This organism may have originated from the food handler and was then transferred to the cheese by cross contamination. Being held at room temperature, the organism had the opportunity to grow in the cheese and produce a heat stable toxin. Even after cooking in the 500°F oven, the toxin was not destroyed. People that complained of illness probably had an intoxication due to *Staphylococcus aureus*. Also, cheddar cheese is drier and salty which provides ideal conditions for *Staphylococcus aureus* while inhibiting other microorganisms that might otherwise compete with the Staph. germs.

Prevention: There are three important prevention steps that could have been taken. The first involves any of several personal hygiene measures. More specifically are proper handwashing and scrubbing under fingernails before handling food; avoiding the transfer of saliva from the mouth to food by eating, talking, or chewing gum; and don't contaminate hands by touching hair, skin, or nose. The second preventive measure is to insure that equipment is clean and sanitary before using. The third and most important preventive measure is making certain that the cheddar cheese is kept in the refrigerator at 41°F (5°C) or below rather than at room temperature. Had the cheese been held at temperatures outside the temperature danger zone, *Staphylococcus aureus* could not have grown and produced the heat stable toxin.

In this case study, cooking could not be used as a preventative measure.

Quiz 2.1

1. d	2. b
3. a	4. c
5. a	6. b
7. c	8. d
9. b	10. a

Chapter 3

Case Study 3.1

Due to her illness, Michelle should not be handling food under any circumstances. Michelle could easily contaminate the food by coughing, sneezing, or simply touching the food. The food manager should advise Michelle not to continue working until she has recovered from the illness. Under special circumstances, the food manager could alternatively assign Michelle to tasks away from food preparation and service, or utensil wash, rinse, and storage areas.

Case Study 3.2

Cameron did not properly clean and sanitize the food thermometer after measuring the temperature of a raw food (meat) followed by a cooked food (eggs). By not cleaning and sanitizing the thermometer, he could contaminate the eggs from the thermometer that may contain juices from the raw meat. Instead, Cameron should have cleaned the thermometer followed by sanitizing it in an in-place sanitizing solution.

Quiz 3.1

1. a	2. d
3. d	4. d
5. b	6. c
7. b	8. a
9. d	10. a

Chapter 4

Case Study 4.1

1. The sanitation hazards in the walk-in refrigerator are:

   a. Turkeys were not covered

   b. Raw products (turkeys) are stored above ready-to-eat food (lettuce).

   c. Containers of food are not properly labeled and dated.

   d. Shelves are lined with aluminum foil which reduces air circulation for cooling.

   e. The thermometer for the walk-in was located near the cooling unit, instead of in the warmest part of the storage compartment.

2. Violations a, b, c, could result in contamination and spoilage.

3. Cover the turkeys during thawing. Store raw foods below containers used for food storage. Remove aluminum foil from the shelves in the walk-in. Relocate the thermometer to the warmest part of the walk-in.

Case Study 4.2

1. Potentially hazardous foods (refrigerated and frozen) are not being stored at proper temperatures upon delivery. Because foods are not being inspected at the time of delivery, defective products may be accepted that would normally be sent back to the supplier.

2. Contact suppliers and request that no deliveries be made during peak periods such as between 11 AM and 2 PM when employees are unable to process them and move to proper storage conditions. Make certain employees know how to inspect incoming shipments and place them in storage in a timely fashion.

Quiz 4.1

1. c	2. c
3. b	4. c
5. b	6. d
7. c	8. c
9. a	10. d
11. c	12. c
13. d	14. a
15.	16. a
17. d	18. c
19. d	20. d

Chapter 5

Case Study 5.1

Ingredients	Amount	Servings		
		25	50	100
Hoisin sauce	Tbsp.	2.5	5.0	10
Bean sauce	Tbsp.	2.5	5.0	10
Apple sauce	Tbsp.	2.5	5.0	10
Catsup	Tbsp.	5.0	10.0	20
Soy sauce	Tbsp.	2.5	5.0	10
Rice wine	Tbsp.	5.0	10.0	20
Peanut oil	Tbsp.	2.5	5.0	10
Ginger, minced	tsp.	1.25	2.5	5
Scallion, minced	1	1.5	5.0	10
Garlic cloves, minced	2	5.0	10.0	20
Sugar	Tbsp.	2.5	5.0	10
Salt	tsp.	1.25	2.5	5
Pork spareribs, trimmed	1 rack	2.6	5.0	10
Honey	Tbsp.	7.5	5.0	30

Pre-preparation

SOP !   1.   Thaw spareribs under refrigeration at 41°F(5°C) for 1 day or until completely thawed.

SOP 2   2.   Wash hands before starting food preparation.

3.   Combine all of the ingredients for the marinade in a large bowl.

Preparation

SOP 3   4.   Score the ribs with a sharp knife. Place the ribs in the marinade. Marinate them for at least 4 hours at a product temperature of 41°F (5°C) or lower in refrigerated storage.

5.   Place the spareribs in a smoker at 425°F (220°C) for 30 minutes.

CCP 1   6.   Reduce the heat to 375°F (190°C) and continue smoking the ribs to a final internal temperature of 155°F (68°C) or higher. This phase of the cooking process should take about 50 minutes. Brush the honey on the spareribs during the last 5 minutes of the smoking process.

Holding/Service

CCP 2 7. Slice the ribs between the bones and maintain at 140°F (60°C) or above while serving.

Cooling

CCP 3 8. Transfer any unused product into clean, 2-inch deep pans. Quick-chill the product from 140°F (60°C) to 70°F (21°C) within 2 hours and from 70°F (21°C) to 41°F (5°C) within 4 hours.

Storage

9. Store the chilled product in a covered container that is properly dated and labeled. Refrigerate at 41°F (5°C) or below.

Reheating

CCP 4 10. Heat spareribs to an internal temperature of 165°F (74°C); or 190°F (88°C) in a microwave oven within 2 hours.

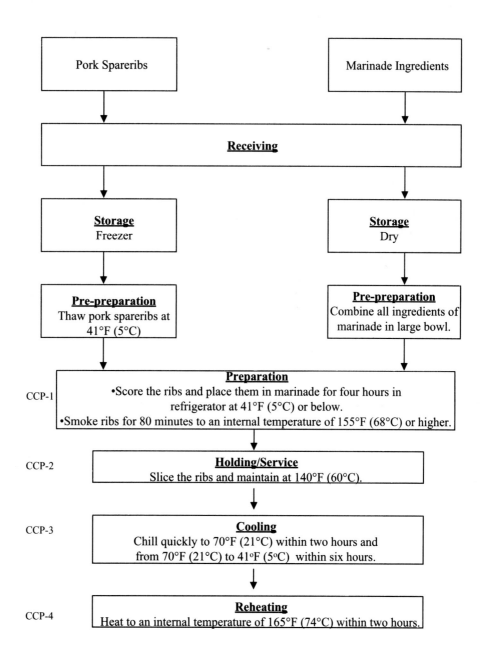

Quiz 5.1

1. d	2. b
3. a	4. c
5. b	6. b
7. d	8. b
9. d	

Chapter 6

Case Study 6.1

1. Wooden cutting boards may harbor disease-causing microbes. Meat is allowed to cool and stay in temperature danger zone. Wiping knife on damp towel transfers microbes on towel onto the blade that then touches the meat.

2. Use approved heat lamps to keep food out of temperature danger zone. Do not use wet kitchen towel to clean equipment.

3. Replace wooden cutting board with board constructed of hard rubber or other approved materials.

Case Study 6.2

1. Contact equipment supplier and get specifications and a price list for different slicers. Compare features and decide which is the best equipment.

2. Does the slicer meet the need and demands of the operation?

   ▼Can the slicer be used for a long period of time?
   ▼Does the slicer require extraordinary repair and upkeep?
   ▼Can the slicer meet future needs of the operation?
   ▼Cost?

Quiz 6.1

1. c	2. b
3. a	4. d
5. d	6. a
7. d	8. b
9. c	10. d

Chapter 7

Case Study 7.1

1. Yes, Ted should be concerned about the suds in the sanitizing solution. Chlorine sanitizers do not work effectively in alkaline conditions. Most detergents are alkaline and therefore, the effectiveness of the sanitizing solution at the Regal supermarket may be lessened by the suds.

2. Drain the sanitizer and refill the compartment of the sink with fresh water and sanitizer measured at 50 ppm.

3. Make certain the detergent is removed by the fresh water rinse that occurs in the second compartment of the sink.

Case Study 7.2

1. Use the three compartment sink to manually wash and sanitize equipment and utensils.

2. The facility could use single-service disposable dishware and tableware until the dishwashing machine can be repaired.

3. It is not necessary to suspend food operations provided the measures described in answers 1 and 2 can be provided.

Quiz 7.1 (Multiple Choice)

1. c	2. a
3. b	4. c
5. a	6. d
7. b	8. d
9. c	10. c

Chapter 8

Case Study 8.1

1. Floors *and* walls should be nonabsorbent, easily cleanable, durable, and smooth. Walls should be light in color.

2. Wood is porous and absorbs water and other liquids. It would not be durable and easy-to-clean.

3. Any light color would be good. A shade of white is often preferred. Light colors show soil and help food workers determine when the surface has been properly cleaned.

4. Grease, oil, blood, and other soils are common in meat departments. It is important to select floor and wall materials that are nonabsorbent and can be effectively cleaned with soap and water. These materials should also stand up under spray type cleaning procedures.

Case Study 8.2

1. The lack of a properly designed and operating handwashing lavatory in the kitchen at Ryan's may pose a health risk for customers. When food workers cannot wash their hands when they become contaminated, risk of food contamination and cross contamination is high. Food workers are more likely to wash their hands correctly when there is a convenient sink and supplies near their work station. By having to walk to customer restrooms, they may be encouraged to wipe their hands on a towel or apron rather then take the time to wash properly.

2. The health department should direct Ryan's to have the lavatory repaired immediately. Until then, food workers should use utensils and disposable gloves to prevent hand contact with food. The infected worker should stay away from work until a physician certifies him or her free of the hepatitis virus.

3. Train employees about proper handwashing and importance of avoiding hand contact with food. Management should also ask food workers to notify them when they have symptoms of a communicable disease that might be transmitted to food.

4. Ryan's will likely receive poor publicity as a result of the outbreak. This will cause consumer confidence to drop and business will likely decline. The short and long-term consequences may ruin the restaurant's reputation and cause financial ruin.

Quiz 8.1 (Multiple Choice)

1. d	2. a
3. a	4. a
5. b	6. b
7. d	8. a
9. a	10. d

Chapter 9

Case Study 9.1

1.

   a. Assist guests and employees to safely evacuate the building.

   b. Call emergency medical and police services to aid victims that have suffered injuries due to the earthquake.

   c. Disconnect gas and electricity to avoid fires and explosions.

    d. To the extent possible, assure the structural safety of the building.

    e. Dispose of all food which are contaminated with glass and other physical hazards.

2. Fire police, ambulance, hospital and other types of emergency services. Public and private utilities including, but not limited to, electric, gas, and water companies.

3. In extreme emergency conditions such as the one descibed in the case study, it is very likely that all food would have to be discarded because of contamination from glass and other physical agents.

It is extremely difficult to serve safe food without an adequate supply of energy and a safe water supply. If the interruption of the power and water service is only temporary, it might be possible to get by with single-service articles (disposable plates, etc.) and temporary sources of heating and cooling for a brief period of time. Consult with your local regulatory agency before attempting to operate under these less than ideal conditions.

Quiz 9.1

1. mesh gloves

2. pressure

3. closed, labeled

4. removed

5. third degree

6. fire extinguishers

7. Hospitals, fire departments, emergency medical systems, insurance companies, professionalassociations, Red Cross, and vendors who supply food supplies, and equipment

8. lie still

9. Heimlich Maneuver

10. Emergency phone numbers

Chapter 10

Quiz 10.1

1. c	2. b
3. d	4. c
5. c	6. a
7. a	8. c
9. d	

Chapter 11

Case Study 11.1

The first thing the waiter should do is be compassionate and understanding. Immediately afterwards, the waiter should contact the food manager—it is the responsibility of the food manager to handle claims of foodborne illness. The food manager should then ensure that the chicken salad is not served to any other customers. The chicken salad should be stored in a separate container in the refrigerator and not be discarded. It is important that the chicken salad be retained so that a health inspector can take a portion to perform tests if necessary. Remember to keep some of the chicken salad in case you decide to perform tests with an independent laboratory. The food manager should then contact the local health department and proceed with the investigation. Once the health inspector and/or other regularity agencies become involved, it is important that the food managers cooperate in any way possible. It may be important to provide records of food suppliers and of handling/preparation practices used regarding the chicken salad.

Quiz 11.1

1. b	2. a
3. c	4. a
5. d	6. d
7. c	8. c
9. d	10. d

GLOSSARY

Abrasive cleaners - cleaning compound containing finely ground minerals used to scour articles; can scratch surfaces.

Acceptable level - within an established range of safety.

Accessible - easy to reach or enter.

Acid - a substance with a pH of less than 7.0.

Additives - natural and man-made substances added to a food for an intended purpose (such as preservatives and colors) or unintentionally (such as pesticides and lubricants).

Adulterated - the deliberate addition of inferior or cheaper material to a supposedly pure food product in order to stretch out supplies and increase profits.

Aerobe - an organism, especially a bacterium, that requires oxygen to live.

Air-dry - to dry in room air after cleaning, washing, or sanitizing.

Air curtain - a window or doorway equipped with jets that force air out and across the opening to keep flying insects from entering.

Air gap - an unobstructed, open vertical distance through air that separates an outlet of the potable water supply from a potentially contaminated source like a drain.

Alkaline - a substance that has a pH of more than 7.0.

Anaerobe - an organism, especially a bacterium, that does not require oxygen or free oxygen to live.

Anisakiasis - disease caused by the anisakis parasite.

Anisakis - roundworm parasite found in fish.

Aseptic packaging - a method in which food is sterilized or commercially sterilized outside the can and then aseptically placed in previously sterilized containers which are then sealed in an aseptic environment. This method may be used for liquid foods such as concentrated milk and soups.

At risk - the term used to describe individuals such as infants, children, pregnant women, and those with weakened immune systems for whom foodborne illness can be very severe, even life threatening.

Backflow - flow of contaminated water into potable supply caused by back pressure.

Backsiphonage - a form of backflow that can occur when pressure in the potable water supply drops below pressure in the flow of contaminated water.

Bacteria - single-celled microscopic organisms.

Bactericide - substance that kills bacteria.

Bacterium - one microorganism.

Bi-metallic stemmed thermometer - food thermometer used to measure product temperatures.

Binary fission - the process by which bacteria grow. One cell divides to form two new cells.

Biofilm - a layer of stubborn soil that develops on surfaces that are improperly cleaned or sanitized; bacteria can accumulate and grow on this surface.

Blast chiller - special refrigerated unit that quickly freezes food items.

Botulism - type of food intoxication caused by *C. botulinum.*

Calibrate - to determine and verify the scale of a measuring instrument with a standard. Thermometers used in food establishments are commonly calibrated using an ice slush method (32°F or 0°C) or a boiling point method (212°F or 100°C).

Campylobacter jejuni - an anaerobic nonsporeforming bacterium that causes a foodborne illness.

Cardiopulmonary resuscitation (CPR) - First aid technique to apply to persons who have stopped breathing.

Chemical sanitizers - products used on equipment and utensils after washing and rinsing to reduce the number of disease causing microbes to safe levels.

Ciguatoxin - a toxin from reef feeding fish that causes foodborne illness.

Clean - free of visible soil but not necessarily sanitized; surface must be clean before it can be sanitized.

Cleaning agent - a chemical compound formulated to remove soil and dirt.

Clean-in-Place (CIP) -equipment designed to be cleaned without moving, usually large or very heavy.

Cleaning - removal of visible soil but not necessarily sanitized. A surface must be cleaned before it can be sanitized.

Code - a systematic collection of regulations, or statutes, and procedures designed to protect the public.

Cold-holding - refers to the safe temperature range (less than 41°F or 5°C) for maintaining foods cold prior to service for consumption.

Competency based training - a job is analyzed and broken down into steps which must be learned to gain mastery of the task. Training should focus on those steps,

Contamination - the unintended presence of harmful substances or conditions in food that can cause illness or injury to people who eat the infected food.

Cooking - the act of providing sufficient heat and time to a given food to effect a change in food texture, aroma, and appearance. More importantly, cooking assures the destruction of foodborne pathogens inherent to that food.

Cooling - the act of reducing the temperature of properly cooked food to 41°F (5°C) or below.

Corrosion resistant - materials which maintain their original surface characteristics under continuous use in food service with normal use of cleaning compounds and sanitizing solutions.

Coving - a curved sealed edge between the floor and wall that makes cleaning easier and inhibits insect harborage.

Critical Control Point (CCP) - means a point or procedure in a specific food system where loss of control may result in an unacceptable health risk.

Critical limit - means the maximum or minimum value to which a physical, biological, or chemical parameter must be controlled at a critical control point to minimize the risk that the identified food safety hazard may occur.

Cross-connection - any physical link through which contaminants from drains, sewers, or waste pipes can enter a potable water supply.

Cross contamination - transfer of harmful organisms between items.

Cumulative - increasing in effect by successive additions. For example, hot food must be cooled from 140°F (60°C) to 70°F (21°C) within 4 hours; it must reach 41°F (5°C) within and additional 2 hours to prevent bacterial growth., therefore, the *cumulative time the food is in this danger zone equals a total of 6 hours.*

Danger zone - temperatures between 41°F (5°C) and 140°F (60°C).

Disinfectant - destroys harmful bacteria.

Dead man's switch - activates equipment when depressed and stops if pressure is relieved.

Detergents - cleaning agent which contains surfactants used with water to break down soil to make it easier to remove.

Deviation - to diverge; go in different directions.

Digital thermometer - a battery-powered thermometer that reveals temperature in a digital numerical display.

Easy to clean - materials and design facilitate cleaning.

Easy-to-move - on wheels, raised on legs, or otherwise designed to facilitate cleaning.

Employee - person working in or for a food establishment who engages in food preparation, service, or other assigned activity.

Equipment - the appliances: stoves, ovens, etc., and storage such as refrigerated units used in food establishments.

Evaluation procedures - systematically checking progress to determine if goals have been met.

Facultative microbe - a microorganism that can survive with or without oxygen.

Facultative anaerobe - an organism that can grow with or without free oxygen.

FATTOM - an acronym used to indicate the six conditions bacteria need for growth. These conditions are **Food**, **Acid**, **Temperature**, **Time**, **Oxygen**, and **Moisture**.

FIFO - acronym for *first in, first out,* used to describe stock rotation procedures of using older products first.

Food establishment - an operation that stores, prepares, packages, serves, vends, or otherwise provides food for human consumption such as a restaurant, food market, institutional feeding location, or vending location.

Foodborne disease outbreak - an incident in which two or more people experience a similar illness after ingesting a common food and epidemiological analysis identifies the food as the source of the illness.

Foodborne illness - an illness caused by the consumption of a contaminated food.

Food-contact surface - any surface of equipment or utensils which food normally touches.

Footcandle - unit of lighting equal to the illumination one foot from a uniform light source.

Fungi - a group of microorganisms that includes mold and yeasts.

Garbage - wet waste matter, usually food product, that cannot be recycled.

Gastroenteritis - an inflammation of the linings of stomach and intestines which can cause nausea, vomiting, abdominal cramping, and diarrhea.

Germicide - kills harmful microbes; germs.

Germs - general term for microorganisms, including bacteria and viruses.

Grade standards - primarily standards of quality to help producers, wholesalers, retailers, and consumers in marketing and purchasing food products. The grade standards are not aimed at protecting the health of the consumer but rather at ensuring value received according to uniform quality standards.

GRAS substances - GRAS stands for generally recognized as safe. These are substances added to foods that have been shown to be safe based on a long history of common usage in food.

Harborage - shelter for pests.

Hazard analysis - identify hazards (problems) that might be introduced into food by practices or the intended use of the product.

Hazard Analysis Critical Control Point (HACCP) - a food safety assurance system that highlights potential problems in food preparation and service.

Hazard - means a biological, chemical, or physical property that may cause an unacceptable consumer health risk.

Hand washing - the proper cleaning of hands with soap and warm water to remove dirt, filth, and disease germs.

Heimlich maneuver - method used to expel foreign body caught in someone's throat.

Hermetic packaging - a container that is sealed completely against the entry of bacteria, molds, yeasts, and filth as long as it remains intact.

Hot-holding - refers to the safe temperature range of 140°F (60°C) and above to maintain properly cooked foods hot until served.

Immunosuppressed - an individual who is susceptible to illness because their immune system is not working properly or is weak.

Impermeable - does not permit passage, especially of fluids.

Infection - illness caused by eating food that contains living disease-causing microorganisms.

Infestation - presence of a large number of pests.

Ingestion - the process of eating and digesting food.

Inherent - being an essential part of something.

Integrated Pest Management (IPO) - a system of preventive and control measures used to control or eliminate pest infestations in food establishments.

Irradiation - exposure of food to low level radiation to prolong shelf life by eliminating pathogens.

Kitchenware - utensils used to prepare food.

Intoxication - Illness caused by eating food that contains a harmful chemical or toxin.

Larva - immature stage of development of insects and parasites.

Leftovers - refers to any food that is prepared for a particular meal and is held over for service at a future meal.

Manager - the individual present at a food service establishment who supervises employees that are responsible for the storage, preparation, display, and service of food to the public.

Measuring device - usually a thermometer that registers the temperature of products and water used for sanitizing.

Media - newspapers, magazines, radio, and television.

Mesophile - microorganisms that grow best at moderate temperatures.

Microbe - a microscopic organism such as a bacterium or a virus.

Microorganism - bacteria, viruses, molds, and other tiny organisms that are too small to be seen with the naked eye. The organisms are also referred to as microbes because they cannot be seen without the aid of a microscope.

Misbranding - falsely or misleadingly packaged or labeled food; may contain ingredients not included on label or does not meet national standards for that food.

Modified Atmosphere Packaging (MAP) - a food processing technique where foods are placed in a flexible container and the air is removed from the package. Gases may be added to help preserve the food.

Mold - any of a various fungi that spoil foods and have a fuzzy appearance.

Monitoring procedures - a defined method of checking foods during receiving, storage, preparation, holding, and serving processes.

Non-food contact surfaces - any area not designed to touch food.

Onset Time - the period between eating a contaminated food and developing symptoms of a foodborne illness.

Palatable - food that has an acceptable taste and flavor.

Parasite - an animal or plant that lives in or on another from whose body it obtains nourishment.

Parts per million (ppm) - unit of measure for water hardness and chemical sanitizing solution concentrations.

Pasteurization - a low heat treatment used to destroy disease-causing organisms and/or extend the shelf life of a product by destroying organisms and enzymes that cause spoilage.

Pathogenic - capable of causing disease; harmful; any disease-causing agent.

Perishable - quick to decay or spoil unless stored properly.

Personal hygiene - health habits including bathing, washing hair, wearing clean clothing, and proper hand washing.

Pest control operator - licensed individual or certified technician who provides pest control services.

pH - The symbol that describes the acidity or alkalinity of a substance, such as food.

Physical hazard - particles or fragments of items not supposed to be in foods.

Potable water - water that is safe to drink.

Potentially hazardous food - a food that is natural or man-made and is in a form capable of supporting the rapid and progressive growth of infectious and toxin-producing microorganisms. The foods usually have high protein and moisture content and low acidity.

Pounds per square inch (psi) - amount of pressure per square inch.

Premises - physical environment of the food establishment; grounds, interior, and exterior of building(s).

Preventive measures - procedures that keep foods from becoming contaminated.

Psychrophile - microorganisms that grow best at cold temperatures.

Quaternary ammonium - a chemical sanitizing compound that is relatively safe for skin contact and is generally noncorrosive, effective in acid and alkaline solutions.

Ready-to-eat foods - foods that do not require cooking or further preparation prior to consumption.

Reconstitute - to combine dehydrated foods with water or other liquids to bring back to original state; example, add water to powdered milk.

Refuse - trash, rubbish, waste.

Reheating - the act of providing sufficient heat (at least 165°F or 74°C) within a two hour time period to assure the destruction of any foodborne pathogens that may be present in that cooked and cooled food.

Risk - the chance of injury, damage, or loss.

Sanitary - Clean and free of harmful microorganisms and other contaminants.

Sanitation - maintenance of conditions which are clean and promote good health.

Sanitizing - application of an agent that reduces microbes to safe levels.

Sanitizer - approved substance or method to use when sanitizing.

Sealed - closed tightly.

Selectivity - chemical sanitizers, especially quats, may kill only certain organisms and not others.

Sensitive ingredient - an ingredient that is prone to support bacterial growth.

Single-use-articles - items for one use then discarded, such as paper cups or plastic eating utensils.

Silicate - salt or ester derived from silica; a hard, glassy material found in sand.

Sneeze guard - a clear, solid barrier which partially covers food in self-service areas to keep customers from coughing, sneezing, or projecting droplets of saliva directly onto food.

Soil - dirt and filth.

Sous vide - A French term for "under vacuum." A method of food processing that involves placing food ingredients in plastic pouches and vacuuming the air out. The pouch is then minimally cooked under precise conditions and refrigerated immediately.

Spoilage - significant food deterioration, usually caused by bacteria and enzymes, that produces a noticeable change in the taste, odor, or appearance of the product.

Splash contact surfaces - areas that are easy-to-clean and designed to catch splashed substances in work areas.

Spore - the inactive or dormant state of some rod-shaped bacteria.

Stationary equipment - equipment that is permanently fastened to the floor, table, or countertop,

Sulfites - preservatives used to maintain freshness and color of fresh fruits and vegetables; subject to state regulations.

Surfactant - chemical agent in detergent that reduces the surface tension, allowing the detergent to penetrate and soak soil loose; wetting agent.

Tableware - plates, cups, bowls, etc.

Task analysis - examining a job task to determine what it takes to do the job.

Temperature abuse - allowing foods to remain in the temperature danger zone (41° and 140°F, 5° and 60°C) for an unacceptable period of time.

Temperature danger zone - temperatures between 41° and 140°F (5° and 60°C) at which bacteria grow best.

Test kit - device that accurately measures the concentration of sanitizing solutions to ensure that they are at proper levels.

Thermophile - microorganisms that grow best at hot temperatures.

Thermometer - a device that measures temperatures.

Toxin-mediated infection - illness caused by eating a food that contains harmful microorganisms that produce a toxin once they get inside the human intestinal tract.

Toxin - a poisonous substance produced by microorganisms, plants, and animals which causes various diseases.

Vacuum breaker - designed for use under continuous supply pressure. Spring loaded device to operate after extended periods of hydrostatic pressure.

Vegetative state - the active state of a bacterium where the cell takes in nourishment, grows, and produces wastes.

Ventilation - air circulation that removes smoke, odors, moisture, and grease laden vapors from a room and replaces with fresh air.

Verification - to prove to be true by evidence, usually a record of time and temperatures of food from receiving to serving or vending.

Viruses - any of a group of infectious microorganisms that reproduce only in living cells. They cause diseases such as mumps and Hepatitis A and can be transmitted through food.

Water activity (Aw) - A measure of the free moisture in a food. Pure water has a water activity of 1.0 and potentially hazardous foods have a water activity of 0.85 and higher.

Wetting agent - breaks down the soil to allow water and soap or detergent to liquefy and remove dirt and grease.

Wholesome - something that is favorable to or promotes health.

Yeast - type of fungus that is not known to cause illness when present in foods but can cause damage to food products and will change taste; useful in making products such as bread and beer.

INDEX

"I'd like to take THE test, please."

By now you have at least glanced at the book *Essentials of Food Safety & Sanitation*. Perhaps you have determined that you are ready to take THE test so that you can become a **certified food safety manager**. Before you sharpen your pencil, there are a couple of additional questions worth thinking about.

First, why do you even need to become a *certified food safety manager*?

▼ You may just love the study and prevention of foodborne illnesses, but certification is probably required by your company, your boss, or to comply with government regulations. Whatever the reason, you need a respected certification to go forward in your career.

Second, what do you get when you successfully complete this exam?

▼ You receive a nationally recognized certification as a **Food Safety Manager**. You have mastered the knowledge needed to successfully manage the safety and sanitation of food establishments.

▼ Additionally, your name will be listed in the **National Registry of Food Safety Professionals**. This will allow your 3-year certification to be verified by contacting the **National Registry of Food Safety Professionals**. This can be a great boost to your career.

"If I could ask anything . . . I'd like to know about the test."

We trust you mean, "What is on the test?"

▼ Here is the examination content list and the number of questions for each:

Ensure Food Protection	12
Purchase and Receive Food	11
Store Foods and Supplies	11
Prepare Foods	9
Serve and Display Foods	9
Use and Maintain Tools and Equipment	2
Clean and Sanitize Equipment, Utensils, and Food Contact Surfaces	4
Select, Monitor, and Maintain Water Sources	1
Monitor and Maintain Plumbing Fixtures	1
Monitor and Maintain Ventilation Systems	1
Select, Monitor, and Maintain Waste Disposal Facilities and Equipment	1
Clean and Maintain Toilet and Hand Washing Equipment and Facilities	1
Perform General Maintenance and Housekeeping Duties	2
Monitor the Location of Equipment and Facilities	1

What about the exam mechanics?

▼ The exam includes 80 multiple-choice questions.

▼ The exam is in easy to understand, simple language and requires an 8th grade reading level.

▼ You will have two hours for the exam.

▼ The exam may be taken in "paper and pencil" form under the supervision of a proctor, or by computer in supervised conditions (this could include an Internet delivery of the test).

▼ The exam is scored and scaled. To pass the exam you must earn **a 75** or higher.

▼ After you take the test, you will be sent a full breakout of how you did. If you don't pass the exam you can use this to analyze where you need to work harder to pass the exam the next time.

How should I prepare for the Certified Food Safety Manager Exam?

It depends . . .

▼ Some states or professional affiliations require attendance in class before sitting for the exam. Seek out your local community college or university for a class or short course.

▼ If you are an independent learner, you should read *Essentials of Food Safety & Sanitation* before you request and take the exam.

▼ You might skip preparing and just keep taking the exam until you get it right. It is possible your professional experience and commitment to preventing foodborne illnesses has equipped you for the exam.

What or who is Professional Testing, Inc.?

▼ Professional Testing, Inc. prepares and administers certification and licensure examinations for national, state and local regulatory and certification agencies.

▼ Over the past 25 years, Professional Testing, Inc. has prepared and administered the certification and licensure exams for such professions as electrical contractors, physicians, architects, real estate agents and airline pilots, to name a few.

▼ In 1995, Professional Testing, Inc. brought together leaders from industry, regulatory agencies, and academia to form an expert panel of food professionals. All questions appearing on the Certified Food Safety Manager exam are written, reviewed, and tested by these experts. An advisory board provides continuous monitoring of changes in the food industry to ensure that the examination reflects current practices. The advisory board adheres to the developing Standards for Food Protection Manager Certification, prepared by the Conference for Food Protection. Professional Testing, Inc. is committed to assuring quality and fairness throughout all of its testing programs, and ascribes to the *Standards for Educational and Psychological Testing*, issued by the American Educational Research Association.

To find out more about the comprehensive *Certified Food Safety Manager* exam just write or call:

Professional Testing, Inc.
National Registry of Food Safety Professionals
1200 E. Hillcrest Street, Suite 300
Orlando Florida 32803-4737

Phone: (407) 228-0909 between 9:00 a.m. – 4:00 p.m. EST
Fax: (407) 894-8164